Solving
Control Engineering Problems
with MATLAB®

KATSUHIKO OGATA
University of Minnesota

MATLAB® Curriculum Series

PRENTICE HALL, Englewood Cliffs, New Jersey 07632

Library of Congress Cataloging-in-Publication Data

Ogata, Katsuhiko.
  Solving control engineering problems with MATLAB / Katsuhiko
Ogata.
    p. cm.
  Includes bibliographical references and index.
  ISBN 0-13-045907-0
  1. Automatic control—Data processing.   2. MATLAB.   I. Title.
TJ213.029   1993
629.8′0285′5369—dc20   93-8443
                                                            CIP

Acquisitions Editor: Don Fowley
Editorial/Production Supervision: Lynda Griffiths
Buyer: Linda Behrens
Cover Design: Perrapin Graphics

Printed in the United States of America

10 9 8 7 6 5 4 3 2

ISBN 0-13-045907-0

PRENTICE-HALL INTERNATIONAL (UK) LIMITED, *London*
PRENTICE-HALL OF AUSTRALIA PTY. LIMITED, *Sydney*
PRENTICE-HALL CANADA INC., *Toronto*
PRENTICE-HALL HISPANOAMERICANA, S.A., *Mexico*
PRENTICE-HALL OF INDIA PRIVATE LIMITED, *New Delhi*
PRENTICE-HALL OF JAPAN, INC., *Tokyo*
SIMON & SCHUSTER ASIA PTE. LTD., *Singapore*
EDITORA PRENTICE-HALL DO BRASIL, LTDA., *Rio de Janeiro*

Contents

Preface

MATLAB® has an excellent collection of commands and functions that are immediately useful for solving control engineering problems. For example, the Student Edition of MATLAB has commands for obtaining the following:

Step response
Root-locus plots
Frequency-response plots (both Bode and Nyquist plots)
Transformation between state-space models and transfer-function models
Eigenvalues and eigenvectors of square matrices
Conversion from continuous-time models to discrete-time models
Design of linear quadratic regulators

among many others. (If you are using the professional version of MATLAB, these commands are included in the Control System Toolbox.) As is shown in this book, plotting step response curves, root loci, and Bode diagrams and finding solutions to many control problems can be done quite easily with MATLAB.

The routines that appear in this book work with the Student Edition of MATLAB and MATLAB versions 3.5 and 4.0. The plots were produced from PostScript files created with version 3.5 of MATLAB. The Student Edition of MATLAB can produce the same plots but only with screen dump hardcopy output.

This book is intended to aid engineering students and practicing engineers in their study of MATLAB for use in solving control engineering problems. The problems discussed in this book are basic in linear control systems and are normally presented in introductory control courses. Many example problems are taken from two of the author's earlier books, *Modern Control Engineering*, 2nd edition (Prentice Hall) and *Discrete-Time Control Systems* (Prentice Hall).

In this book the discussions are limited to linear, time-invariant control systems. Both continuous- and discrete-time systems are treated. All input signals considered are deterministic.

Once the theoretical aspects of control problems are studied through standard control courses, MATLAB can be used with advantage to obtain numerical solutions that involve various types of vector–matrix operations.

Many of the MATLAB programs presented in this book are written with user-friendly comments so that the reader can follow each step easily. Thus those readers who are not yet familiar with MATLAB will find this book to be very useful in that it presents details of how to write MATLAB programs to obtain solutions of control engineering problems. Since this book provides detailed explanations to answer a variety of questions that were raised by students in my courses on control systems, I trust that it will also answer many of the questions that the reader might have.

Finally, I would like to thank The MathWorks, Inc. for their permission to use some of the basic MATLAB materials presented in *Student Edition of MATLAB* (published by Prentice Hall) in this book.

Katsuhiko Ogata

Chapter 1 Introductory Materials

1-1 INTRODUCTION

MATLAB (an abbreviation for MATrix LABoratory) is a matrix-based system for mathematical and engineering calculations. We may think of MATLAB as a kind of language designed solely to do matrix manipulations. All variables handled in MATLAB are matrices. That is, MATLAB has only one data type, a matrix, or a rectangular array of numbers. MATLAB has an extensive set of routines for obtaining graphical outputs.

This chapter presents an introduction to MATLAB. We first introduce MATLAB commands and mathematical functions that may be used in solving control engineering problems with MATLAB. Then we present matrix operators, relational and logical operators, and special characters used in MATLAB. The reader should become familiar with all materials in this chapter before studying MATLAB programs.

MATLAB has an on-line help facility that may be invoked whenever need arises. The command help will display a list of predefined functions and operators for which on-line help is available. The command

help 'function name'

will give information on the specific function named as to its purpose and use. The command

help help

will give information as to how to use the on-line help.

Many important and useful features are not discussed in this book. For those features the reader is referred to *The Student Edition of MATLAB* and *MATLAB User's Guide* listed in the references.

1-2 COMMANDS AND MATRIX FUNCTIONS USED IN MATLAB

We shall first list various types of MATLAB commands and matrix functions that are frequently used in solving control engineering problems. Then we shall briefly present mathematical model conversions, matrix operators, relational and logical operators, and special characters used in MATLAB.

MATLAB commands and matrix functions that are frequently used in solving control engineering problems

MATLAB has many predefined functions that can be called by the user to solve many different types of problems. In this book we shall discuss only those commands and matrix functions that are used in solving control engineering problems.

In Table 1-1, we list such commands and matrix functions.

Table 1-1 MATLAB COMMANDS AND MATRIX FUNCTIONS

Commands and matrix functions commonly used in solving control engineering problems	Explanations of what commands do, matrix functions mean, or statements mean
abs	Absolute value, complex magnitude
angle	Phase angle
ans	Answer when expression is not assigned
atan	Arctangent
axis	Manual axis scaling
bode	Plot Bode diagram
clear	Clear workspace
clg	Clear graph screen
computer	Type of computer
conj	Complex conjugate
conv	Convolution, multiplication
corrcoef	Correlation coefficients
cos	Cosine
cosh	Hyperbolic cosine
cov	Covariance
deconv	Deconvolution, division
det	Determinant
diag	Diagonal matrix
eig	Eigenvalues and eigenvectors
exit	Terminate program
exp	Exponential base e
expm	Matrix exponential
eye	Identity matrix
filter	Direct filter implementation
format long	15-Digit scaled fixed point (Example: 1.33333333333333)
format long e	15-Digit floating point (Example: 1.33333333333333e+000)
format short	5-Digit scaled fixed point (Example: 1.3333)
format short e	5-Digit floating point (Example: 1.3333e+000)
freqs	Laplace transform frequency response
freqz	z-Transform frequency response
grid	Draw grid lines
hold	Hold current graph on the screen

i	$\sqrt{-1}$
imag	Imaginary part
inf	Infinity (∞)
inv	Inverse

j	$\sqrt{-1}$

length	Vector length
linspace	Linearly spaced vectors
log	Natural logarithm
loglog	Loglog $x-y$ plot
logm	Matrix logarithm
logspace	Logarithmically spaced vectors
log10	Log base 10
lqe	Linear quadratic estimator design
lqr	Linear quadratric regulator design

max	Maximum value
mean	Mean value
median	Median value
min	Minimum value

NaN	Not-a-number
nyquist	Plot Nyquist frequency response

ones	constant

pi	Pi (π)
plot	Linear $x-y$ plot
polar	Polar plot
poly	Characteristic polynomial
polyfit	Polynomial curve fitting
polyval	Polynomial evaluation
polyvalm	Matrix polynomial evaluation
prod	Product of elements

quit	Terminate program

rand	Generate random numbers and matrices
rank	Calculate the rank of a matrix
real	Real part
rem	Remainder or modulus
residue	Partial-fraction expansion
rlocus	Plot root loci
roots	Polynomial roots

semilogx	Semilog $x-y$ plot (x-axis logarithmic)
semilogy	Semilog $x-y$ plot (y-axis logarithmic)
sign	Signum function
sin	Sine
sinh	Hyperbolic sine
size	Row and column dimensions
sqrt	Square root
sqrtm	Matrix square root
std	Standard deviation
step	Plot unit-step response
sum	Sum of elements

(*Continued*)

Table 1-1 (*Continued*)

Commands and matrix functions commonly used in solving control engineering problems	Explanations of what commands do, matrix functions mean, or statements mean
tan tanh text title trace	Tangent Hyperbolic tangent Arbitrarily positioned text Plot title Trace of a matrix
who	Lists all variables currently in memory
xlabel	x-Axis label
ylabel	y-Axis label
zeros	Zero

Model conversions

MATLAB has commands for the following model conversions:

> State-space to transfer-function conversion   (ss2tf)
> Transfer-function to state-space conversion   (tf2ss)
> State-space to zero-pole conversion   (ss2zp)
> Zero-pole to state-space conversion   (zp2ss)
> Transfer-function to zero-pole conversion   (tf2zp)
> Zero-pole to transfer-function conversion   (zp2tf)
> Continuous-time to discrete-time conversion   (c2d)

In this book we shall treat ss2tf, tf2ss, and c2d in detail.

Matrix operators

The following notations are used in the matrix operations:

> +   Addition
> −   Subtraction
> *   Multiplication
> ∧   Power
> '   Conjugate transpose

Relational and logical operators

The following relational and logical operators are used in MATLAB:

> <   Less than
> <=   Less than or equal
> >   Greater than
> >=   Greater than or equal
> ==   Equal
> ~=   Not equal

Note that '=' is used in an assignment statement, while '==' is used in a relation. The logical operators are

                    &   AND
                    | OR
                    ~   NOT

Special characters

The following special characters are used in MATLAB:

[ ]	Used to form vectors and matrices
( )	Arithmetic expression precedence
,	Separate subscripts and function arguments
;	End rows, suppress printing (see following details)
:	Subscripting, vector generation (see following details)
!	Execute operating system command
%	Comments (see following details)

Use of semicolon operator

The semicolon is used to suppress printing. If the last character of a statement is a semicolon, the printing is suppressed; but the command is still executed, only the result is not displayed. This is a useful feature, since printing of intermediate results may not be needed. Also, in entering a matrix, a semicolon is used to indicate the end of the row, except at the last row.

Use of colon operator

The colon operator plays an important role in MATLAB. This operator may be used to create vectors, to subscript matrices, and to specify *for* iterations. For example, j:k is the same as $[j \quad j + 1 \quad . . . \quad k]$, A(:,j) is the *j*th column of **A** and A(i,:) is the *i*th row of **A**.

Program line beginning with '%'

Throughout this book, many MATLAB programs are written with comments and remarks that explain particular steps taken in the programs. Program lines in MATLAB beginning with '%' are comments or remarks. The notation '%' is similar to 'REM' in BASIC. A line beginning with % is used to store the programmer's comments or remarks, and such comments or remarks are not executed. That is, everything appearing after % on a MATLAB program line is ignored. If comments or remarks require more than one program line, each line must begin with %. (See, for example, MATLAB Program 3-1.)

1-3 OUTLINE OF THE BOOK

The outline of the book is as follows: This book is designed primarily to discuss in detail how to present the results of control systems analysis in graphical forms.

    The contents of each chapter are summarized next. Chapter 1 has presented introductory material. Chapter 2 gives background materials concerning matrix operations with MATLAB.

Chapters 3 and 4 present transient-response analysis of control systems with MATLAB. Chapter 3 is concerned with continuous-time systems and Chapter 4 with discrete-time systems. Chapter 5 deals with the root locus plots. We discuss problems that may arise in plotting root loci with MATLAB. Plotting of root loci for discrete-time control systems is also included. Frequency-response analyses of closed-loop systems are presented in Chapter 6. We treat both continuous-time and discrete-time control systems. Simple design problems based on the Bode diagram approach are treated in this chapter.

Chapter 2   Basic Background Materials

2-1 INTRODUCTION

This chapter deals with the necessary background materials for solving control engineering problems with MATLAB.

If you need to clock and date

Statement clock gives year, month, day, hour, minute, and second. That is, clock returns a six-element row vector containing the current time and date in decimal form.

$$clock = [year\ month\ day\ hour\ minute\ second]$$

Also, statement date gives the current date.

date

ans =

1-Jan-94

Accessing and exiting MATLAB

On most systems, once MATLAB has been installed, to invoke MATLAB execute the command MATLAB. To exit MATLAB, execute the command exit or quit.

How MATLAB is used

MATLAB is usually used in a command-driven mode. When single-line commands are entered, MATLAB processes them immediately and displays the results. MATLAB is also capable of executing sequences of command that are stored in files.

The commands that are typed may be accessed later by using the *up-arrow* key. It is possible to scroll through some of the latest commands that are entered and recall a particular command line.

Variables in MATLAB

A convenient feature of MATLAB is that the variables need not be dimensioned before use. In MATLAB, variables are generated automatically once they are used. (The dimensions of the variables can be altered later if necessary.) Such variables remain in memory until the command exit or quit is entered.

To obtain a list of the variables in the workspace, simply type the command who. Then all variables currently in the workspace appear on the screen.

The command clear will clear all nonpermanent variables from the workspace. If it is desired to clear only a particular variable, say 'x', from the workspace, enter the command clear x.

How to enter comments in a MATLAB program

As stated in Chapter 1, if it is desired to enter comments that are not to be executed, use the % symbol at the start of the line. That is, the % symbol indicates that the rest of the line is a comment and should be ignored.

How to save variables when exiting from MATLAB

When 'exit' or 'quit' is typed, all variables in MATLAB are lost. If the command save is entered before exiting, all variables can be kept in a disk file named matlab.mat. When we later reenter MATLAB, the command load will restore the workspace to its former state.

Outline of the chapter

Section 2-1 has provided introductory material. Section 2-2 discusses how to enter matrices in MATLAB programs. Section 2-3 presents vector generation, matrix operations, eigenvalues, and related subjects. Section 2-4 shows how to plot response curves, and Section 2-5 discusses mathematical models and linear system transformations.

2-2 ENTERING MATRICES IN MATLAB PROGRAMS

Entering sampled data signals in MATLAB programs

Vectors, which are $1 \times n$ or $n \times 1$ matrices, are used to hold ordinary one-dimensional sampled data signals, or sequences. One way to introduce a sequence into MATLAB is to enter it as an explicit list of elements. Note that the elements must be separated by blank spaces or commas, as follows:

$$x = \begin{bmatrix} 1 & 2 & 3 & -4 & -5 \end{bmatrix}$$

or

$$x = [1,2,3,-4,-5]$$

For readability, it is better to provide spaces between elements. As shown, the values must be entered within square brackets.

The statement

$$x = [1 \quad 2 \quad 3 \quad -4 \quad -5]$$

creates a simple five-element real sequence in a row vector. The sequence can be turned into a column vector by transposition. That is,

$$x = x'$$

results in

$$x =$$

$$
\begin{matrix}
1 \\
2 \\
3 \\
-4 \\
-5
\end{matrix}
$$

How to enter matrices in MATLAB programs

A matrix

$$
\mathbf{A} = \begin{bmatrix} 1.2 & 10 & 15 \\ 3 & 5.5 & 2 \\ 4 & 6.8 & 7 \end{bmatrix}
$$

may be entered by a row vector as follows:

$$A = [1.2 \quad 10 \quad 15; 3 \quad 5.5 \quad 2; 4 \quad 6.8 \quad 7]$$

As shown, the values must be entered within square brackets. The elements of any row must be separated by blanks (or by commas). The end of each row, except the last row, is indicated by a semicolon.

A large matrix may be spread across several input lines. For example, consider the following matrix **B**:

$$
\mathbf{B} = \begin{bmatrix} 1.5630 & 2.4572 & 3.1113 & 4.1051 \\ 3.2211 & 1.0000 & 2.5000 & 3.2501 \\ 1.0000 & 2.0000 & 0.6667 & 0.0555 \\ 0.2345 & 0.9090 & 1.0000 & 0.3333 \end{bmatrix}
$$

This matrix may be spread across four input lines, as follows:

$$
\begin{aligned}
B = [&1.5630 \quad 2.4572 \quad 3.1113 \quad 4.1051 \\
&3.2211 \quad 1.0000 \quad 2.5000 \quad 3.2501 \\
&1.0000 \quad 2.0000 \quad 0.6667 \quad 0.0555 \\
&0.2345 \quad 0.9090 \quad 1.0000 \quad 0.3333]
\end{aligned}
$$

Note that carriage returns replace the semicolons.

As another example, matrix **C** given by

$$
\mathbf{C} = \begin{bmatrix} 1 & e^{-0.02} \\ \sqrt{2} & 3 \end{bmatrix}
$$

may be entered as follows:

$$C = [1 \quad \exp(-0.02); \operatorname{sqrt}(2) \quad 3]$$

Then the following matrix will be shown on the screen:

$$C =$$

$$\begin{matrix} 1.0000 & 0.9802 \\ 1.4142 & 3.0000 \end{matrix}$$

Transpose and conjugate transpose

The apostrophe (prime) ' denotes the conjugate transpose of a matrix. If the matrix is real, the conjugate transpose is simply a transpose. An entry like

$$A = [1 \quad 2 \quad 3;4 \quad 5 \quad 6;7 \quad 8 \quad 9]$$

will produce the following matrix on the screen:

$$A =$$

$$\begin{matrix} 1 & 2 & 3 \\ 4 & 5 & 6 \\ 7 & 8 & 9 \end{matrix}$$

Also, if

$$B = A'$$

is entered, then we see on the screen

$$B =$$

$$\begin{matrix} 1 & 4 & 7 \\ 2 & 5 & 8 \\ 3 & 6 & 9 \end{matrix}$$

Entering complex numbers

Complex numbers may be entered using function i or j. For example, a number $1 + j\sqrt{3}$ may be entered as

$$x = 1 + \operatorname{sqrt}(3) * i$$

or

$$x = 1 + \operatorname{sqrt}(3) * j$$

This complex number $1 + j\sqrt{3} = 2 \exp[(\pi/3)j]$ may also be entered as

$$x = 2 * \exp((\operatorname{pi}/3) * j)$$

It is important to note that, when complex numbers are entered as matrix elements within brackets, we avoid any blank spaces. For example, $1 + 5*j$ should be entered as follows:

$$x = 1+5*j$$

If spaces are provided around the $+$ sign, such as

$$x = 1 \quad + \quad 5*j$$

it represents two separate numbers.

If i and j are used as variables, a new complex unit may be generated as follows:

$$ii = sqrt(-1)$$

or

$$jj = sqrt(-1)$$

Then $-1 + j\sqrt{3}$ may be entered as

$$x = -1+sqrt(3)*ii$$

or

$$x = -1+sqrt(3)*jj$$

Entering complex matrices

If matrix **X** is a complex matrix such as

$$\mathbf{X} = \begin{bmatrix} 1 & j \\ -j5 & 2 \end{bmatrix}$$

then an entry like

$$X = [1 \quad j; -j*5 \quad 2]$$

will produce the following matrix on the screen:

X =

    1.0000   0 + 1.0000i
    0 - 5.0000i   2.0000

Note that

$$Y = X'$$

will yield

Y =

    1.0000   0 + 5.0000i
    0 - 1.0000i   2.0000

which is

$$\mathbf{Y} = \begin{bmatrix} 1 & j5 \\ -j & 2 \end{bmatrix}$$

Since the prime, ', gives the complex conjugate transpose, for an unconjugated transpose use one of the following two entries:

$$Y.' \qquad or \qquad conj(Y')$$

If we type

$$Y.'$$

then the screen shows

ans =

    1.0000   0 − 1.0000i
        0 + 5.0000i   2.0000

Also, if

$$conj(Y')$$

is entered, then the screen shows

ans =

    1.0000   0 − 1.0000i
        0 + 5.0000i   2.0000

Addition and subtraction

Matrices of the same dimension may be added or subtracted. Consider the following matrices **A** and **B**:

$$\mathbf{A} = \begin{bmatrix} 2 & 3 \\ 4 & 5 \\ 6 & 7 \end{bmatrix}, \qquad \mathbf{B} = \begin{bmatrix} 1 & 0 \\ 2 & 3 \\ 0 & 4 \end{bmatrix}$$

If we enter

$$A = [2 \quad 3;4 \quad 5;6 \quad 7]$$

then the screen shows

A =

    2   3
    4   5
    6   7

If matrix **B** is entered as

$$B = [1 \quad 0;2 \quad 3;0 \quad 4]$$

then the screen shows

$$B =$$

$$
\begin{matrix}
1 & 0 \\
2 & 3 \\
0 & 4
\end{matrix}
$$

For the addition of two matrices such as **A** + **B**, we enter

$$C = A + B$$

Then matrix **C** appears on the screen as

$$C =$$

$$
\begin{matrix}
3 & 3 \\
6 & 8 \\
6 & 11
\end{matrix}
$$

If a vector **x** is given by

$$\mathbf{x} = \begin{bmatrix} 5 \\ 4 \\ 6 \end{bmatrix}$$

then we enter this vector as

$$x = [5;4;6]$$

The screen shows the column vector as follows:

$$x =$$

$$
\begin{matrix}
5 \\
4 \\
6
\end{matrix}
$$

The following entry will subtract 1 from each element of vector **x**.

$$y = x - 1$$

The screen will show

$$y =$$

$$
\begin{matrix}
4 \\
3 \\
5
\end{matrix}
$$

Matrix multiplication

Multiplication of matrices is denoted by $*$. Consider

$$x = [1;2;3]; \quad y = [4;5;6]; \quad A = [1 \quad 1 \quad 2;3 \quad 4 \quad 0;1 \quad 2 \quad 5]$$

The entry

$$x' * y$$

will give

$$ans =$$

$$32$$

Also, the entry

$$x * y'$$

will give

$$ans =$$

4	5	6
8	10	12
12	15	18

Similarly, if we enter

$$y * x'$$

then the screen shows

$$ans =$$

4	8	12
5	10	15
6	12	18

Matrix–vector products are a special case of general matrix–matrix products. For example, an entry like

$$b = A * x$$

will produce

$$b =$$

$$9$$
$$11$$
$$20$$

Note that a scalar can multiply, or be multiplied by, any matrix. For example, entering

$$5 * A$$

gives

ans =

$$\begin{array}{rrr} 5 & 5 & 10 \\ 15 & 20 & 0 \\ 5 & 10 & 25 \end{array}$$

and an entry like

A ∗ 5

will also give

ans =

$$\begin{array}{rrr} 5 & 5 & 10 \\ 15 & 20 & 0 \\ 5 & 10 & 25 \end{array}$$

Matrix exponential

expm(A) is the matrix exponential of an $n \times n$ matrix **A**. That is,

$$\mathrm{expm}(\mathbf{A}) = \mathbf{I} + \mathbf{A} + \mathbf{A}^2/2! + \mathbf{A}^3/3! + \cdots$$

Note that a transcendental function is interpreted as a matrix function if an "m" is appended to the function name, as in expm(A) or sqrtm(A).

Absolute values

abs(A) gives the matrix consisting of the absolute value of each element of **A**. If **A** is complex, abs returns the complex modulus (magnitude):

$$\mathrm{abs(A)} = \mathrm{sqrt(real(A)}.^2 + \mathrm{imag(A)}.^2)$$

angle(A) returns the phase angles, in radians, of the elements of complex matrix **A**. The angles lie between $-\pi$ and π. See the following example.

```
A = [2+2*i   1+3*i;4+5*i   6−i];
abs(A)

ans =

    2.8284        3.1623
    6.4031        6.0828

angle(A)

ans =

    0.7854        1.2490
    0.8961       −0.1651
```

Magnitude and phase angle of a complex number

The magnitude and phase angle of a complex number $z = x + iy = re^{i\theta}$ are given by

$$r = \text{abs}(z)$$
$$\text{theta} = \text{angle}(z)$$

and the statement

$$z = r * \exp(i * \text{theta})$$

converts back to the original complex number z.

Obtaining squares of entries of vector x

For a vector **x**, $x.^2$ gives the vector of the square of each element. For example, for

$$\mathbf{x} = \begin{bmatrix} 1 & 2 & 3 \end{bmatrix}$$

$x.^2$ is given as shown in the following MATLAB output:

```
x = [1   2   3];
x.^2

ans =

          1     4     9
```

Also, for the vector **y**,

$$\mathbf{y} = \begin{bmatrix} 2 + 5j & 3 + 4j & 1 - j \end{bmatrix}$$

$y.^2$ is given as follows:

```
y = [2+5*i   3+4*i   1−i];
y.^2

ans =

  −21.0000 + 20.0000i   −7.0000 + 24.0000i          0 − 2.0000i
```

Obtaining squares of entries of matrix A

For a matrix **A**, $A.^2$ gives the matrix consisting of the square of each element. For example, for matrices **A** and **B**, where

$$\mathbf{A} = \begin{bmatrix} 1 & 2 \\ 3 & 4 \end{bmatrix}, \qquad \mathbf{B} = \begin{bmatrix} 1 + j & 2 - 2j \\ 3 + 4j & 5 - j \end{bmatrix}$$

A.$^\wedge$2 and B.$^\wedge$2 are given as follows:

```
A = [1   2;3   4];
A.^2

ans =

      1       4
      9      16

B = [1+i   2−2*i;3+4*i   5−i];
B.^2

ans =

          0 +   2.0000i           0 −   8.0000i
     −7.0000 + 24.0000i      24.0000 − 10.0000i
```

Array multiplication and division

Array, or element by element, multiplication is denoted by '.$*$'. If **x** and **y** have the same dimensions, then

$$x.*y$$

denotes the array whose elements are simply the products of the individual elements of **x** and **y**. For example, if

$$x = [1 \quad 2 \quad 3], \qquad y = [4 \quad 5 \quad 6]$$

then

$$z = x.*y$$

results in

$$z = [4 \quad 10 \quad 18]$$

Similarly, if matrices **A** and **B** have the same dimensions, than A.$*$B denotes the array whose elements are simply the products of the corresponding elements of **A** and **B**. For example, if

$$A = \begin{bmatrix} 1 & 2 & 3 \\ 0 & 9 & 8 \end{bmatrix}, \qquad B = \begin{bmatrix} 4 & 5 & 6 \\ 7 & 6 & 5 \end{bmatrix}$$

then

$$C = A.*B$$

results in

$$C = \begin{bmatrix} 4 & 10 & 18 \\ 0 & 54 & 40 \end{bmatrix}$$

The expressions x./y, x.\y, A./B, and A.\B give the quotients of the individual elements. Thus, for

$$\mathbf{x} = [1 \quad 2 \quad 3], \qquad \mathbf{y} = [4 \quad 5 \quad 6]$$

the statement

$$u = x./y$$

gives

$$\mathbf{u} = [0.25 \quad 0.4 \quad 0.5]$$

and the statement

$$v = x.\backslash y$$

results in

$$\mathbf{v} = [4 \quad 2.5 \quad 2]$$

Similarly, for matrices **A** and **B**, where

$$\mathbf{A} = \begin{bmatrix} 1 & 2 & 3 \\ 1 & 9 & 8 \end{bmatrix}, \qquad \mathbf{B} = \begin{bmatrix} 4 & 5 & 6 \\ 7 & 6 & 5 \end{bmatrix}$$

the statement

$$C = A./B$$

gives

$$\mathbf{C} = \begin{bmatrix} 0.2500 & 0.4000 & 0.5000 \\ 0.1429 & 1.5000 & 1.6000 \end{bmatrix}$$

And the statement

$$D = A.\backslash B$$

gives

$$\mathbf{D} = \begin{bmatrix} 4.0000 & 2.5000 & 2.0000 \\ 7.0000 & 0.6667 & 0.6250 \end{bmatrix}$$

Correcting mistyped letters and numbers

Use the arrow keys on the keypad to edit mistyped commands or to recall previous command lines. For example, if we enter

$$A = (1 \quad 1 \quad 2]$$

then the first parenthesis must be corrected. Instead of retyping the entire line, hit the *up-arrow* key. This incorrect line will be displayed again. Using the *left-arrow* key, move the cursor over (and then type [and hit the *delete* key.

MATLAB is case sensitive

It is important to remember that MATLAB is case sensitive in the names of commands, functions, and variables. MATLAB distinguishes between upper- and lower-case letters. Thus, x and X are not the same variable.

All function names must be in lowercase; inv(A) will invert **A**, eig(A) will give eigenvalues. Note, however, that if the command casesen off is entered MATLAB becomes insensitive to the case of letters and INV(A) is the same as inv(A). In using the command casesen off, a certain caution is necessary, however.

Consider the following example. Suppose that matrix **A** is given as

$$\mathbf{A} = \begin{bmatrix} 0 & 1 & 0 \\ 0 & 0 & 1 \\ -6 & -11 & -6 \end{bmatrix}$$

Entering the command inv(A) produces the inverse of matrix **A**. If we enter the command INV(A), MATLAB output shows an error message. If we subsequently enter the command casesen off, MATLAB output again shows an error message. See the following MATLAB output:

```
A = [0   1   0;0   0   1;−6   −11   −6];
inv(A)

ans =

   −1.8333       −1.0000       −0.1667
    1.0000             0             0
         0        1.0000             0

INV(A)
[[[ Undefined function or variable.
Symbol in question MM INV

casesen off
INV(A)
[[[ Undefined function or variable.
Symbol in question MM a
```

To avoid such error messages, enter the statement

$$a = [A];$$

before the command casesen off is entered. Then the command INV(A) will produce the inverse of matrix **A**. See the following MATLAB output:

```
A = [0   1   0;0   0   1;−6   −11   −6];
INV(A)
[[[ Undefined function or variable.
Symbol in question MM INV

a = [A];
casesen off
INV(A)

ans =

   −1.8333       −1.0000       −0.1667
    1.0000             0             0
         0        1.0000             0
```

Entering a long statement that will not fit on one line

A statement is normally terminated with the carriage return or enter key. If the statement being entered is too long for one line, an ellipsis consisting of three or more periods, . . ., followed by the carriage return, can be used to indicate that the statement continues on the next line. An example is

$$x = 1.234 + 2.345 + 3.456 + 4.567 + 5.678 + 6.789 \ldots$$
$$+ 7.890 + 8.901 - 9.012;$$

Note that the blank spaces around the =, +, and − signs are optional. Such spaces are often provided to improve readability.

Entering several statements on one line

Several statements can be placed on one line if they are separated by commas or semicolons. Examples are

plot(x,y,'o'), text(1,20,'System 1'), text(1,15,'System 2')

and

plot(x,y,'o'); text(1,20,'System 1'); text(1,15,'System 2')

Selecting output format

All computations in MATLAB are performed in double precision. However, the displayed output may have a fixed point with four decimal places. For example, for the vector

$$\mathbf{x} = [1/3 \quad 0.00002]$$

MATLAB exhibits the following output:

x =

0.3333   0.0000

If at least one element of a matrix is not an exact integer, there are four possible output formats. The displayed output can be controlled by use of the following commands:

format short
format long
format short e
format long e

Once invoked, the chosen format remains in effect until changed.

For control systems analysis, format short and format long are commonly used. Whenever MATLAB is invoked and no format command is entered, MATLAB shows the numerical results in format short, as follows:

```
x = [1/3   0.00002];
x

x =

     0.3333     0.0000

format short; x

x =

     0.3333     0.0000

format long; x

x =

     0.33333333333333     0.00002000000000
```

If all elements of a matrix or vector are exact integers, then format short and format long yield the same result, as follows:

```
y = [2   5   40];
y

y =

     2   5   40

format short; y

y =

     2   5   40

format long; y

y =

     2   5   40
```

2-3 VECTOR GENERATION, MATRIX OPERATIONS, EIGENVALUES, AND RELATED SUBJECTS

Generating vectors

The colon, :, is an important character in MATLAB. The statement

$$t = 1:5$$

generates a row vector containing the numbers from 1 to 5 with unit increment. It produces

$$t =$$

$$1 \quad 2 \quad 3 \quad 4 \quad 5$$

An increment of other than 1 can be used. For example,

$$t = 1:0.5:3$$

will result in

$$t =$$

$$1.0000 \quad 1.50000 \quad 2.0000 \quad 2.5000 \quad 3.0000$$

Negative increments may be used. For example, the statement

$$t = 5:-1:2$$

gives

$$t =$$

$$5 \quad 4 \quad 3 \quad 2$$

Other vector generation functions include linspace, which allows the number of points, rather than the increments, to be specified.

$$x = \text{linspace}(-10,10,5)$$

gives

$$x =$$

$$-10 \quad -5 \quad 0 \quad 5 \quad 10$$

Next, consider a vector $\mathbf{x}$ given by

$$\mathbf{x} = [2 \quad 4 \quad 6 \quad 8 \quad 10]$$

Individual vector or matrix entries can be referenced with indexes inside parentheses. For example, $x(3)$ is the third element of $\mathbf{x}$ and $x([1 \quad 2 \quad 3])$ is the first three elements of $\mathbf{x}$ (that is, 2, 4, 6). Also, for a matrix $\mathbf{A}$, $A(3,1)$ denotes the entry in the third row, first column of matrix $\mathbf{A}$.

Norms

The norm of a matrix is a scalar that gives some measure of the size of the matrix. Several different definitions are commonly used. One such definition is

$$\text{norm}(\mathbf{A}) = \text{largest singular value of } \mathbf{A}$$

Similarly, several definitions are available for the norm of a vector. One commonly used definition for the norm of a vector **x** is

$$\text{norm(x)} = \text{sum(abs(x)}.\wedge 2)\wedge 0.5$$

See the following example:

```
x = [2   3   6];
norm(x)

ans =

      7
```

Eigenvalues and eigenvectors

If **A** is an $n \times n$ matrix, then the n numbers λ that satisfy

$$\mathbf{Ax} = \lambda\mathbf{x}$$

are the eigenvalues of **A**. They are found using the command

$$\text{eig(A)}$$

which returns the eigenvalues in a column vector.

If **A** is real and symmetric, the eigenvalues will be real. But if **A** is not symmetric, the eigenvalues are frequently complex numbers.

For example, with

$$\mathbf{A} = \begin{bmatrix} 0 & 1 \\ -1 & 0 \end{bmatrix}$$

the command

$$\text{eig(A)}$$

produces

$$\text{ans} =$$

$$0 + 1.0000i$$
$$0 - 1.0000i$$

MATLAB functions may have single- or multiple-output arguments. For example, as seen above, eig(A) produces a column vector consisting of the eigenvalues of **A**, while a double-assignment statement

$$[\text{X,D}] = \text{eig(A)}$$

produces eigenvalues and eigenvectors. The diagonal elements of diagonal matrix **D** are the eigenvalues, and the columns of **X** are the corresponding eigenvectors such that

$$\mathbf{AX} = \mathbf{XD}$$

For example, if

$$\mathbf{A} = \begin{bmatrix} 0 & 1 & 0 \\ 0 & 0 & 1 \\ -6 & -11 & -6 \end{bmatrix}$$

then the statement

$$[X,D] = \text{eig}(A)$$

gives the following result:

```
[X,D] = eig(A)

X =

        -0.5774      0.2182     -0.1048
         0.5774     -0.4364      0.3145
        -0.5774      0.8729     -0.9435


D =

        -1.0000           0            0
              0     -2.0000            0
              0           0      -3.0000
```

The eigenvectors are scaled so that the norm of each is 1.

   If the eigenvalues of a matrix are distinct, the eigenvectors are always independent, and the eigenvector matrix **X** will diagonalize the original matrix **A** if applied as a similarity transformation. However, if a matrix has repeated eigenvalues, it is not diagonalizable unless it has a full (independent) set of eigenvectors. If the eigenvectors are not independent, the original matrix is said to be defective. Even if a matrix is defective, the solution from eig satisfies the relationship $\mathbf{AX} = \mathbf{XD}$.

Generalized eigenvalues and generalized eigenvectors

If **A** and **B** are square matrices, then the command

$$\text{eig}(A,B)$$

returns a vector containing the generalized eigenvalues solving the equation

$$\mathbf{Ax} = \lambda\mathbf{Bx}$$

where λ is a scalar. The values of λ that satisfy the equation are the generalized eigenvalues, and the corresponding values of **x** are the generalized eigenvectors.

   To obtain eigenvectors, use the double-assignment command as follows:

$$[X,D] = \text{eig}(A,B)$$

This produces a diagonal matrix **D** of generalized eigenvalues and a square matrix **X** whose columns are corresponding eigenvectors so that

$$\mathbf{AX} = \mathbf{BXD}$$

For example, if

$$A = \begin{bmatrix} 1 & 1 & 0 & 0 \\ 1 & 0 & 0 & 0 \\ -1 & 0 & 1 & 0 \\ 0 & -1 & 0 & 1 \end{bmatrix}$$

$$B = \begin{bmatrix} 1 & 0 & 1 & 0 \\ 0 & 1 & 0 & 0 \\ 0 & 0 & 1 & 1 \\ 0 & 0 & 1 & 0 \end{bmatrix}$$

then eig(A,B) gives

```
eig(A,B)

ans =

    2.1889 − 0.0000i
   −2.1889 − 0.0000i
   −0.4569 − 0.0000i
    0.4569 − 0.0000i
```

and [X,D] = eig(A,B) gives

```
[X,D] = eig(A,B)

X =

    0.8463 + 0.0000i   −0.3548 − 0.0000i    0.2433 + 0.0000i    0.1233 − 0.0000i
    0.3866 + 0.0000i    0.1621 + 0.0000i   −0.5326 − 0.0000i    0.2699 − 0.0000i
   −0.2830 − 0.0000i    0.4429 + 0.0000i    0.3899 + 0.0000i    0.7374 − 0.0000i
   −0.2329 − 0.0000i   −0.8073 − 0.0000i   −0.7107 − 0.0000i    0.6068 − 0.0000i


D =

    2.1889 − 0.0000i          0                  0                  0
         0            −2.1889 − 0.0000i          0                  0
         0                  0           −0.4569 − 0.0000i          0
         0                  0                  0            0.4569 − 0.0000i
```

The eigenvectors are scaled so that the norm of each is 1.0.

Characteristic equation

The roots of the characteristic equation are the same as the eigenvalues of matrix **A**. The characteristic equation of matrix **A** is computed with

$$p = poly(A)$$

For example, if matrix **A** is given by

$$A = \begin{bmatrix} 0 & 1 & 0 \\ 0 & 0 & 1 \\ -6 & -11 & -6 \end{bmatrix}$$

then the command poly(A) will yield

```
p = poly(A)

p =

        1.0000    6.0000    11.0000    6.0000
```

This is the MATLAB representation of the polynomial

$$s^3 + 6s^2 + 11s + 6 = 0$$

The roots of the characteristic equation $p = 0$ can be obtained by entering the command r = roots(p):

```
r = roots(p)

r =

        −3.0000
        −2.0000
        −1.0000
```

The roots of the characteristic equation may be reassembled back into the original polynomial with the command q = poly(r).

```
q = poly(r)

q =

        1.0000    6.0000    11.0000    6.0000
```

Product of polynomials

Consider

$$a(s) = s^2 - 20.6$$
$$b(s) = s^2 + 19.6s + 151.2$$

The product of the polynomials is the convolution of the coefficients. The product of polynomials $a(s)$ and $b(s)$ can be obtained by entering the command c = conv(a, b).

```
a = [1  0  −20.6]; b = [1  19.6  151.2];
c = conv(a,b)

c =

  1.0e+003 *

    0.0010    0.0196    0.1306    −0.4038    −3.1147
```

This is the MATLAB representation of the polynomial

$$c(s) = s^4 + 19.6s^3 + 130.6s^2 - 403.8s - 3114.7$$

Deconvolution (division of polynomials)

To divide polynomial $c(s)$ by $a(s)$, use the deconvolution command $[q,r] =$ deconv(c,a).

```
[q,r] = deconv(c,a)

q =

        1.0000    19.6000   151.2000


r =

        0      0      0      0      0
```

Polynomial evaluation

If p is a vector whose elements are the coefficients of a polynomial in descending powers, then polyval(p,s) is the value of the polynomial evaluated at s. For example, to evaluate the polynomial

$$p(s) = 3s^2 + 2s + 1$$

at $s = 5$, enter the command

```
p = [3   2   1];
polyval(p,5)
```

Then we get

```
ans =

86
```

The command polyvalm(p,A) evaluates the polynomial p in a matrix sense. Consider the following matrix $\mathbf{J}$:

$$\mathbf{J} = \begin{bmatrix} -2 + j2\sqrt{3} & 0 & 0 \\ 0 & -2 - j2\sqrt{3} & 0 \\ 0 & 0 & -10 \end{bmatrix}$$

The command poly(J) gives the characteristic polynomial for $\mathbf{J}$.

```
p = poly(J)

p =

        1.0000    14.0000    56.0000    160.0000
```

This is the MATLAB expression for the characteristic polynomial for $\mathbf{J}$.

$$\text{poly}(\mathbf{J}) = \phi(\mathbf{J}) = \mathbf{J}^3 + 14\mathbf{J}^2 + 56\mathbf{J} + 160\mathbf{I}$$

where $\mathbf{I}$ is the identity matrix. For the matrix

$$\mathbf{A} = \begin{bmatrix} 0 & 1 & 0 \\ 0 & 0 & 1 \\ -6 & -11 & -6 \end{bmatrix}$$

the command polyvalm(poly(J),A) evaluates the following $\phi(\mathbf{A})$:

$$\phi(\mathbf{A}) = \mathbf{A}^3 + 14\mathbf{A}^2 + 56\mathbf{A} + 160\mathbf{I} = \begin{bmatrix} 154 & 45 & 8 \\ -48 & 66 & -3 \\ 18 & -15 & 84 \end{bmatrix}$$

See the following MATLAB output.

```
polyvalm(poly(J),A)

ans =

   154.0000     45.0000      8.0000
   -48.0000     66.0000     -3.0000
    18.0000    -15.0000     84.0000
```

Utility matrices

In MATLAB, the functions

```
ones(n)
ones(m,n)
ones(A)
zeros
```

generate special matrices. That is, ones(n) produces an $n \times n$ matrix of ones. ones(m,n) produces an $m \times n$ matrix of ones. Similarly, zeros(n) produces an $n \times n$ matrix of zeros, while zeros(m,n) produces an $m \times n$ matrix of zeros. zeros(A) produces a matrix of zeros of the same size as $\mathbf{A}$.

Identity matrix

We often need to enter an identity matrix $\mathbf{I}$ in MATLAB programs. A statement eye(n) gives an $n \times n$ identity matrix. That is,

```
eye(5)

ans =

     1     0     0     0     0
     0     1     0     0     0
     0     0     1     0     0
     0     0     0     1     0
     0     0     0     0     1
```

Diagonal matrix

If **x** is a vector, a statement diag(x) produces a diagonal matrix with **x** on the diagonal line. For example, for a vector

$$x = [ones(1,n)]$$

diag([ones(1,n)]) gives an $n \times n$ identity matrix as follows:

```
diag([ones(1,5)])

ans =

     1    0    0    0    0
     0    1    0    0    0
     0    0    1    0    0
     0    0    0    1    0
     0    0    0    0    1
```

If **A** is a square matrix, then diag(A) is a vector consisting of the diagonal of **A**, and diag(diag(A)) is a diagonal matrix with elements of diag(A) appearing on the diagonal line. See the following MATLAB output.

```
A = [1   2   3;4   5   6;7   8   9];
diag(A)

ans =

     1
     5
     9

diag(diag(A))

ans =

     1    0    0
     0    5    0
     0    0    9
```

Note that diag(1:5) gives

```
diag(1:5)

ans =

     1    0    0    0    0
     0    2    0    0    0
     0    0    3    0    0
     0    0    0    4    0
     0    0    0    0    5
```

Also, diag(0:4) gives

```
diag(0:4)

ans =

     0     0     0     0     0
     0     1     0     0     0
     0     0     2     0     0
     0     0     0     3     0
     0     0     0     0     4
```

Hence diag(1:5) − diag(0:4) is an identity matrix.

```
[diag(1:5)−diag(0:4)]

ans =

     1     0     0     0     0
     0     1     0     0     0
     0     0     1     0     0
     0     0     0     1     0
     0     0     0     0     1
```

Similarly, diag(3:7) − diag(2:6) is an identity matrix.

It is important to note that diag(0,n) is quite different from diag(0:n). diag(0,n) is an $(n + 1) \times (n + 1)$ matrix consisting of all zero elements. See the following MATLAB output.

```
diag(0,4)

ans =

     0     0     0     0     0
     0     0     0     0     0
     0     0     0     0     0
     0     0     0     0     0
     0     0     0     0     0
```

2-4 PLOTTING RESPONSE CURVES

MATLAB has an extensive set of routines for obtaining graphical output. The plot command creates linear x–y plots. (Logarithmic and polar plots are created by substituting the words loglog, semilogx, semilogy, or polar for plot.) All such commands are used the same way: they only affect how the axis is scaled and how the data are displayed.

x–y plot

If **x** and **y** are vectors of the same length, the command

plot(x,y)

plots the values in y against the values in x.

Plotting multiple curves

To plot multiple curves on a single graph, use the plot command with multiple arguments.

plot(X1, Y1, X2, Y2, ..., Xn, Yn)

The variables X1, Y1, X2, Y2, and so on, are pairs of vectors. Each x–y pair is graphed, generating multiple curves on the plot. Multiple arguments have the benefit of allowing vectors of different lengths to be displayed on the same graph. Each pair uses a different line type.

Plotting more than one curve on a single graph may also be accomplished by using the command hold. The hold command freezes the current plot and inhibits erasure and rescaling. Hence subsequent curves will be overplotted on the original curve. Entering the command hold again releases the current plot.

Adding grid lines, title of the graph,
x-axis label, and y-axis label

Once a graph is on the screen, grid lines may be drawn, the graph may be titled, and x and y axes may be labeled. MATLAB commands for grid, title, x-axis label, and y-axis label are

grid   (grid lines)
title   (graph title)
xlabel (*x*-axis label)
ylabel (*y*-axis label)

Note that, once the command display has been brought back, grid lines, graph title, and x and y labels can be put on the plot by successively entering the commands.

Writing text on the graphic screen

To write text beginning at point (X, Y) on the graphic screen, use the command

text(X,Y,'text')

For example, the statement

text(3,0.45, 'sin t')

will write sin t horizontally beginning at point (3, 0.45). Also, the statements

plot(x1,y1,x2,y2), text(x1,y1,'1'), text(x2,y2,'2')

mark two curves so that they can be distinguished easily. (See Examples 2-1 and 2-2 for writing text on the graphics screen.)

Getting a hard copy

A hard copy of the graph on the screen can be obtained by pressing *Print-Scrn* key.

EXAMPLE 2-1

Enter the following MATLAB command program and show the resulting plot.

```
t = 0:0.05:10;
y = sin(t);
z = cos(t);
plot(t,y,'o',t,z,'x')
grid
title('Sine and Cosine Curves')
xlabel('Sec')
ylabel('y = sin t ; z = cos t')
text(3,0.45, 'sin t')
text(0.8,−0.3, 'cos t')
```

Note that the vector *t* is a partition of the domain $0 \leq t \leq 10$ with mesh size 0.05, while *y* and *z* are vectors giving the values of sine and cosine at the nodes of the partition. Figure 2-1 shows the resulting plot of sine and cosine curves.

When in the graphics screen, note that pressing any key will cause MATLAB to show the command screen. By using the *up-arrow* key, enter any one of the last seven commands (plot, grid, title, xlabel, ylabel, text, text). MATLAB will then show the current graphics screen. Also, if the command shg (show graph) is entered, MATLAB will show the current graphics screen.

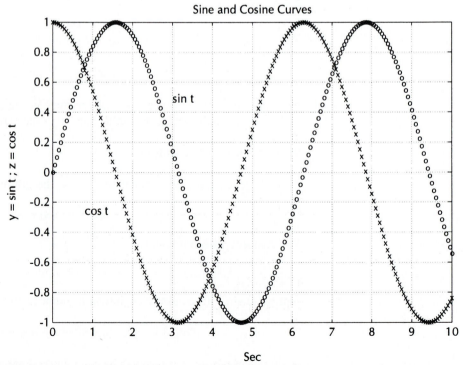

Figure 2-1

EXAMPLE 2-2

Enter the following MATLAB command program and show the resulting plot.

```
t = 0:0.25:10;
y = sin(t);
z = cos(t);
plot(t,y,t,z),text(t,y,'y'),text(t,z,'z')
grid
title('Sine and Cosine Curves')
xlabel('Sec')
ylabel('y = sin t ; z = cos t')
```

Figure 2-2 shows the resulting plot of the sine and cosine curves.

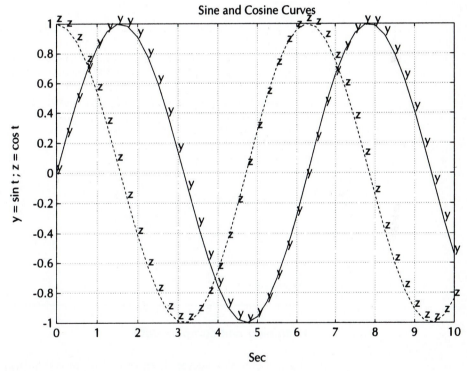

Figure 2-2

EXAMPLE 2-3

Plot the graph of

$$y = x^2$$

over the interval $0 \le x \le 3$ with increments of 0.1. The MATLAB program for this example problem is

```
x = 0:0.1:3;
y = x.^2;
plot(x,y)
grid
title('Plot of y = x^2')
xlabel('x')
ylabel('y')
```

Note that it is necessary that '$^\wedge 2$' is preceded by a period to ensure that it operates entrywise. Figure 2-3 shows the resulting plot.

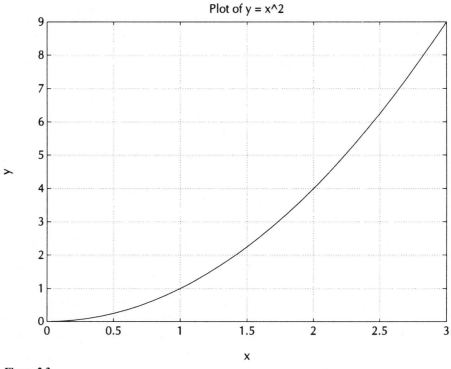

Figure 2-3

Imaginary and complex data

If **z** is a complex vector, then plot(z) is equivalent to plot(real(z),imag(z)).

Polar plots

polar(theta,rho) will give a plot in polar coordinates of the angle theta (in radians) versus radius rho. Subsequent use of the grid command draws polar grid lines.

Logarithmic plots

log log:	a plot using $\log_{10}$–$\log_{10}$ scales
semilogx:	a plot using semilog scales; the x axis is $\log_{10}$, while the y axis is linear
semilogy:	a plot using semilog scales; the y axis is $\log_{10}$, while the x axis is linear

Other types of plots

bar(x):   displays a bar chart of the elements of vector **x**; bar does not accept multiple arguments

stairs: similar to bar, but missing the vertical lines; this produces a stairstep plot useful for graphing signals in discrete-time (samples data) systems

Automatic plotting algorithms

In MATLAB the plot is automatically scaled. This plot remains as the current plot until another is plotted, in which case the old plot is erased and the axis is automatically rescaled. The automatic plotting algorithms for transient-response curves, root loci, Bode diagrams, Nyquist plots, and the like, are designed to work with a wide range of systems but are not always perfect. Thus, in certain situations, it may become desirable to override the automatic axis scaling feature of the plot command and to manually select the plotting limits.

Manual axis scaling

If it is desired to plot a curve in a region specified by

$$v = [\text{x-min} \quad \text{x-max} \quad \text{y-min} \quad \text{y-max}]$$

enter the command axis(v). axis(v), where v is a four-element vector, sets the axis scaling to the prescribed limits. For logarithmic plots, the elements of v are $\log_{10}$ of the minimums and maximums.

Executing axis(v) freezes the current axis scaling for subsequent plots. Typing axis again resumes autoscaling.

axis('square') sets the plot region on the screen to be square. With a square aspect ratio, a line with slope 1 is at a true 45°, not skewed by the irregular shape of the screen. axis('normal') sets the aspect ratio back to normal.

Plot type

$$\text{plot}(X,Y,'x')$$

draws a point plot using ×-mark symbols, while

$$\text{plot}(X1, Y1, ':', X2, Y2, '+')$$

uses a dotted line for the first curve and the plus symbol + for the second curve. Other line and point types are as follows:

Line types		Point types	
solid	–	point	•
dashed	– –	plus	+
dotted	:	star	*
dash-dot	–•	circle	○
		×-mark	×

Color

Statements

$$\text{plot}(X,Y,\text{'r'})$$
$$\text{plot}(X,Y,\text{'+g'})$$

indicate the use of a red line on the first graph and green + marks on the second. Other colors are

red	r
green	g
blue	b
white	w
invisible	i

2-5 MATHEMATICAL MODELS OF LINEAR SYSTEMS

MATLAB has useful commands to transform a mathematical model of a linear system to another model. Such linear system transformations useful for solving control engineering problems are listed in the following.

Transfer function to state space

The command

$$[A,B,C,D] = \text{tf2ss}(\text{num},\text{den})$$

converts the system in the transfer function form

$$\frac{Y(s)}{U(s)} = \frac{\text{num}}{\text{den}} = \mathbf{C}(s\mathbf{I} - \mathbf{A})^{-1}\mathbf{B} + D$$

to the state-space form

$$\dot{\mathbf{x}} = \mathbf{A}\mathbf{x} + \mathbf{B}u$$
$$y = \mathbf{C}\mathbf{x} + Du$$

State space to transfer function

If the system has one input and one output, the command

$$[\text{num, den}] = \text{ss2tf}(A,B,C,D)$$

yields the transfer function $Y(s)/U(s)$.

If the system involves more than one input, use the following command:

$$[\text{num,den}] = \text{ss2tf}(A,B,C,D,iu)$$

This command converts the system in state space

$$\dot{\mathbf{x}} = \mathbf{A}\mathbf{x} + \mathbf{B}\mathbf{u}$$
$$y = \mathbf{C}\mathbf{x} + \mathbf{D}\mathbf{u}$$

to the transfer function

$$\frac{Y(s)}{U_i(s)} = \mathbf{C}(s\mathbf{I} - \mathbf{A})^{-1}\mathbf{B} + \mathbf{D}$$

Note that the scalar 'iu' is an index into the inputs of the system and specifies which input is to be used for the response.

Consider, for example, the following system, which has two inputs, u_1 and u_2.

$$\begin{bmatrix} \dot{x}_1 \\ \dot{x}_2 \end{bmatrix} = \begin{bmatrix} 0 & 1 \\ -2 & -3 \end{bmatrix}\begin{bmatrix} x_1 \\ x_2 \end{bmatrix} + \begin{bmatrix} 1 & 0 \\ 0 & 1 \end{bmatrix}\begin{bmatrix} u_1 \\ u_2 \end{bmatrix}$$

$$y = \begin{bmatrix} 1 & 0 \end{bmatrix}\begin{bmatrix} x_1 \\ x_2 \end{bmatrix} + \begin{bmatrix} 0 & 0 \end{bmatrix}\begin{bmatrix} u_1 \\ u_2 \end{bmatrix}$$

Two transfer functions may be obtained for this system. One relates the output y and input u_1, and the other relates the output y and input u_2. (When considering input u_1, we assume that input u_2 is zero, and vice versa.) See the following MATLAB output.

```
A = [0   1;−2   −3];
B = [1   0;0   1];
C = [1   0];
D = [0   0];

[num,den] = ss2tf(A,B,C,D,1)

num =

        0    1    3


den =

        1    3    2

[num,den] = ss2tf(A,B,C,D,2)

num =

        0    0    1


den =

        1    3    2
```

From the MATLAB output, we have

$$\frac{Y(s)}{U_1(s)} = \frac{s + 3}{s^2 + 3s + 2}$$

and

$$\frac{Y(s)}{U_2(s)} = \frac{1}{s^2 + 3s + 2}$$

(For further discussion of systems having multiple inputs and multiple outputs, refer to Section 3-5.)

Partial-fraction expansion of the transfer function

Consider the transfer function

$$\frac{B(s)}{A(s)} = \frac{\text{num}}{\text{den}} = \frac{b(1)s^n + b(2)s^{n-1} + \cdots + b(n)}{a(1)s^n + a(2)s^{n-1} + \cdots + a(n)}$$

where $a(1) \neq 0$, but some of $a(i)$ and $b(j)$ may be zero.

Row vectors num and den specify the coefficients of the numerator and denominator of the transfer function. That is,

$$\text{num} = [b(1) \quad b(2) \quad \cdots \quad b(n)]$$
$$\text{den} = [a(1) \quad a(2) \quad \cdots \quad a(n)]$$

The command

$$[\text{r,p,k}] = \text{residue(num,den)}$$

finds the residues, poles, and direct terms of a partial-fraction expansion of the ratio of two polynomials $B(s)$ and $A(s)$. The partial-fraction expansion of $B(s)/A(s)$ is given by

$$\frac{B(s)}{A(s)} = \frac{r(1)}{s - p(1)} + \frac{r(2)}{s - p(2)} + \cdots + \frac{r(n)}{s - p(n)} + k(s)$$

As an example, consider the following transfer function:

$$\frac{B(s)}{A(s)} = \frac{2s^3 + 5s^2 + 3s + 6}{s^3 + 6s^2 + 11s + 6}$$

For this function,

$$\text{num} = [2 \quad 5 \quad 3 \quad 6]$$
$$\text{den} = [1 \quad 6 \quad 11 \quad 6]$$

The command

$$[\text{r,p,k}] = \text{residue(num,den)}$$

gives the following result:

```
[r,p,k] = residue(num,den)

r =

        −6.0000
        −4.0000
         3.0000


p =

        −3.0000
        −2.0000
        −1.0000


k =

     2
```

(Note that the residues are returned in column vector r, the pole locations in column vector p, and the direct term in row vector k.) This is the MATLAB representation of the following partial-fraction expansion of $B(s)/A(s)$;

$$\frac{B(s)}{A(s)} = \frac{2s^3 + 5s^2 + 3s + 6}{(s + 1)(s + 2)(s + 3)}$$

$$= \frac{-6}{s + 3} + \frac{-4}{s + 2} + \frac{3}{s + 1} + 2$$

The command

$$[num,den] = residue(r,p,k)$$

where r, p, k are as given in the previous MATLAB output, converts the partial-fraction expansion back to the polynomial ratio $B(s)/A(s)$, as follows:

```
[num,den] = residue(r,p,k)

num =

     2.0000    5.0000    3.0000    6.0000


den =

     1.0000    6.0000   11.0000    6.0000
```

Conversion from continuous time to discrete time

The command

$$[G,H] = c2d(A,B,Ts)$$

where Ts is the sampling time in seconds, converts the state-space model from continuous time to discrete time, assuming a zero-order hold on the inputs. That is, with this command

$$\dot{\mathbf{x}} = \mathbf{A}\mathbf{x} + \mathbf{B}\mathbf{u}$$

is converted to

$$\mathbf{x}(k + 1) = \mathbf{G}\mathbf{x}(k) + \mathbf{H}\mathbf{u}(k)$$

Chapter 3   Transient-Response Analysis of Continuous-Time Systems

3-1 INTRODUCTION

Transient responses (such as step response, impulse response, and ramp response) are used frequently to investigate the time-domain characteristics of control systems. Transient-response characteristics such as rise time, peak time, maximum overshoot, settling time, and steady-state error can be determined from the step response.

If num and den (the numerator and denominator of the closed-loop transfer function) are known, commands such as

$$step(num,den), \qquad step(num,den,t)$$

will generate plots of unit-step responses. (t in the step command is the user-specified time.)

For a control system defined in a state-space form, where state matrix **A**, control matrix **B**, output matrix **C**, and direct transmission matrix **D** of state-space equations are known, the command

$$step(A,B,C,D)$$

will generate plots of unit-step responses. The time vector is automatically determined when t is not explicitly included in the step commands.

Note that when step commands have left-hand arguments such as

$$[y,x,t] = step(num,den,t)$$
$$[y,x,t] = step(A,B,C,D,iu)$$
$$[y,x,t] = step(A,B,C,D,iu,t) \qquad (3-1)$$

no plot is shown on the screen. Hence it is necessary to use a *plot* command to see the response curves. The matrices y and x contain the output and state response of the system, respectively, evaluated at the computation time points t. (y has as many columns as outputs and one row for each element in t. x has as many columns as states and one row for each element in t.)

Note in Eq. (3-1) that the scalar iu is an index into the inputs of the system and specifies which input is to be used for the response, and t is the user-specified time. If the system involves multiple inputs and multiple outputs, the *step* command, such as given by Eq. (3-1), produces a series of step response plots, one for each input and output combination of

$$\dot{x} = Ax + Bu$$
$$y = Cx + Du$$

The impulse response or ramp response of the control system may be obtained by multiplying or dividing the closed-loop transfer function by s and using the step command. (See Sections 3-3 and 3-4.)

MATLAB representation of linear systems

The transfer function of a system (in the s or z domain) is represented by two arrays of numbers. Consider the system

$$G(s) = \frac{2s + 4}{s^3 + 1.3s^2 + 7s + 4}$$

This system is represented as two arrays each containing the coefficients of the polynomials in decreasing powers of s as follows:

$$\text{num} = \begin{bmatrix} 0 & 0 & 2 & 4 \end{bmatrix}$$
$$\text{den} = \begin{bmatrix} 1 & 1.3 & 7 & 4 \end{bmatrix}$$

Note that zeros must be padded where necessary.

It is important to note that if, by mistake, we enter the denominator of this transfer function as

$$\text{den} = \begin{bmatrix} 1 & 1,3 & 7 & 4 \end{bmatrix}$$

this denominator is completely different from the correct one. Because of the presence of a comma between 1 and 3, this denominator means

$$\text{den} = \begin{bmatrix} 1 & 1 & 3 & 7 & 4 \end{bmatrix}$$

Therefore, the response of the original system and the mistyped system are completely different. Always avoid such an innocent mistake as typing a comma instead of a period.

Outline of the chapter

Section 2-1 has presented an introduction to step response. Sections 3-2, 3-3, and 3-4 treat in detail the step response, impulse response, and ramp response, respectively. Section 3-5 discusses transformations of the system model from state space to transfer function, and vice versa.

3-2 STEP RESPONSE

We shall begin this section with a simple case.

Obtaining the unit-step response of the transfer-function system

Consider the system

$$\frac{C(s)}{R(s)} = \frac{25}{s^2 + 4s + 25}$$

Obtain a plot of the unit-step response curve.

MATLAB Program 3-1 will yield a plot of the unit-step response of this system. A plot of the unit-step-response curve is shown in Figure 3-1.

```
MATLAB Program 3–1

% ---------- Unit-step response ----------

% ***** Unit-step response of transfer-function system *****

% ***** Enter the numerator and denominator of the transfer
% function *****

num = [0   0   25];
den = [1   4   25];

% ***** Enter the following step-response command *****

step(num,den)

% ***** Enter grid and title of the plot *****

grid
title('Unit-Step Response of G(s) = 25/(s^2 + 4s + 25)')
```

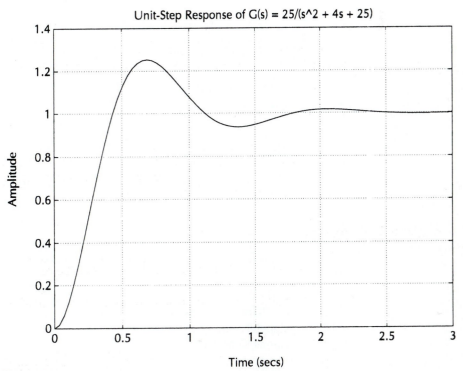

Figure 3-1

EXAMPLE 3-1

Obtain the unit-step response of the system shown in Figure 3-2. The closed-loop transfer function can be obtained as follows:

$$\frac{C(s)}{R(s)} = \frac{6.3223s^2 + 18s + 12.8112}{s^4 + 6s^3 + 11.3223s^2 + 18s + 12.8112}$$

Obtain a plot of the response curve marked with 'o'.

To obtain a plot of the response curve marked with 'o', enter MATLAB Program 3-2 into the computer. The resulting response curve is shown in Figure 3-3.

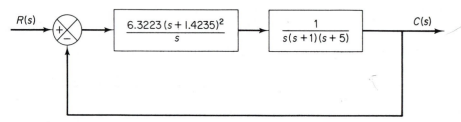

Figure 3-2

MATLAB Program 3–2

```
% ---------- Unit-step response ----------

% ***** If it is desired to plot the unit-step response
% curve with marks 'o', 'x', '--', etc., use the program
% shown below *****

% ***** Enter the numerator and denominator of the
% closed-loop transfer function *****

num = [0  0  6.3223  18  12.8112];
den = [1  6  11.3223  18  12.8112];

% ***** Enter the following step-response command and
% plot command *****

[c,x,t] = step(num,den); plot(t,c,'o')

% ***** Add grid, title, xlabel, and ylabel *****

grid
title('Unit-Step Response')
xlabel('t Sec')
ylabel('Output c')
```

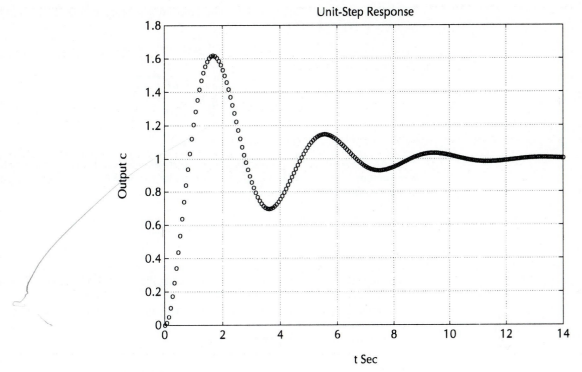

Figure 3-3

EXAMPLE 3-2

Consider the control system shown in Figure 3-4. In this system the proportional controller delivers torque T to position the load element, which consists of moment of inertia and viscous friction. The torque disturbance to the system is denoted by N.

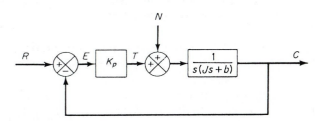

Figure 3-4

Assuming that the reference input is zero or $R(s) = 0$, the transfer function between $C(s)$ and $N(s)$ is given by

$$\frac{C(s)}{N(s)} = \frac{1}{Js^2 + bs + K_p}$$

Hence

$$\frac{E(s)}{N(s)} = -\frac{C(s)}{N(s)} = -\frac{1}{Js^2 + bs + K_p}$$

The steady-state error due to a step disturbance torque of magnitude T_n is given by

$$e_{ss} = \lim_{s \to 0} sE(s)$$

$$= \lim_{s \to 0} \frac{-s}{Js^2 + bs + K_p} \frac{T_n}{s}$$

$$= -\frac{T_n}{K_p}$$

At steady state, the proportional controller provides the torque $-T_n$, which is equal in magnitude but opposite in sign to the disturbance torque T_n. The steady-state output due to the step disturbance torque is

$$c_{ss} = -e_{ss} = \frac{T_n}{K_p}$$

The steady-state error can be reduced by increasing the value of the gain K_p. Increasing this value, however, will cause the system response to be more oscillatory.

Obtain step-response curves for a small value of K_p and a large value of K_p. Plot two step-response curves on one diagram.

We shall consider two cases:

Case 1 $J = 1, b = 0.5, K_p = 1$ (system 1):

$$\frac{C(s)}{N(s)} = \frac{1}{s^2 + 0.5s + 1}$$

Case 2 $J = 1, b = 0.5, K_p = 4$ (system 2):

$$\frac{C(s)}{N(s)} = \frac{1}{s^2 + 0.5s + 4}$$

Note that for system 1

$$\text{num1} = [0 \quad 0 \quad 1]$$
$$\text{den1} = [1 \quad 0.5 \quad 1]$$

For system 2

$$\text{num2} = [0 \quad 0 \quad 1]$$
$$\text{den2} = [1 \quad 0.5 \quad 4]$$

MATLAB Program 3-3 will give plots of two step-response curves on one diagram. In this program we have used notations y1 and y2 for the response. y1 is the response $c(t)$ of system 1, and y2 is the response $c(t)$ of System 2.

When plotting multiple curves on one diagram, we may use the *hold* command. If we enter the command hold in the computer, the screen will show

```
hold

Current plot held
```

MATLAB Program 3–3

```
% ---------- Plotting two step-response curves on one
% diagram ----------
%
% ***** Enter numerators and denominators of two
% transfer functions *****

num1 = [0   0   1];
den1 = [1   0.5   1];
num2 = [0   0   1];
den2 = [1   0.5   4];

% ***** To plot two step-response curves y1 versus t
% and y2 versus t on one diagram, enter the following
% commands *****

step(num1,den1);
hold

Current plot held

step(num2,den2);
grid
title('Step Responses of Two Systems')

% ***** Clear hold on graphics *****

hold

Current plot released
```

To release the held plot, enter the command hold again. Then the current plot will be released. See the following statements:

```
hold

Current plot held

hold

Current plot released
```

The two step-response curves obtained are shown in Figure 3-5.

Notice in Figure 3-5 that the x-axis and y-axis labels are automatically determined. If it is desired to label the x axis and y axis differently, we need to modify the step command. For example, if it is desired to label the x axis as 't Sec' and the y axis as 'Outputs y1 and y2', then use the step-response command with left-hand arguments, such as

$$[y, x, t] = step(num, den, t)$$

See MATLAB Program 3-4.

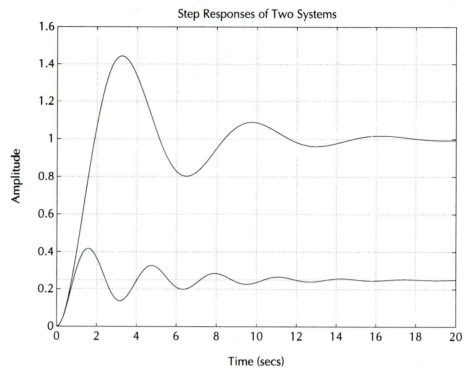

Figure 3-5

If it is desired to indicate which curves represent system 1 and system 2, respectively, we may enter the *text* command. In what follows we shall consider two cases.

a. *Write text on the graphics screen*   To write text on the graphics screen, enter, for example, the following statements:

$$\text{text(9, 0.9, 'System 1')}$$

and

$$\text{text(9, 0.15, 'System 2')}$$

The first statement tells the computer to write 'System 1' beginning at the coordinates $x = 9$, $y = 0.9$. Similarly, the second statement tells the computer to write 'System 2' beginning at the coordinates $x = 9$, $y = 0.15$. See MATLAB Program 3-4. The resulting plot is shown in Figure 3-6.

In MATLAB Program 3-4, note that we have used the *plot* command with multiple arguments, rather than using the *hold* command. (We get the same result either way.) To use the *plot* command with multiple arguments, the sizes of the y1 and y2 vectors need not be the same. However, it is convenient if the two vectors are of the same length. Hence, we specify the same number of computing points by specifying the computing time points (such as t = 0:0.1:20). The *step* command must include this user-specified time t. Thus, in MATLAB Program 3-4 we have used the following *step* command:

$$[y, x, t] = \text{step(num, den, t)}$$

b. *Mark entire curves with text*   To mark the entire curves with text, use the following statements:

$$\text{text(t,y1,'1'),}\qquad \text{text(t,y2,'2')}$$

MATLAB Program 3–4

```
% ---------- Plotting two step-response curves on one
% diagram ----------

% ***** Enter numerators and denominators of two
% transfer functions *****

num1 = [0   0   1];
den1 = [1   0.5   1];
num2 = [0   0   1];
den2 = [1   0.5   4];

% ***** To plot two step-response curves y1 versus t
% and y2 versus t on one diagram and write texts
% 'System 1' and 'System 2' to distinguish two curves,
% enter the following commands *****

t = 0:0.1:20;
[y1,x1,t] = step(num1,den1,t);
[y2,x2,t] = step(num2,den2,t);
plot(t,y1,t,y2)
grid
text(9,0.9,'System 1'), text(9,0.15,'System 2')

% ***** Add title of the plot, xlabel, and ylabel *****

title('Step Responses of Two Systems')
xlabel('t Sec')
ylabel('Outputs y1 and y2')
```

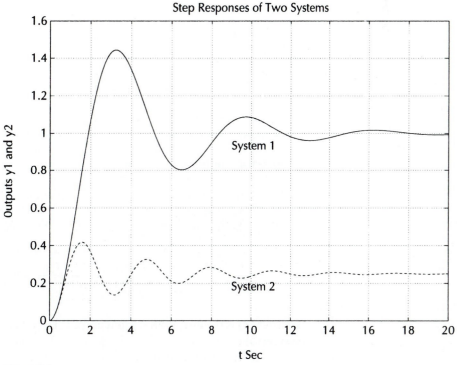

Figure 3-6

Using these statements, the curves will be marked with 1 and 2, respectively, so that they can be distinguished easily. For this case, see MATLAB Program 3-5. (In this program we used the *plot* command with multiple arguments.) The resulting plot is shown in Figure 3-7.

MATLAB Program 3–5

```
% ---------- Plotting two step-response curves on one
% diagram ----------

% ***** Enter numerators and denominators of two
% transfer functions *****

num1 = [0   0   1];
den1 = [1   0.5   1];
num2 = [0   0   1];
den2 = [1   0.5   4];

% ***** To plot two step-response curves y1 versus t and
% y2 versus t on one diagram with curves marked '1' and '2',
% respectively, enter the following commands *****

t = 0:0.4:20;
[y1,x1,t] = step(num1,den1,t);
[y2,x2,t] = step(num2,den2,t);
plot(t,y1,'o',t,y2,'o')
text(t,y1,'1'), text(t,y2,'2')

% ***** Add grid, title of the plot, xlabel, and ylabel *****

grid
title('Step Responses of Two Systems')
xlabel('t Sec')
ylabel('Outputs y1 and y2')
```

Step response (singular case)

In obtaining the unit-step response, some singular cases will cause division by zero in MATLAB computations. An example of such a singular case is discussed here. Consider the following closed-loop transfer function system:

$$\frac{C(s)}{N(s)} = \frac{s}{2s^2 + 2s + 1}$$

where $N(s)$ is the disturbance input and $C(s)$ is the corresponding output. In control systems the effect of the disturbance must be made as small as possible. (In this system for a step disturbance input, the output due to this step disturbance becomes zero at steady state.)

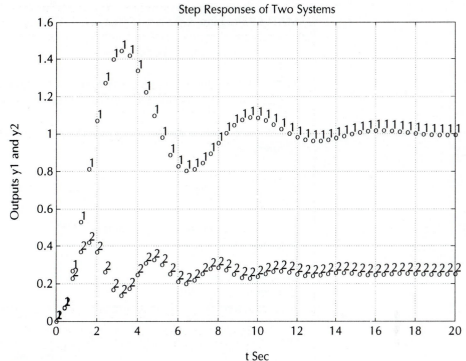

Figure 3-7

Let us obtain the response $c(t)$ to the unit-step disturbance input. Since $N(s) = 1/s$, we obtain

$$C(s) = \frac{s}{2s^2 + 2s + 1} \frac{1}{s} = \frac{1}{2s^2 + 2s + 1}$$

The inverse Laplace transform of $C(s)$ gives

$$c(t) = e^{-0.5t} \sin 0.5t$$

The response $c(t)$ damps out to zero.

Now, let us obtain this step response with MATLAB. MATLAB Program 3-6 may be used to obtain the response to the unit-step disturbance input. Note that the command

$$\text{step(num, den)}$$

may not give the step response. The warning message 'Divide by zero' may appear on the screen. When such a warning message appears, enter the specific computing time points (such as $t = 0{:}0.1{:}12$) and enter the user-specified time t in the *step* command as follows:

$$\text{step(num, den, t)}$$

Then the response $c(t)$ can be obtained. The plot generated by MATLAB Program 3-6 is shown in Figure 3-8.

An alternative way to avoid this type of difficulty (division by zero) is to change num and/or den slightly. For example, in this example problem, if we change the denominator polynomial from $2s^2 + 2s + 1$ to $2s^2 + 2s + 0.9999$ (or, say, $2s^2 + 1.9999s + 1$, or the like), we can eliminate this difficulty.

```
MATLAB Program 3–6
```

```
% ---------- Unit-step response ----------

% ***** We shall obtain unit-step response of singular case
% that will cause 'division by zero' in MATLAB computation *****

% ***** Enter numerator and denominator of the transfer
% function *****

num = [0   1   0];
den = [2   2   1];

% ***** Enter step-response command *****
step (num, den)

Warning: Divide by zero
[[[ Error using MM ltitr
Student system limit on maximum variable size exceeded.

Error in MM \MATLAB\SIGSYS\step.m
On line 85 MM x = ltitr(aa,bb,ones(n,l),zeros(nb,mb));

% ***** If this type of warning/error message appears, then
% specify the computing time points (such as t = 0:0.1:12)
% and enter the following step-response command:
% step(num,den,t) *****

t = 0:0.1:12;
step(num,den,t)

% ***** Add grid and title of the plot *****

grid
title('Unit-Step Response')
```

EXAMPLE 3-3

Consider the system shown in Figure 3-9. Obtain the responses of the system to the unit-step reference input and unit-step disturbance input.

Response to unit-step reference input The closed-loop transfer function for the system, assuming $U_d(s) = 0$, is obtained as follows:

$$\frac{C(s)}{R(s)} = \frac{\dfrac{10.4(s^2 + 4.5192s + 15.385)}{s}\dfrac{1}{s^2 + 3.6s + 9}}{1 + \dfrac{10.4(s^2 + 4.5192s + 15.385)}{s(s^2 + 3.6s + 9)}}$$

$$= \frac{10.4s^2 + 47s + 160}{s^3 + 14s^2 + 56s + 160}$$

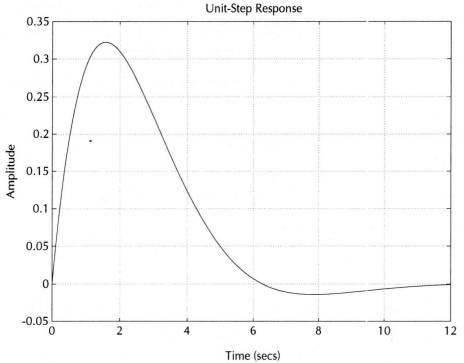

Figure 3-8

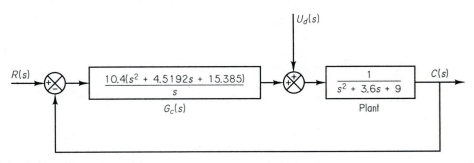

Figure 3-9

Hence, the unit-step response of this system, when there is no disturbance input, can be obtained by entering MATLAB Program 3-7 into the computer. A plot of this response is shown in Figure 3-10.

Response to unit-step disturbance input The response to a unit-step disturbance input may be obtained by assuming the reference input to be zero. The closed-loop transfer function between $C(s)$ and $U_d(s)$ is obtained as follows:

$$\frac{C(s)}{U_d(s)} = \frac{\dfrac{1}{s^2 + 3.6s + 9}}{1 + \dfrac{10.4(s^2 + 4.5192s + 15.385)}{s} \dfrac{1}{s^2 + 3.6s + 9}}$$

$$= \frac{s}{s^3 + 14s^2 + 56s + 160}$$

MATLAB Program 3–7

% ---------- Response to unit-step rererence input ----------

num = [0   10.4   47   160];
den = [1   14   56   160];
v = [0   5   0   1.4];
axis(v);
t = 0:0.05:5;
step(num,den,t)
grid
title('Response to Unit-Step Reference Input')

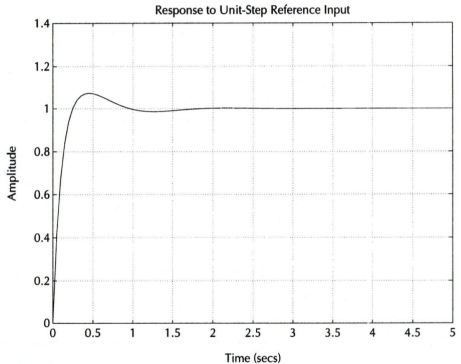

Figure 3-10

MATLAB Program 3-8 may be entered into the computer to obtain a plot of the response to a unit-step disturbance input. A plot of this response is shown in Figure 3-11.

MATLAB Program 3–8

```
% ---------- Response to unit-step disturbance input ----------

num = [0  0  1  0];
den = [1  14  56  160];
v = [0  10  -0.04  0.04];
axis(v);
t = 0:0.1:10;
step(num,den,t)
grid
title('Response to Unit-Step Disturbance Input')
```

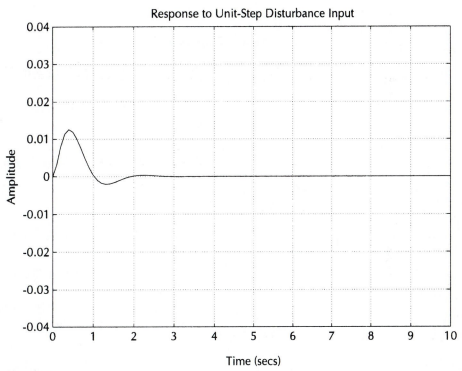

Figure 3-11

EXAMPLE 3-4

In this example, we shall consider a system subjected only to an initial condition.

Consider the mechanical system shown in Figure 3-12, where $m = 1$ kg, $b = 3$ N-s/m, and $k = 2$ N/m. Assume that at $t = 0$ the mass m is pulled downward such that $x(0) = 0.1$ m and $\dot{x}(0) = 0.05$ m/s. Obtain the motion of the mass subjected to the initial condition. (Assume no external forcing function.)

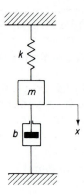

Figure 3-12

The system equation is

$$m\ddot{x} + b\dot{x} + kx = 0$$

with the initial conditions $x(0) = 0.1$ m and $\dot{x}(0) = 0.05$ m/s. The Laplace transform of the system equation gives

$$m[s^2X(s) - sx(0) - \dot{x}(0)] + b[sX(s) - x(0)] + kX(s) = 0$$

or

$$(ms^2 + bs + k)X(s) = mx(0)s + m\dot{x}(0) + bx(0)$$

Solving this last equation for $X(s)$ and substituting the given numerical values, we obtain

$$X(s) = \frac{mx(0)s + m\dot{x}(0) + bx(0)}{ms^2 + bs + k}$$

$$= \frac{0.1s + 0.35}{s^2 + 3s + 2}$$

This equation can be written as

$$X(s) = \frac{0.1s^2 + 0.35s}{s^2 + 3s + 2}\frac{1}{s}$$

Hence the motion of the mass m may be obtained as the unit-step response of the following system:

$$G(s) = \frac{0.1s^2 + 0.35s}{s^2 + 3s + 2}$$

MATLAB Program 3-9 will give a plot of the motion of the mass. The plot is shown in Figure 3-13.

MATLAB Program 3–9

```
% ---------- Response to initial conditions ----------

% ***** System response to inital conditions is converted to
% a unit-step response by modifying the numerator polynomial *****

% ***** Enter the numerator and denominator of the transfer
% function G(s) *****

num = [0.1   0.35   0];
den = [1   3   2];

% ***** Enter the following step-response command *****

step(num,den)

% ***** Enter grid and title of the plot *****

grid
title('Response of Spring-Mass-Damper System to Initial Conditions')
```

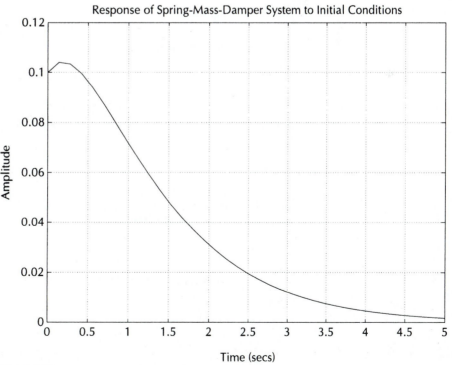

Figure 3-13

**Obtaining the unit-step response of the system
in state-space form**

Obtain the unit-step response of the following system:

$$\dot{\mathbf{x}} = \mathbf{A}\mathbf{x} + \mathbf{B}u$$
$$y = \mathbf{C}\mathbf{x} + Du$$

where

$$\mathbf{A} = \begin{bmatrix} 0 & 1 & 0 & 0 \\ 0 & 0 & 1 & 0 \\ 0 & 0 & 0 & 1 \\ -100 & -80 & -32 & -8 \end{bmatrix}, \quad \mathbf{B} = \begin{bmatrix} 0 \\ 0 \\ 5 \\ 60 \end{bmatrix}, \quad \mathbf{C} = \begin{bmatrix} 1 & 0 & 0 & 0 \end{bmatrix}, \quad D = 0$$

MATLAB Program 3-10 will produce a plot of the unit-step response curve. The resulting curve is shown in Figure 3-14.

MATLAB Program 3–10

```
% ---------- Unit-step response ----------

% ***** Enter matrices A, B, C, and D of the state-space
% equations *****

A = [0  1  0  0;0  0  1  0;0  0  0  1; -100  -80  -32  -8];
B = [0;0;5;60];
C = [1  0  0  0];
D = [0];

% ***** To obtain unit-step response y versus t, enter the
% following command *****

step(A,B,C,D)
grid
title('Unit-Step Response')
```

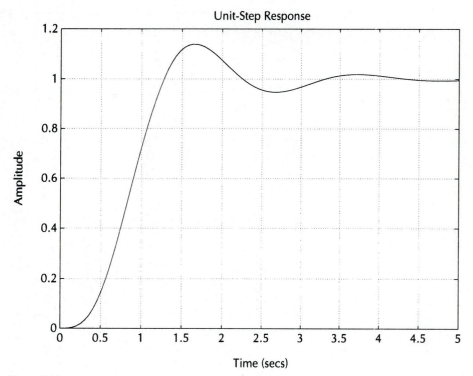

Figure 3-14

EXAMPLE 3-5

Obtain the unit-step response of the system described by the following state-space equations:

$$\begin{bmatrix} \dot{x}_1 \\ \dot{x}_2 \\ \dot{x}_3 \end{bmatrix} = \begin{bmatrix} 0 & 1 & 0 \\ 0 & 0 & 1 \\ -5.008 & -25.1026 & -5.0325 \end{bmatrix} \begin{bmatrix} x_1 \\ x_2 \\ x_3 \end{bmatrix} + \begin{bmatrix} 0 \\ 25.04 \\ -121.005 \end{bmatrix} u$$

$$y = \begin{bmatrix} 1 & 0 & 0 \end{bmatrix} \begin{bmatrix} x_1 \\ x_2 \\ x_3 \end{bmatrix}$$

MATLAB Program 3-11 will give a plot of the unit-step response of the system. A plot of the output $y(t)$ versus t is shown in Figure 3-15. It is important to note that, if we give the command

$$\text{plot(y)}$$

instead of plot(t,y), then y is plotted against computation points (280 points = 10 seconds in this example). See Figure 3-16 for the plot of y versus computation points. To plot y(t) versus t, it is necessary to enter the command plot(t,y).

To plot curves x1 versus t, x2 versus t, and x3 versus t on one diagram, simply enter the command plot(t,x).

In plotting x2 versus t and x3 versus t on separate diagrams, notice that

$$x2 = \begin{bmatrix} 0 & 1 & 0 \end{bmatrix} * x'$$
$$x3 = \begin{bmatrix} 0 & 0 & 1 \end{bmatrix} * x'$$

MATLAB Program 3–11

```
% ---------- Unit-step response ----------

% ***** Enter matrices A, B, C, and D of the state-space
% equations *****

A = [0  1  0 ;0  0  1;-5.008  -25.1026  -5.0325];
B = [0;25.04;-121.005];
C = [1  0  0];
D = [0];

% ***** Enter the following step-response command *****

[y,x,t] = step(A,B,C,D);
plot(t,y)
grid
title('Unit-Step Response')
xlabel('t Sec')
ylabel('Output y')
```

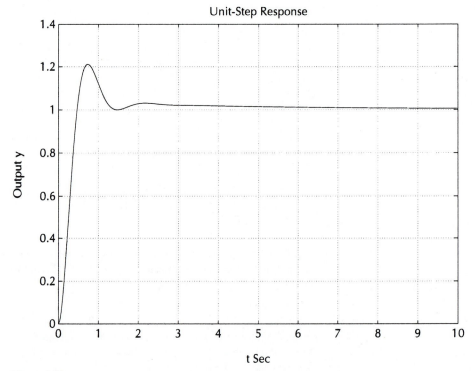

Figure 3-15

A MATLAB program to plot all three curves, x1 versus t, x2 versus t, and x3 versus t, on one diagram as well as to plot them on separate diagrams is given in MATLAB Program 3-12. A plot of three curves, x1 versus t, x2 versus t, and x3 versus t, on one diagram is shown in Figure 3-17. Separate plots of x2 versus t and x3 versus t are shown in Figures 3-18 and 3-19, respectively.

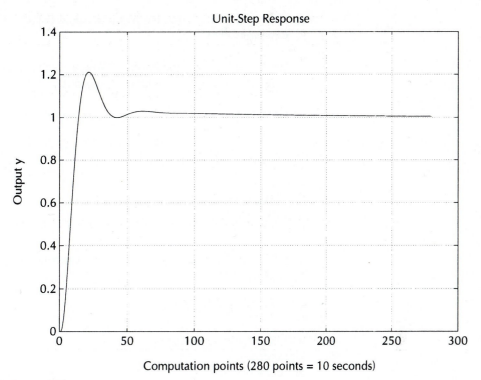

Figure 3-16

MATLAB Program 3–12

```
% ----------Step responses ----------

% ***** This program is a continuation of Program 3-11.
% See Program 3-11 for matrices A, B, C, D, and vectors y
% and x *****

% ***** To plot curves x1 versus t, x2 versus t, and
% x3 versus t on one digaram, enter the following
% plot command and text command *****

plot(t,x)
text(5,1.3,'x1')
text(5,-1.8,'x2')
text(5,-24.5,'x3')

% ***** Add grid, title, xlabel, and ylabel *****

grid
title('Step-Response Curves for x1, x2, and x3')
xlabel('t Sec')
ylabel('x1, x2, and x3')
```

```
% ***** In the following, we plot individual curves
% separately *****

% ***** Since x1 = y, the curve x1 versus t is the same
% as the curve y versus t obtained previously *****

% ***** To plot curve x2 versus t, enter the following
% command *****

x2 = [0   1   0]*x'; plot(t,x2)
grid
title('Response x2 versus t')
xlabel('t Sec')
ylabel('x2')

% ***** To plot curve x3 versus t, enter the following
% command *****

x3 = [0   0   1]*x'; plot(t,x3)
grid
title('Response x3 versus t')
xlabel('t Sec')
ylabel('x3')
```

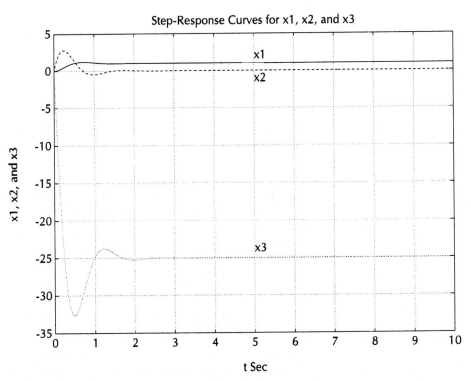

Figure 3-17

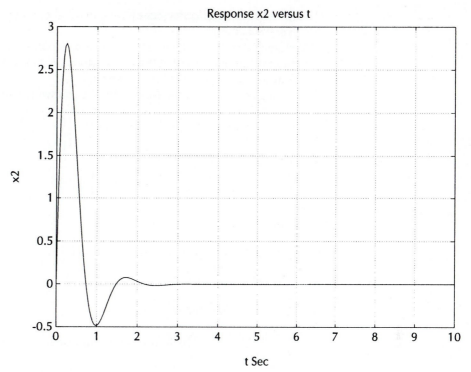

Figure 3-18

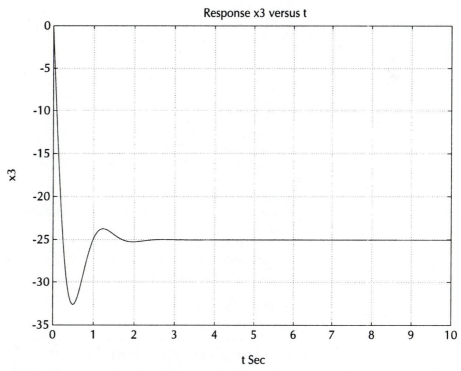

Figure 3-19

Step response (singular case)

As stated earlier, in obtaining the unit-step response, some singular cases will cause division by zero in MATLAB computations. We shall discuss again such a singular case here.

Consider the system defined by the following state-space equations:

$$\begin{bmatrix} \dot{x}_1 \\ \dot{x}_2 \end{bmatrix} = \begin{bmatrix} -1 & -0.5 \\ 1 & 0 \end{bmatrix} \begin{bmatrix} x_1 \\ x_2 \end{bmatrix} + \begin{bmatrix} 0.5 \\ 0 \end{bmatrix} u$$

$$y = \begin{bmatrix} 1 & 0 \end{bmatrix} \begin{bmatrix} x_1 \\ x_2 \end{bmatrix} + [0]u$$

```
MATLAB Program 3–13

% ---------- Unit-step response ----------

% ***** We shall obtain unit-step response of system
% defined in state space *****

% ***** Enter matrices A, B, C, and D *****

A = [-1  -0.5;1  0];
B = [0.5;0];
C = [1  0];
D = [0];

% ***** Enter step-response command *****

step(A,B,C,D);

Warning: Divide by zero
[[[ Error using MM ltitr
Student system limit on maximum variable size exceeded.

Error in MM \MATLAB\SIGSYS\step.m
On line 85 MM x = ltitr(aa,bb,ones(n,l),zeros(nb,mb));

% ***** If this type of warning message appears, then specify
% the computing time points (such as t = 0:0.1:12) and enter
% the following step-response command:  step(A,B,C,D,1,t) *****

t = 0:0.1:12;
step(A,B,C,D,1,t);

% ***** Add grid and title of the plot *****

grid
title('Unit-Step Response of System Defined in State Space')
```

MATLAB Program 3-13 may be used to obtain the response $y(t)$ versus t when the input u is a unit-step function. Note that the command

step(A,B,C,D)

will not give the step response. In this case a warning message, 'Divide by zero', may appear on the screen. If this happens, to obtain the response curve on the screen, enter a set of specific computing time points (such as t = 0:0.1:12) and enter the user-specified time t in the step command as follows:

step(A,B,C,D,1,t)

The resulting response curve is shown in Figure 3-20.
Note that if we enter the command

step(A,B,C,D,t)

a warning message, 'Index into matrix is negative or zero', will appear on the screen. Since this system involves only one input function u, enter the index '1' in the step command such that step(A,B,C,D,1,t).
An alternative way to avoid division by zero is to make a small change in one (or more) element of matrix **A**. For example, changing matrix **A** to

$$\begin{bmatrix} -1 & -0.4999 \\ 1 & 0 \end{bmatrix}, \qquad \begin{bmatrix} -1 & -0.5 \\ 0.9999 & 0 \end{bmatrix}$$

will eliminate the difficulty.

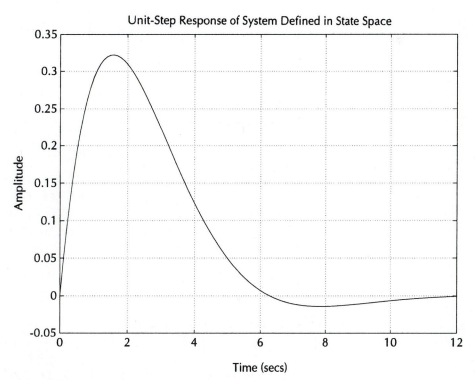

Figure 3-20

EXAMPLE 3-6

Consider the following system:

$$\begin{bmatrix} \dot{x}_1 \\ \dot{x}_2 \end{bmatrix} = \begin{bmatrix} -1 & -1 \\ 6.5 & 0 \end{bmatrix} \begin{bmatrix} x_1 \\ x_2 \end{bmatrix} + \begin{bmatrix} 1 & 1 \\ 1 & 0 \end{bmatrix} \begin{bmatrix} u_1 \\ u_2 \end{bmatrix}$$

$$\begin{bmatrix} y_1 \\ y_2 \end{bmatrix} = \begin{bmatrix} 1 & 0 \\ 0 & 1 \end{bmatrix} \begin{bmatrix} x_1 \\ x_2 \end{bmatrix} + \begin{bmatrix} 0 & 0 \\ 0 & 0 \end{bmatrix} \begin{bmatrix} u_1 \\ u_2 \end{bmatrix}$$

Obtain the unit-step response curves.

We shall first obtain the transfer matrix expression for the system:

$$\dot{x} = Ax + Bu$$
$$y = Cx + Du$$

The transfer matrix $G(s)$ is a matrix that relates $Y(s)$ and $U(s)$ as follows:

$$Y(s) = G(s)U(s)$$

Taking Laplace transforms of the state-space equations, we obtain

$$sX(s) - x(0) = AX(s) + BU(s) \tag{3-2}$$
$$Y(s) = CX(s) + DU(s) \tag{3-3}$$

In deriving the transfer matrix, we assume that $x(0) = 0$. Then, from Eq. (3-2), we get

$$X(s) = (sI - A)^{-1}BU(s) \tag{3-4}$$

By substituting Eq. (3-4) into Eq. (3-3), we obtain

$$Y(s) = [C(sI - A)^{-1}B + D]U(s)$$

Thus the transfer matrix $G(s)$ is given by

$$G(s) = C(sI - A)^{-1}B + D$$

The transfer matrix $G(s)$ for the given system becomes

$$G(s) = C(sI - A)^{-1}B$$

$$= \begin{bmatrix} 1 & 0 \\ 0 & 1 \end{bmatrix} \begin{bmatrix} s+1 & 1 \\ -6.5 & s \end{bmatrix}^{-1} \begin{bmatrix} 1 & 1 \\ 1 & 0 \end{bmatrix}$$

$$= \frac{1}{s^2 + s + 6.5} \begin{bmatrix} s & -1 \\ 6.5 & s+1 \end{bmatrix} \begin{bmatrix} 1 & 1 \\ 1 & 0 \end{bmatrix}$$

$$= \frac{1}{s^2 + s + 6.5} \begin{bmatrix} s-1 & s \\ s+7.5 & 6.5 \end{bmatrix}$$

Hence

$$\begin{bmatrix} Y_1(s) \\ Y_2(s) \end{bmatrix} = \begin{bmatrix} \dfrac{s-1}{s^2+s+6.5} & \dfrac{s}{s^2+s+6.5} \\ \dfrac{s+7.5}{s^2+s+6.5} & \dfrac{6.5}{s^2+s+6.5} \end{bmatrix} \begin{bmatrix} U_1(s) \\ U_2(s) \end{bmatrix}$$

Since this system involves two inputs and two outputs, four transfer functions may be defined depending on which signals are considered as the input and output. Note that, when considering the signal u_1 as the input, we assume that signal u_2 is zero, and vice versa. The four transfer function are

$$\frac{Y_1(s)}{U_1(s)} = \frac{s-1}{s^2+s+6.5}, \qquad \frac{Y_2(s)}{U_1(s)} = \frac{s+7.5}{s^2+s+6.5}$$

$$\frac{Y_1(s)}{U_2(s)} = \frac{s}{s^2+s+6.5}, \qquad \frac{Y_2(s)}{U_2(s)} = \frac{6.5}{s^2+s+6.5}$$

The four individual step-response curves can be plotted by use of the command

$$step(A,B,C,D)$$

MATLAB Program 3-14 produces four such step-response curves. The curves are shown in Figure 3-21.

MATLAB Program 3–14

```
A = [-1  -1;6.5   0];
B = [1   1;1   0];
C = [1   0;0   1];
D = [0   0;0   0];
step(A,B,C,D)
```

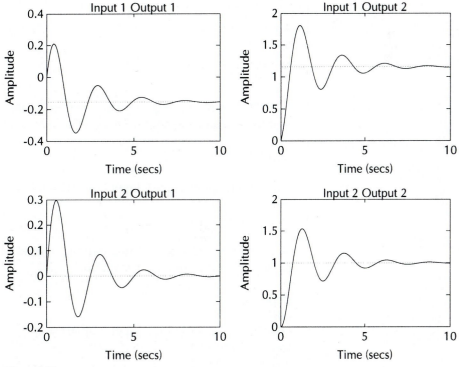

Figure 3-21

To plot two step-response curves for the input u_1 in one diagram and two step-response curves for the input u_2 in another diagram, we may use the commands

$$\text{step(A,B,C,D,1)}$$

and

$$\text{step(A,B,C,D,2)}$$

respectively. MATLAB Program 3-15 is a program to plot two step-response curves for the input u_1 in one diagram and two step-response curves for the input u_2 in another diagram. Figure 3-22 shows the two diagrams, each consisting of two step-response curves.

MATLAB Program 3–15

```
% ---------- Step-response curves for system defined in state
% space ----------

% ***** In this program we plot step-response curves of a system
% having two inputs (u1 and u2) and two outputs (y1 and y2) *****

% ***** We shall first plot step-response curves when the input is
% u1.  Then we shall plot step-response curves when the input is
% u2 *****

% ***** Enter matrices A, B, C, and D *****

A = [-1  -1;6.5   0];
B = [1   1;1   0];
C = [1   0;0   1];
D = [0   0;0   0];

% ***** To plot step-response curves when the input is u1, enter
% the command 'step(A,B,C,D,1)' *****

step(A,B,C,D,1)
grid
title('Step-Response Plots:  Input = u1 (u2 = 0)')
text(3.5,-0.1,'Y1')
text(3.5,1.35,'Y2')

% ***** Next, we shall plot step-response curves when the input is
%  u2.  Enter the command 'step(A,B,C,D,2)' *****

step(A,B,C,D,2);
grid
title('Step-Response Plots:  Input = u2 (u1 = 0)')
text(3.5,0.06,'Y1')
text(3,1.1,'Y2')
```

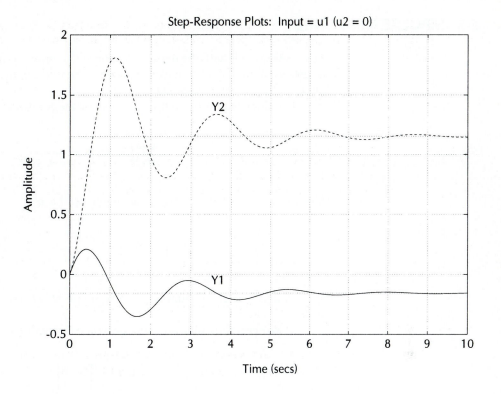

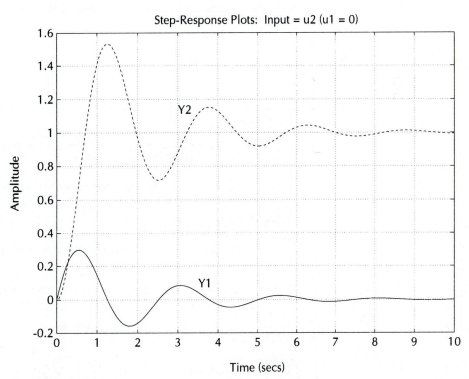

Figure 3-22

3-3 IMPULSE RESPONSE

This section deals with the impulse response of control systems. The basic idea here is that, when the initial conditions are zero, the unit-impulse response of $G(s)$ is the same as the unit-step response of $sG(s)$.

Consider the unit-impulse response of the following system:

$$\frac{C(s)}{R(s)} = G(s) = \frac{1}{s+1}$$

Since $R(s) = 1$ for the unit-impulse input, we have

$$C(s) = G(s) = \frac{1}{s+1} = \left(\frac{s}{s+1}\right)\frac{1}{s}$$

We can thus convert the unit-impulse response of $G(s)$ to the unit-step response of $sG(s)$.

If we enter the following numerator and denominator into MATLAB program

$$\text{num} = [1 \quad 0]$$
$$\text{den} = [1 \quad 1]$$

and use the step-response command, as given in MATLAB Program 3-16, we can obtain a plot of the unit-impulse response of the system as shown in Figure 3-23.

MATLAB Program 3–16

```
% ---------- Unit-impulse response ----------

% ***** To obtain unit-impulse response of first-order
% system G(s) = 1/(s + 1), multiply s to G(s) and use
% step-response command *****

% ***** Enter the numerator and denominator of sG(s) *****

num = [1   0];
den = [1   1];

% ***** Enter step-response command *****

step(num,den)
grid
title('Unit-Impulse Response of G(s) = 1/(s+1)')
```

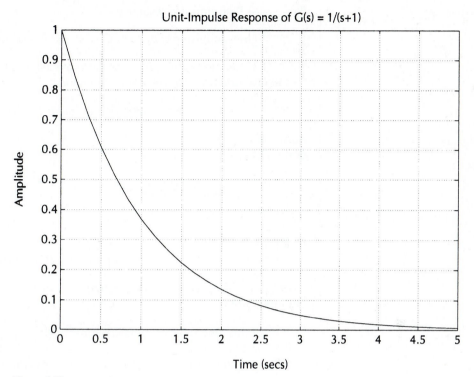

Figure 3-23

EXAMPLE 3-7

Consider the unit-impulse response of the second-order system

$$\frac{C(s)}{R(s)} = G(s) = \frac{1}{s^2 + 0.2s + 1}$$

For the unit-impulse input, $R(s) = 1$. Hence

$$C(s) = \frac{1}{s^2 + 0.2s + 1} = \frac{s}{s^2 + 0.2s + 1}\frac{1}{s}$$

Considering the unit-impulse response of $G(s)$ as the unit-step response of $sG(s)$, enter the following numerator and denominator in the program:

$$num = \begin{bmatrix} 0 & 1 & 0 \end{bmatrix}$$
$$den = \begin{bmatrix} 1 & 0.2 & 1 \end{bmatrix}$$

A complete MATLAB program for obtaining the unit-impulse response of this system is given in MATLAB Program 3-17. A plot of the unit-impulse response of the system is shown in Figure 3-24.

MATLAB Program 3–17

```
% ---------- Unit-impulse response ----------

% ***** Unit-impulse response of G(s) = 1/(s^2 + 0.2s + 1) *****

% ***** To obtain unit-impulse response of G(s), multiply
% s to G(s) and use step-response command *****

% ***** Enter the numerator and denominator of sG(s) *****

num = [0   1   0];
den = [1   0.2   1];

% ***** Enter the step-response command *****

step(num,den)

[[[ Error using MM ltitr
Student system limit on maximum variable size exceeded.

Error in MM \MATLAB\SIGSYS\step.m
On line 85 MM x = ltitr(aa,bb,ones(n,l),zeros(nb,mb));

% ***** If this type of error message appears, then specify
% the computing time points (such as t = 0:0.1:50) and enter the
% following step-response command:  step(num,den,t) *****

t = 0:0.1:50;
step(num,den,t);
grid
title('Unit-Impulse Response of G(s) = 1/(s^2+0.2s+1)')
```

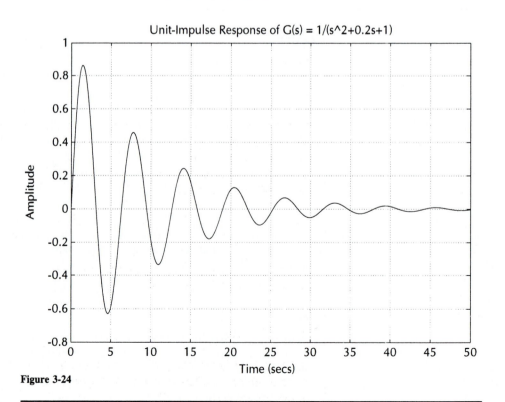

Figure 3-24

EXAMPLE 3-8

Consider the impulse response of the standard second-order system defined by

$$\frac{C(s)}{R(s)} = \frac{\omega_n^2}{s^2 + 2\zeta\omega_n s + \omega_n^2}$$

For a unit-impulse input, $R(s) = 1$. Thus

$$C(s) = \frac{\omega_n^2}{s^2 + 2\zeta\omega_n s + \omega_n^2} = \frac{\omega_n^2 s}{s^2 + 2\zeta\omega_n s + \omega_n^2} \frac{1}{s}$$

Consider the normalized system where $\omega_n = 1$. Then

$$C(s) = \frac{s}{s^2 + 2\zeta s + 1} \frac{1}{s}$$

To obtain the unit-impulse response, enter the following numerator and denominator in the program.

$$\text{num} = [0 \quad 1 \quad 0]$$
$$\text{den} = [1 \quad 2*(\text{zeta}) \quad 1]$$

Here we shall consider five different values of zeta: $\zeta = 0.1, 0.3, 0.5, 0.7$, and 1.0.

A MATLAB program for plotting the five unit-impulse response curves in one diagram is given in MATLAB Program 3-18. The resulting diagram is shown in Figure 3-25.

```
MATLAB Program 3–18

% ---------- Unit-impulse response ----------

% ***** Unit-impulse response curves for the normalized
% second-order system G(s) = 1/[s^2 + 2(zeta)s + 1] *****

% ***** The unit-impulse response is obtained as the
% unit-step response of sG(s) *****

% ***** The values of zeta considered here are 0.1, 0.3,
% 0.5, 0.7, and 1.0 *****

% ***** Enter the numerator and denominator of sG(s) for
% zeta = 0.1 *****

num = [0   1   0];
den1 = [1   0.2   1];

% ***** Specify the computing time points (such as t = 0:0.1:10).
% Then enter the step-response command step(num,den,t) and text
% command text( , ,' ') *****
```

```
t = 0:0.1:10;
step(num,den1,t);
text(1.5,0.86,'Zeta = 0.1')

% ***** Hold this plot and add other unit-impulse response
% curves to it *****

hold

Current plot held

% ***** Enter denominators of sG(s) for zeta = 0.3, 0.5,
% 0.7, and 1.0 *****

den2 = [1   0.6   1]; den3 = [1   1   1]; den4 = [1   1.4   1];
den5 = [1   2   1];

% ***** Superimpose on the held plot the unit-impulse response
% curves for zeta = 0.3, 0.5, 0.7, and 1.0 by entering
% successively the step-response command step(num,den,t)
% and text command text( , ,' ') *****

step(num,den2,t);
text(1.4,0.65,'0.3')
step(num,den3,t);
text(1.2,0.55,'0.5')
step(num,den4,t);
text(1.0,0.45,'0.7')
step(num,den5,t);
text(0.8,0.35,'1.0')

% ***** Enter grid and title of the plot *****

grid
title('Impulse-Response Curves for G(s) = 1/[s^2+2(zeta)s+1]')

% ***** Clear hold on graphics *****

hold

Current plot released
```

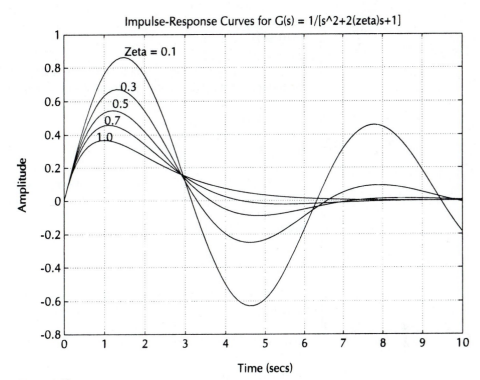

Figure 3-25

If it is desired to use different marks for different curves (such as 'o', '×', or ':'), modify the previous MATLAB program. The modified version is given as MATLAB Program 3-19. The resulting plots of curves are shown in Figure 3-26.

From the unit-impulse response curves for different values of zeta, we may conclude that if the impulse response $c(t)$ does not change sign the system is either critically damped or overdamped, in which case the corresponding step response does not overshoot but increases or decreases monotonically and approaches a constant value.

```
MATLAB Program 3–19

% ----------Unit-impulse response ----------

% ***** Unit-impulse response curves for the normalized
% second-order system G(s) = 1/[s^2 + 2(zeta)s + 1] *****

% ***** The unit-impulse response is obtained as the
% unit-step response of sG(s) *****

% ***** The values of zeta considered here are 0.1, 0.3,
% 0.5, 0.7, and 1.0 *****

% ***** Enter the numerator and denominator of sG(s) for
% zeta = 0.1 *****
```

```
num = [0  1   0];
den1 = [1  0.2  1];

% ***** Specify the computing time points (such as t = 0:0.1:10)
% and then enter step-response command c = step(num,den,t) *****

t = 0:0.1:10;
c1 = step(num,den1,t);
plot(t,c1,'o')

% ***** Hold this plot and add other unit-impulse response
% curves to it *****

hold

Current plot held

% ***** Enter denominators of sG(s) for zeta = 0.3, 0.5,
% 0.7, and 1.0 *****

den2 = [1   0.6   1];
den3 = [1   1   1];
den4 = [1   1.4   1];
den5 = [1   2   1];

% ***** Superimpose on the held plot the unit-impulse
% response curves for zeta = 0.3, 0.5, 0.7, and 1.0 by
% entering successively step-response command and plot
% command *****

c2 = step(num,den2,t); plot(t,c2,'x')
c3 = step(num,den3,t); plot(t,c3,'--')
c4 = step(num,den4,t); plot(t,c4,'-')
c5 = step(num,den5,t); plot(t,c5,':')

% ***** Enter grid, title, xlabel, and ylabel *****

grid
title('Impulse-Response Curves for G(s) = 1/[s^2+2(zeta)s+1])
xlabel('t Sec')
ylabel('Outputs c1, c2, c3, c4, c5')

% ***** Clear hold on graphics *****

hold

Current plot released
```

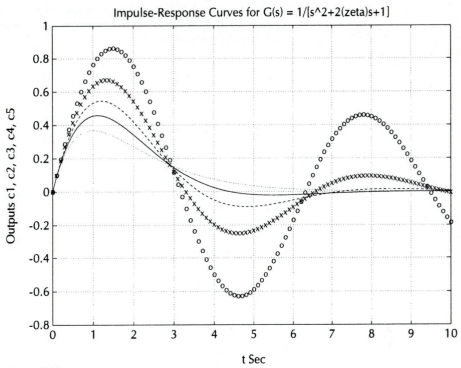

Figure 3-26

EXAMPLE 3-9

Obtain the unit-step response and unit-impulse response of the following system:

$$
\begin{bmatrix} \dot{x}_1 \\ \dot{x}_2 \\ \dot{x}_3 \\ \dot{x}_4 \end{bmatrix} =
\begin{bmatrix}
0 & 1 & 0 & 0 \\
0 & 0 & 1 & 0 \\
0 & 0 & 0 & 1 \\
-0.0073 & -0.0878 & -0.4791 & -1.4791
\end{bmatrix}
\begin{bmatrix} x_1 \\ x_2 \\ x_3 \\ x_4 \end{bmatrix} +
\begin{bmatrix} 0 \\ 0.0878 \\ -0.0347 \\ 0.0166 \end{bmatrix} u
$$

$$
y = \begin{bmatrix} 1 & 0 & 0 & 0 \end{bmatrix} \begin{bmatrix} x_1 \\ x_2 \\ x_3 \\ x_4 \end{bmatrix}
$$

To obtain the unit-step response of this system, use the command

$$[y,x,t] = \text{step}(A,B,C,D)$$

Since the unit-impulse response is the derivative of the unit-step response, the derivative of the output $(y = x1)$ will give the unit-impulse response. From the state equation, we see that the derivative of y is $x2$. Hence $x2$ versus t will give the unit-impulse response. $x2$ can be obtained from

$$x2 = \begin{bmatrix} 0 & 1 & 0 & 1 \end{bmatrix} * x'$$

MATLAB Program 3-20 will give both the unit-step and unit-impulse responses.

Figure 3-27 gives the plot of the unit-step response curve and Figure 3-28 is the plot of the unit-impulse response curve.

```
MATLAB Program 3–20

% -------- Unit-step response and unit-impulse response --------

% ***** Unit-step response and unit-impulse response of system
% defined in state space *****

% ***** Enter matrices A, B, C, and D of the state-space
% equations *****

A = [0          1         0         0
     0          0         1         0
     0          0         0         1
    -0.0073   -0.0878   -0.4791   -1.4791];
B =  [0;0.0878;-0.0347;0.0166];
C =  [1  0  0  0];
D =  [0];

% ***** Enter the following step-response command *****

[y,x,t] = step(A,B,C,D);
plot(t,y)
grid
title('Unit-Step Response')
xlabel('t Sec')
ylabel('Output y')

% ***** The unit-impulse response of the system is the
% same as the derivative of the unit-step response.  Hence,
% the unit-impulse response of this system is given by
% ydot = x2.  To plot the unit-impulse response curve,
% enter the following command *****

x2 = [0  1  0  0]*x'; plot(t,x2)
grid
title('Unit-Impulse Response')
xlabel('t Sec')
ylabel('Output to Unit-Impulse Input, x2')
```

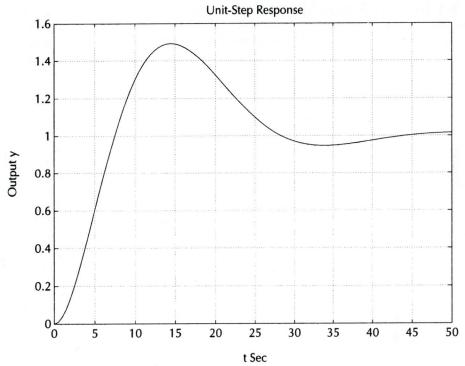

Figure 3-27

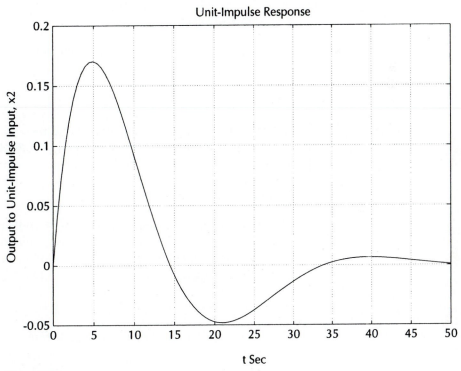

Figure 3-28

3-4 RAMP RESPONSE

To obtain the ramp response of the transfer-function system $G(s)$, divide $G(s)$ by s and use the step-response command. For example, consider the closed-loop system

$$\frac{C(s)}{R(s)} = \frac{1}{s^2 + s + 1}$$

For a unit-ramp input, $R(s) = 1/(s^2)$. Hence

$$C(s) = \frac{1}{s^2 + s + 1} \frac{1}{s^2} = \frac{1}{(s^2 + s + 1)s} \frac{1}{s}$$

To obtain the unit-ramp response, enter the following numerator and denominator into the MATLAB program,

$$\text{num} = [0 \quad 0 \quad 0 \quad 1];$$
$$\text{den} = [1 \quad 1 \quad 1 \quad 0];$$

and use the step-response command. See MATLAB Program 3-21. The plot obtained by using this program is shown in Figure 3-29.

MATLAB Program 3–21

```
% ----------Unit-ramp response ----------

% ***** The unit-ramp response is obtained as the unit-step
% response of G(s)/s *****

% ***** Enter the numerator and denominator of G(s)/s *****

num = [0   0   0   1];
den = [1   1   1   0];

% ***** Specify the computing time points (such as t = 0:0.1:7)
% and then enter step-response command:  c = step(num,den,t) *****

t = 0:0.1:7;
c = step(num, den, t);

% ***** In plotting the ramp-response curve, add the reference
% input to the plot.  The reference input is t.  Add to the
% argument of the plot command with the following:  t,t,'-'.  Thus
% the plot command becomes as follows:  plot(t,c,'o',t,t,'-') *****

plot(t,c,'o',t,t,'-')

% ***** Add grid, title, xlabel, and ylabel *****

grid
title('Unit-Ramp Response Curve for system G(s) = 1/ (s^2 + s + 1)')
xlabel('t Sec')
ylabel('Output c')
```

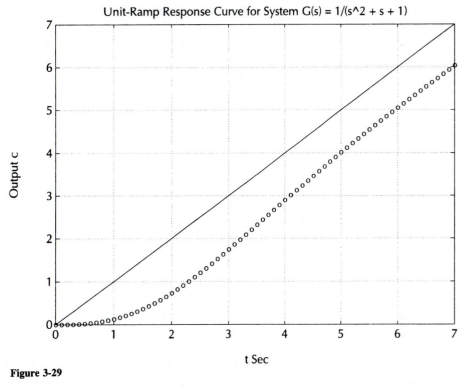

Figure 3-29

Next, we shall treat the unit-ramp response of the system in state-space form. Consider the system described by

$$\dot{\mathbf{x}} = \mathbf{A}\mathbf{x} + \mathbf{B}u$$
$$y = \mathbf{C}\mathbf{x} + Du$$

where

$$\mathbf{A} = \begin{bmatrix} 0 & 1 \\ -1 & -1 \end{bmatrix}, \qquad \mathbf{B} = \begin{bmatrix} 0 \\ 1 \end{bmatrix}, \qquad \mathbf{x}(0) = \mathbf{0}$$

$$\mathbf{C} = [1 \quad 0], \qquad D = [0]$$

When the initial conditions are zeros, the unit-ramp response is the integral of the unit-step response. Hence the unit-ramp response can be given by

$$z = \int_0^t y \, dt \tag{3-5}$$

From Eq. (3-5), we obtain

$$\dot{z} = y = x_1 \tag{3-6}$$

Let us define

$$z = x_3$$

Then Eq. (3-6) becomes

$$\dot{x}_3 = x_1 \tag{3-7}$$

Combining Eq. (3-7) with the original state-space equation, we obtain

$$\begin{bmatrix} \dot{x}_1 \\ \dot{x}_2 \\ \dot{x}_3 \end{bmatrix} = \begin{bmatrix} 0 & 1 & 0 \\ -1 & -1 & 0 \\ 1 & 0 & 0 \end{bmatrix} \begin{bmatrix} x_1 \\ x_2 \\ x_3 \end{bmatrix} + \begin{bmatrix} 0 \\ 1 \\ 0 \end{bmatrix} u$$

$$z = \begin{bmatrix} 0 & 0 & 1 \end{bmatrix} \begin{bmatrix} x_1 \\ x_2 \\ x_3 \end{bmatrix}$$

which can be written as

$$\dot{\mathbf{x}} = \mathbf{AA}\mathbf{x} + \mathbf{BB}u$$
$$z = \mathbf{CC}\mathbf{x} + DDu$$

where

$$\mathbf{AA} = \begin{bmatrix} 0 & 1 & 0 \\ -1 & -1 & 0 \\ 1 & 0 & 0 \end{bmatrix} = \begin{bmatrix} \mathbf{A} & \vdots & 0 \\ \cdots & \vdots & 0 \\ \mathbf{C} & \vdots & 0 \end{bmatrix}$$

$$\mathbf{BB} = \begin{bmatrix} 0 \\ 1 \\ 0 \end{bmatrix} = \begin{bmatrix} \mathbf{B} \\ \cdots \\ 0 \end{bmatrix}, \qquad \mathbf{CC} = \begin{bmatrix} 0 & 0 & 1 \end{bmatrix}, \qquad DD = \begin{bmatrix} 0 \end{bmatrix}$$

Note that x_3 is the third element of $\mathbf{x}$. A plot of the unit-ramp response curve $z(t)$ can be obtained by entering MATLAB Program 3-22 into the computer. A plot of the unit-ramp response curve obtained from this MATLAB program is shown in Figure 3-30.

MATLAB Program 3–22

```
% ---------- Unit-ramp response ----------

% ***** The unit-ramp response is obtained by adding a new
% state variable x3.  The dimension of the state
% equation is enlarged by one *****

% ***** Enter matrices A, B, C, and D of the original
% state equation and output equation *****

A = [0  1;-1  -1];
B = [0;1];
C = [1  0];
D = [0];

% ***** Enter matrices AA, BB, CC, and DD of the new,
% enlarged state equation and output equation *****

AA = [A  zeros(2,1); C  0];
BB = [B;0];
CC = [0  0  1];
DD = [0];
```

```
% ***** Enter step-response command:  [z,x,t] = step(AA,BB,CC,DD)
% *****

[z,x,t] = step(AA,BB,CC,DD);

Warning: Matrix is singular to working precision.

% ***** In plotting x3 add the unit-ramp input t in the plot
% by entering the following command:  plot(t,x3,t,t,'--') *****

x3 = [0   0   1]*x'; plot(t,x3,t,t,'--')

% ***** Add grid, title, xlabel, and ylabel *****

grid
title('Unit-Ramp Response')
xlabel('t Sec')
ylabel('Output')
```

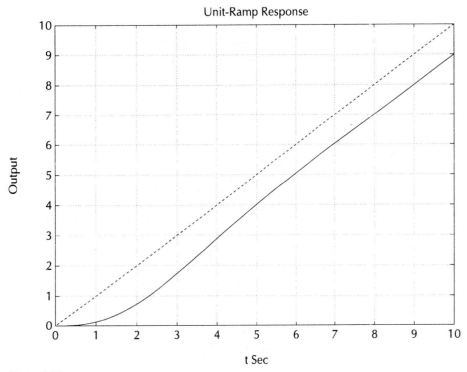

Figure 3-30

EXAMPLE 3-10

Figure 3-31 shows three systems. System I is a positional servo system. System II is a positional servo system utilizing proportional-plus-derivative control action. System III is a positional servo system utilizing velocity feedback or tachometer feedback. Let us compare the unit-step, unit-impulse, and unit-ramp responses of the three systems.

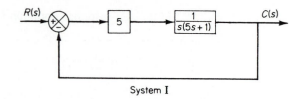

System I

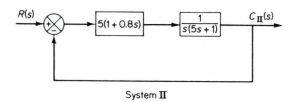

System II

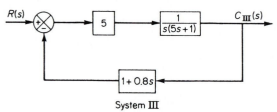

System III

Figure 3-31

The closed-loop transfer function for system I is

$$\frac{C_I(s)}{R(s)} = \frac{1}{s^2 + 0.2s + 1}$$

The closed-loop transfer function for system II is

$$\frac{C_{II}(s)}{R(s)} = \frac{0.8s + 1}{s^2 + s + 1}$$

The closed-loop transfer function for system III is

$$\frac{C_{III}(s)}{R(s)} = \frac{1}{s^2 + s + 1}$$

We shall first compare the unit-step responses of systems I, II, and III. The unit-step responses can be obtained by entering MATLAB Program 3-23. The resulting unit-step response curves are shown in Figure 3-32. Notice from this plot that the system utilizing proportional-plus-derivative control action exhibits the shortest rise time. The system with velocity feedback has the least maximum overshoot, or the best relative stability, of the three systems.

If it is desired to plot the three unit-step response curves as continuous curves, enter MATLAB Program 3-24. The resulting plots are shown in Figure 3-33.

Next, we shall obtain the unit-impulse response curves of these three systems. Unit-impulse response curves can be plotted by using MATLAB Program 3-25. The resulting plot is shown in Figure 3-34.

```
MATLAB Program 3–23

% ---------- Step response ----------

% ***** Enter the numerators and denominators of Systems I,
% II, and III *****

num1 = [0   0   1];
den1 = [1   0.2   1];
num2 = [0   0.8   1];
den2 = [1   1   1];
num3 = [0   0   1];
den3 = [1   1   1];

% ***** Specify the computing time points (such as t = 0:0.1:10)
% and then enter step-response command c = step(num,den,t) *****

t = 0:0.1:10;
c1 = step(num1,den1,t);
plot(t,c1,'o')

% ***** Hold this plot and add other unit-step response
% curves to it *****

hold

Current plot held

c2 = step(num2,den2,t);
plot(t,c2,'x')
c3 = step(num3,den3,t);
plot(t,c3,'--')

% ***** add grid, title, xlabel, and ylabel *****

grid
title('Unit-Step Response Curves for Systems I, II, and III')
xlabel('t Sec')
ylabel('Outputs c1, c2, c3')

% ***** Clear hold on graphics *****

hold

Current plot released
```

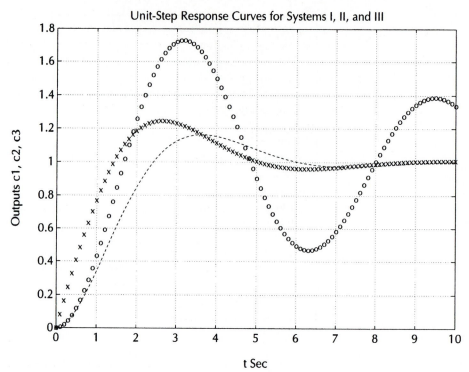

Figure 3-32

```
MATLAB Program 3–24

% ---------- Step responses ----------

% ***** Enter the numerators and denominators of the three
% systems *****

num1 = [0   0   1];
den1 = [1   0.2   1];
num2 = [0   0.8   1];
den2 = [1   1   1];
num3 = [0   0   1];
den3 = [1   1   1];

% ***** Specify the computing time points (such as t = 0:0.1:10)
% and then enter step-response command step(num,den,t) and text
% command text( , ,' ') *****

t = 0:0.1:10;
step(num1,den1,t);
text(4.5,1.5,'System I')

% ***** Hold this plot and add other unit-step response
% curves to it *****
```

```
hold

Current plot held

step(num2,den2,t);
text(2.3,1.27,'System II')
step(num3,den3,t);
text(2,0.7,'System III')

% ***** Add grid and title of the plot *****

grid
title('Unit-Step Response Curves for Systems I, II, and III')

% ***** Clear hold on graphics *****

hold

Current plot released
```

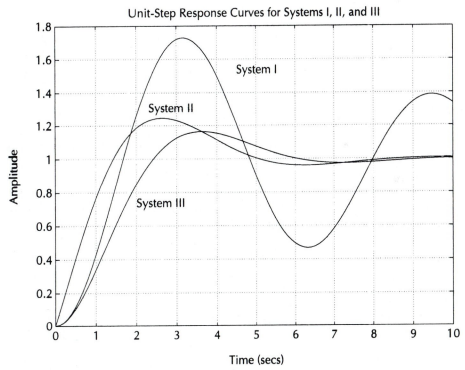

Figure 3-33

```
MATLAB Program 3–25

% --------- Unit-impulse responses ---------

% ***** Unit-impulse response is obtained as the unit-step
% response of sG(s) *****
```

```
% ***** Enter the numerators and denominators of sG1(s),
% sG2(s), and sG3(s) *****

num1 = [0   1   0];
den1 = [1   0.2   1];
num2 = [0.8   1   0];
den2 = [1   1   1];
num3 = [0   1   0];
den3 = [1   1   1];

% ***** Specify the computing time points (such as t = 0:0.1:10)
% and then enter step-response command c = step(num,den,t) and
% plot command *****

t = 0:0.1:10;
c1 = step(num1,den1,t);
c2 = step(num2,den2,t);
c3 = step(num3,den3,t);
plot(t,c1,'o',t,c2,'x',t,c3,'--')

% ***** Add grid, title, xlabel, and ylabel *****

grid
title('Unit-Impulse Response Curves for Systems I, II, and III')
xlabel('t Sec')
ylabel('Outputs c1, c2, c3')
```

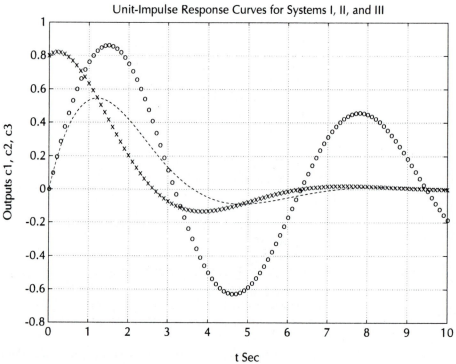

Figure 3-34

Finally, to obtain a plot of unit-ramp response curves, enter MATLAB Program 3-26 into the computer. The resulting plot of these three unit-ramp response curves is shown in Figure 3-35. From this plot, we see that system II has the advantage of quicker response and less steady-state error to a ramp input.

The main reason why the system utilizing proportional-plus-derivative control action has superior response characteristics is that derivative control responds to the rate of change of the error signal and can produce early corrective action before the magnitude of the error becomes large.

Notice that the output of system III is the output of system II delayed by a first-order lag term $1/(1 + 0.8s)$. Figure 3-36 shows the relationship between the outputs of system II and system III.

MATLAB Program 3–26

```
% --------- Unit-ramp responses ---------

% ***** Unit-ramp response is obtained as the unit-step
% response of G(s)/s *****

% ***** Enter the numerators and denominators of G1(s)/s,
% G2(s)/s, and G3(s)/s *****

num1 = [0   0   0   1];
den1 = [1   0.2   1   0];
num2 = [0   0   0.8   1];
den2 = [1   1   1   0];
num3 = [0   0   0   1];
den3 = [1   1   1   0];

% ***** Specify the computing time points (such as t = 0:0.1:7)
% and then enter step-response command c = step(num,den,t).
% Add the input ramp function in the plot by entering
% command plot(t,t,'-') *****

t = 0:0.1:7;
c1 = step(num1,den1,t);
c2 = step(num2,den2,t);
c3 = step(num3,den3,t);
plot(t,c1,'o',t,c2,'x',t,c3,'--',t,t,'-')

% ***** Add grid, title, xlabel, and ylabel *****

grid
title('Unit-Ramp Response Curves for Systems I, II, and III')
xlabel('t Sec')
ylabel('Outputs c1, c2, c3')
```

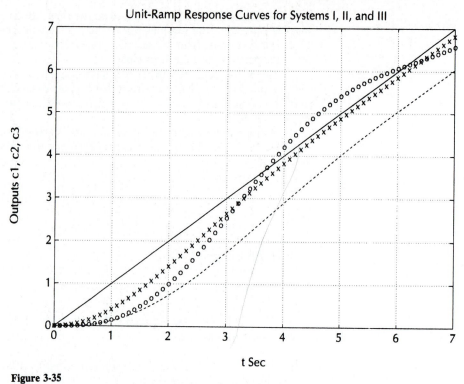

Figure 3-35

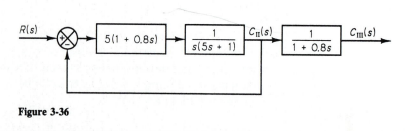

Figure 3-36

3-5 TRANSFORMATION OF SYSTEM MODELS

In this section we shall consider transformation of the system model from transfer function to state space, and vice versa. We shall begin our discussion with transformation from transfer function to state space.

Let us write the closed-loop transfer function as

$$\frac{Y(s)}{U(s)} = \frac{\text{numerator polynomial in } s}{\text{denominator polynomial in } s} = \frac{\text{num}}{\text{den}}$$

Once we have this transfer-function expression, the following MATLAB command

$$[A,B,C,D] = tf2ss(num,den)$$

will give a state-space representation. It is important to note that the state-space representation for any system is not unique. There are many (infinitely many) state-space representations for the same system. The MATLAB command gives one possible such state-space representation.

State-space formulation of transfer-function systems

Consider the transfer-function system

$$\frac{Y(s)}{U(s)} = \frac{s}{(s + 10)(s^2 + 4s + 16)}$$

$$= \frac{s}{s^3 + 14s^2 + 56s + 160} \tag{3-8}$$

There are many (infinitely many) possible state-space representations for this system. One possible state-space representation is

$$\begin{bmatrix} \dot{x}_1 \\ \dot{x}_2 \\ \dot{x}_3 \end{bmatrix} = \begin{bmatrix} 0 & 1 & 0 \\ 0 & 0 & 1 \\ -160 & -56 & -14 \end{bmatrix} \begin{bmatrix} x_1 \\ x_2 \\ x_3 \end{bmatrix} + \begin{bmatrix} 0 \\ 1 \\ -14 \end{bmatrix} u$$

$$y = \begin{bmatrix} 1 & 0 & 0 \end{bmatrix} \begin{bmatrix} x_1 \\ x_2 \\ x_3 \end{bmatrix} + [0]u$$

Another possible state-space representation (among infinitely many alternatives) is

$$\begin{bmatrix} \dot{x}_1 \\ \dot{x}_2 \\ \dot{x}_3 \end{bmatrix} = \begin{bmatrix} -14 & -56 & -160 \\ 1 & 0 & 0 \\ 0 & 1 & 0 \end{bmatrix} \begin{bmatrix} x_1 \\ x_2 \\ x_3 \end{bmatrix} + \begin{bmatrix} 1 \\ 0 \\ 0 \end{bmatrix} u \tag{3-9}$$

$$y = \begin{bmatrix} 0 & 1 & 0 \end{bmatrix} \begin{bmatrix} x_1 \\ x_2 \\ x_3 \end{bmatrix} + [0]u \tag{3-10}$$

MATLAB transforms the transfer function given by Eq. (3-8) into the state-space representation given by Eqs. (3-9) and (3-10). For the example system considered here, MATLAB Program 3-27 will produce matrices **A**, **B**, **C**, and D.

MATLAB Program 3–27

```
num = [0  0  1  0];
den = [1  14  56  160];
[A,B,C,D] = tf2ss(num,den)

A =

  -14   -56   -160
    1     0      0
    0     1      0


B =

    1
    0
    0


C =

    0     1     0


D =

    0
```

EXAMPLE 3-11

Consider the system

$$\frac{Y(s)}{U(s)} = \frac{25.04s + 5.008}{s^3 + 5.03247s^2 + 25.1026s + 5.008}$$

This transfer function can be transformed into a state-space form by entering MATLAB Program 3-28. The state-space equations for the system obtained by the use of this program are

$$\begin{bmatrix} \dot{x}_1 \\ \dot{x}_2 \\ \dot{x}_3 \end{bmatrix} = \begin{bmatrix} -5.0325 & -25.1026 & -5.008 \\ 1 & 0 & 0 \\ 0 & 1 & 0 \end{bmatrix} \begin{bmatrix} x_1 \\ x_2 \\ x_3 \end{bmatrix} + \begin{bmatrix} 1 \\ 0 \\ 0 \end{bmatrix} u$$

$$y = \begin{bmatrix} 0 & 25.04 & 5.008 \end{bmatrix} \begin{bmatrix} x_1 \\ x_2 \\ x_3 \end{bmatrix} + [0]u$$

MATLAB Program 3–28

```
% ---------- Transform transfer function to state-space
% form ----------

% ***** Transfer function can be transformed into state-
% space form by entering the following transformation
% command:   [A,B,C,D] = tf2ss(num,den)   *****

% ***** Enter the numerator and denominator of the transfer
% function *****

num = [0   0   25.04   5.008];
den = [1   5.03247   25.1026   5.008];

% ***** Enter the transformation command *****

[A,B,C,D] = tf2ss(num,den)

A =

    -5.0325   -25.1026   -5.0080
     1.0000          0          0
          0     1.0000          0


B =

     1
     0
     0


C =

          0    25.0400     5.0080


D =

     0
```

Transformation from state space to transfer function

To obtain the transfer function from the state-space equations, use the following command:

$$[\text{num},\text{den}] = \text{ss2tf}(A,B,C,D,iu)$$

iu must be specified for systems with more than one input. For example, if the system has three inputs ($u1$, $u2$, $u3$), then iu must be either 1, 2, or 3, where 1 implies $u1$, 2 implies $u2$, and 3 implies $u3$.

If the system has only one input, then either

$$[\text{num},\text{den}] = \text{ss2tf}(A,B,C,D)$$

or

$$[\text{num},\text{den}] = \text{ss2tf}(A,B,C,D,1)$$

may be used. (See Example 3-12 and MATLAB Program 3-29.)

For the case when the system has multiple inputs and multiple outputs, see Example 3-13.

EXAMPLE 3-12

Obtain the transfer function of the system defined by the following state-space equations:

$$\begin{bmatrix} \dot{x}_1 \\ \dot{x}_2 \\ \dot{x}_3 \end{bmatrix} = \begin{bmatrix} 0 & 1 & 0 \\ 0 & 0 & 1 \\ -5.008 & -25.1026 & -5.03247 \end{bmatrix} \begin{bmatrix} x_1 \\ x_2 \\ x_3 \end{bmatrix} + \begin{bmatrix} 0 \\ 25.04 \\ -121.005 \end{bmatrix} u$$

$$y = \begin{bmatrix} 1 & 0 & 0 \end{bmatrix} \begin{bmatrix} x_1 \\ x_2 \\ x_3 \end{bmatrix}$$

MATLAB Program 3-29 will produce the transfer function for the given system. The transfer function obtained is given by

$$\frac{Y(s)}{U(s)} = \frac{25.04s + 5.008}{s^3 + 5.0325s^2 + 25.1026s + 5.008}$$

MATLAB Program 3–29

```
% ---------- Transform state-space equations into transfer
% function ----------

% ***** Transformation of state-space equations into
% transfer function is accomplished by entering transformation
% command    [num,den] = ss2tf(A,B,C,D) or
% [num,den] = ss2tf(A,B,C,D,1) *****

% ***** Enter matrices A, B, C, and D of state-space
% equations *****

A = [0  1  0;0  0  1;-5.008  -25.1026  -5.03247];
B = [0;25.04;-121.005];
C = [1  0  0];
D = [0];

% ***** Enter the following transformation command *****

[num,den] = ss2tf(A,B,C,D)

num =

          0      -0.0000      25.0400       5.0080


den =

     1.0000       5.0325      25.1026       5.0080

% ***** The same result can be obtained by entering the
% following command *****

[num,den] = ss2tf(A,B,C,D,1)

num =

          0      -0.0000      25.0400       5.0080


den =

     1.0000       5.0325      25.1026       5.0080
```

EXAMPLE 3-13

Consider a system with multiple inputs and multiple outputs. When the system has more than one output, the command

$$[NUM, den] = ss2tf(A, B, C, D, iu)$$

produces transfer functions for all outputs to each input. (The numerator coefficients are returned to matrix NUM with as many rows as there are outputs.)

Consider the system defined by

$$\begin{bmatrix} \dot{x}_1 \\ \dot{x}_2 \end{bmatrix} = \begin{bmatrix} 0 & 1 \\ -25 & -4 \end{bmatrix} \begin{bmatrix} x_1 \\ x_2 \end{bmatrix} + \begin{bmatrix} 1 & 1 \\ 0 & 1 \end{bmatrix} \begin{bmatrix} u_1 \\ u_2 \end{bmatrix}$$

$$\begin{bmatrix} y_1 \\ y_2 \end{bmatrix} = \begin{bmatrix} 1 & 0 \\ 0 & 1 \end{bmatrix} \begin{bmatrix} x_1 \\ x_2 \end{bmatrix} + \begin{bmatrix} 0 & 0 \\ 0 & 0 \end{bmatrix} \begin{bmatrix} u_1 \\ u_2 \end{bmatrix}$$

This system involves two inputs and two outputs. Four transfer functions are involved: $Y_1(s)/U_1(s)$, $Y_2(s)/U_1(s)$, $Y_1(s)/U_2(s)$, and $Y_2(s)/U_2(s)$. (When considering input u_1, we assume that input u_2 is zero, and vice versa.) See the following MATLAB output.

```
A = [0   1;  -25   -4];
B = [1   1;0   1];
C = [1   0;0   1];
D = [0   0;0   0];
[NUM,den] = ss2tf(A,B,C,D,1)

NUM =

        0    1     4
        0    0   -25


den =

        1    4    25

[NUM,den] = ss2tf(A,B,C,D,2)

NUM =

            0     1.0000      5.0000
            0     1.0000    -25.0000


den =

        1    4    25
```

This is the MATLAB representation of the following four transfer functions:

$$\frac{Y_1(s)}{U_1(s)} = \frac{s + 4}{s^2 + 4s + 25}, \qquad \frac{Y_2(s)}{U_1(s)} = \frac{-25}{s^2 + 4s + 25}$$

$$\frac{Y_1(s)}{U_2(s)} = \frac{s + 5}{s^2 + 4s + 25}, \qquad \frac{Y_2(s)}{U_2(s)} = \frac{s - 25}{s^2 + 4s + 25}$$

Chapter 4   Transient-Response Analysis of Discrete-Time Systems

4-1 INTRODUCTION

This chapter deals with the transient response of discrete-time systems. The command for transient response is different from the continuous-time case. For discrete-time systems, one commonly used command for transient response is

$$y = \text{filter(num,den,x)}$$

where x is the input and y is the filtered output.

Before we obtain plots of transient response for discrete-time systems, we shall summarize how to generate input functions to discrete-time systems. The input functions considered here are the Kronecker delta function (which corresponds to the unit-impulse function for continuous-time systems), step function, ramp function, acceleration function, and arbitrary input function.

Generating input functions

Kronecker delta input

The Kronecker delta function is defined by

$$u(0) = 1$$
$$u(k) = 0, \qquad \text{for } k = 1, 2, 3, \ldots$$

The Kronecker delta input such that

$$u(0) = 1$$
$$u(k) = 0, \qquad \text{for } k = 1, 2, 3, \ldots, 60$$

may be entered in the MATLAB program as

$$u = [1 \quad \text{zeros}(1, 60)]$$

A Kronecker delta input of magnitude 8 such that

$$u(0) = 8$$
$$u(k) = 0, \qquad \text{for } k = 1, 2, 3, \ldots, 40$$

may be entered in the program as

$$u = [8 \quad \text{zeros}(1, 40)]$$

Step input

A unit-step input such as

$$u(k) = 1(k) = 1, \qquad \text{for } k = 0, 1, 2, \ldots, 100$$

may be entered in the MATLAB program as

$$u = \text{ones}(1, 101)$$

or

$$u = [1 \quad \text{ones}(1, 100)]$$

Similarly, a step input of magnitude 5, or

$$u(k) = 5 \cdot 1(k) = 5, \qquad \text{for } k = 0, 1, 2, \ldots, 50$$

may be entered in the MATLAB program as

$$u = 5 * \text{ones}(1,51)$$

or

$$u = [5 \quad 5 * \text{ones}(1, 50)]$$

Ramp input

The unit-ramp input is defined by

$$u = t, \qquad \text{for } 0 \le t$$

For discrete-time systems, $t = kT$, where T is the sampling period (sec). Hence the ramp input can be written as

$$u(k) = kT, \qquad \text{for } k = 0, 1, 2, \ldots$$

If the ramp input is given by

$$u(k) = kT, \qquad \text{for } k = 0, 1, 2, \ldots, 50$$

then use either of the following forms:

$$u = 0{:}T{:}50 * T \qquad (T = \text{sampling period, sec})$$

or

$$k = 0{:}50; \qquad u = [k * T]$$

That is, if $T = 0.2$ sec and $k = 50$, then use either

$$u = 0:0.2:10$$

or

$$k = 0:50; \qquad u = [0.2 * k]$$

Acceleration input

Before we consider the acceleration input, consider the following signal:

$$h = [0 \quad 1 \quad 2 \quad 3 \quad 4 \quad 5 \quad 6]$$

The square of this signal at each sampling point is given by

$$w = [0 \quad 1 \quad 4 \quad 9 \quad 16 \quad 25 \quad 36]$$

The signal w can be generated in the MATLAB as follows:

```
h = 0:6

h =

      0    1    2    3    4    5    6

w = h.^2

w =

      0    1    4    9    16    25    36
```

Note that it is necessary to put a period after h to get each sampled value squared.

Now consider the acceleration input in general. Suppose that the input is given by

$$u(k) = \frac{1}{2}(kT)^2, \qquad \text{for } k = 0, 1, 2, \ldots$$

where T is the sampling period. Assume, for example, that $T = 0.2$ sec, or

$$u(0) = 0$$
$$u(1) = \frac{1}{2}T^2 = \frac{1}{2}(0.2)^2$$
$$u(2) = \frac{1}{2}(2T)^2 = \frac{1}{2}(0.4)^2$$
$$u(k) = \frac{1}{2}(kT)^2 = \frac{1}{2}(0.2k)^2, \qquad \text{for } k = 3, 4, 5, \ldots$$

This acceleration input may be entered in the MATLAB program as follows: If $k = 0, 1, 2, 3, 4$, then we may enter the following statement:

$$k = 0:4; \qquad u = [0.5 * (0.2 * k).^2]$$

Then the screen will exhibit the following:

```
k = 0:4;   u = [0.5 * (0.2 * k). ^ 2]

u =

            0    0.0200    0.0800    0.1800    0.3200
```

We may also enter the following statement:

$$k = 0:4; \quad m = [0.5 * (0.2 * k)' * (0.2 * k)]; \quad u = [diag(m)]'$$

The computer screen will show the following:

```
k = 0:4;    m = [0.5 * (0.2 * k)' * (0.2 * k)]

m =

            0         0         0         0         0
            0    0.0200    0.0400    0.0600    0.0800
            0    0.0400    0.0800    0.1200    0.1600
            0    0.0600    0.1200    0.1800    0.2400
            0    0.0800    0.1600    0.2400    0.3200

u = [diag(m)]'

u =

            0    0.0200    0.0800    0.1800    0.3200
```

To summarize, if k is to run from 0 to 40, we may use one of the following forms:

a. $k = 0:40; \quad u = [0.5 * (0.2 * k). ^ 2]$
b. $k = 0:40; \quad u = [diag(0.5 * (0.2 * k)' * (0.2 * k))]'$

Arbitrary input

If an arbitrary input is specified such that

$$u(0) = 3$$
$$u(1) = 2.5$$
$$u(2) = 1.2$$
$$u(k) = 0, \qquad \text{for } k = 3, 4, 5, \ldots 80$$

the following form may be used as the input:

$$u = [3 \quad 2.5 \quad 1.2 \quad zeros(1, 78)]$$

Outline of the chapter

The outline of this chapter is as follows: Section 4-1 has presented introductory material. Section 4-2 gives a brief discussion of digital filters. Section 4-3 deals with the response of discrete-time systems to the Kronecker delta input. Section 4-4 treats the response to step inputs and arbitrary inputs. Section 4-5 presents the ramp response. Section 4-6 discusses the transient-response characteristics of a PID-controlled digital system and of deadbeat control systems. Finally, Section 4-7 presents the transformation of system models from continuous time to discrete time.

4-2 DIGITAL FILTERS

Consider a digital filter whose pulse transfer function is

$$\frac{Y(z)}{X(z)} = \frac{b(z)}{a(z)}$$

where $b(z)$ is the numerator polynomial in z and $a(z)$ is the denominator polynomial in z. The command

$$y = \text{filter(b,a,x)} \qquad \text{or} \qquad y = \text{filter(num,den,x)}$$

filters the data in vector x with the filter described by vectors b and a (vectors num and den), creating filtered data y. Consider the response of the following digital filter to an input x.

$$\frac{Y(z)}{X(z)} = \frac{10z + 2}{10z^3 + 5z^2 + 2z + 1} = \frac{10z^{-2} + 2z^{-3}}{10 + 5z^{-1} + 2z^{-2} + z^{-3}}$$

Notice that the filter coefficients are ordered in descending powers of z or in ascending powers of z^{-1}.

The dynamics of the system are described in terms of b and a (or in terms of num and den). Thus the dynamics of the system are entered in the MATLAB as

$$b = [0 \quad 0 \quad 10 \quad 2];$$
$$a = [10 \quad 5 \quad 2 \quad 1];$$

or

$$\text{num} = [0 \quad 0 \quad 10 \quad 2];$$
$$\text{den} = [10 \quad 5 \quad 2 \quad 1];$$

Since the numerator polynomial is of smaller degree than the denominator polynomial, the former must be padded with leading zeros. (The numerator polynomial must be of the same size as the denominator polynomial.)

Once the numerator and denominator are entered in MATLAB, enter the input x, filter command, and plot command. Then the response to the input x will appear on the screen. We shall discuss in Sections 4-3 through 4-5 the response of the digital filter to various input signals.

Some remarks on digital filter

Note that in $Y(z)/X(z)$, where

$$\frac{Y(z)}{X(z)} = \frac{b(1) + b(2)z^{-1} + \cdots + b(n + 1)z^{-n}}{a(1) + a(2)z^{-1} + \cdots + a(n + 1)z^{-n}}$$

if $a(1) \neq 1$, the filter coefficients may be normalized by dividing all coefficients by $a(1)$. If $a(1) = 0$, the command filter produces the following error message:

First denominator filter coefficient must be non-zero.

If this type of error message appears, make corrections as needed.

4-3 RESPONSE TO THE KRONECKER DELTA INPUT

Consider the following discrete-time control system:

$$\frac{Y(z)}{X(z)} = \frac{0.4673z^{-1} - 0.3393z^{-2}}{1 - 1.5327z^{-1} + 0.6607z^{-2}}$$
$$= \frac{0.4673z - 0.3393}{z^2 - 1.5327z + 0.6607}$$

We shall consider the response $y(k)$ of this system to the Kronecker delta input.

Kronecker delta input

The Kronecker delta input is defined by

$$x(k) = 1, \qquad \text{for } k = 0$$
$$= 0, \qquad \text{for } k \neq 0$$

The z transform of the Kronecker delta input is

$$X(z) = 1$$

The input $x(k)$ to the MATLAB program can be written as

$$x = [1 \quad \text{zeros}(1,N)]$$

where N corresponds to the end of the discrete-time duration of the process considered.

Finding the inverse z transform of G(z)

Finding the inverse z transform of $G(z)$ is the same as finding the response of $G(z)$ to the Kronecker delta input. For the system being considered, we have

$$\frac{Y(z)}{X(z)} = G(z) = \frac{0.4673z^{-1} - 0.3393z^{-2}}{1 - 1.5327z^{-1} + 0.6607z^{-2}}$$

Since the z transform of the Kronecker delta input $X(z)$ is equal to unity, the response of the system to this input is

$$Y(z) = G(z) = \frac{0.4673z^{-1} - 0.3393z^{-2}}{1 - 1.5327z^{-1} + 0.6607z^{-2}}$$

Hence the inverse z transform of $G(z)$ is given by $y(0), y(1), y(2), \ldots$.

To obtain the inverse z transform of $G(z)$, we proceed as follows: Enter the numerator and denominator as follows:

$$\text{num} = [0 \quad 0.4673 \quad -0.3393]$$
$$\text{den} = [1 \quad -1.5327 \quad 0.6607]$$

Enter the Kronecker delta input.

$$x = [1 \quad \text{zeros}(1,40)]$$

Then enter the command

$$y = \text{filter(num,den,x)}$$

to obtain the response $y(k)$ from $k = 0$ to $k = 40$.

Summarizing the above, the MATLAB program to obtain the inverse z transform or the response to the Kronecker delta input is as shown in MATLAB Program 4-1. The screen will show the output $y(k)$ from $k = 0$ to 40 as follows:

```
y =
Columns 1 through 7
         0      0.4673    0.3769    0.2690    0.1632    0.0725    0.0032
Columns 8 through 14
    -0.0429   -0.0679   -0.0758   -0.0712   -0.0591   -0.0436   -0.0277
Columns 15 through 21
    -0.0137   -0.0027    0.0050    0.0094    0.0111    0.0108    0.0092
Columns 22 through 28
     0.0070    0.0046    0.0025    0.0007   -0.0005   -0.0013   -0.0016
Columns 29 through 35
    -0.0016   -0.0014   -0.0011   -0.0008   -0.0004   -0.0002    0.0000
Columns 36 through 41
     0.0002    0.0002    0.0002    0.0002    0.0002    0.0001
```

```
MATLAB Program 4-1

% ---------- Finding inverse z transform ----------

% ***** Finding the inverse z transform of G(z) is the same as
% finding the response of the system Y(z)/X(z) = G(z) to the
% Kronecker delta input *****

% ***** Enter the numerator and denominator of G(z) *****

num = [0   0.4673   -0.3393];
den = [1   -1.5327   0.6607];

% ***** Enter the Kronecker delta input x and filter command
% y = filter(num,den,x) *****

x = [1   zeros(1,40)];
y = filter(num,den,x)
```

(Note that MATLAB computations begin from column 1 and end at column 41, rather than from column 0 to column 40.) These values give the inverse z transform of $G(z)$. That is,

$$y(0) = 0$$
$$y(1) = 0.4673$$
$$y(2) = 0.3769$$
$$y(3) = 0.2690$$
$$\vdots$$
$$y(40) = 0.0001$$

To plot the values of the inverse z transform of $G(z)$, proceed as follows. Since we have chosen $0 \le k \le N = 40$, and the range of response $y(k)$ may be estimated to be between -1 and 1 (if this estimation is found to be unsatisfactory, change the range after a trial run), enter the ranges for the x axis ($0 \le x \le 40$) and the y axis ($-1 \le y \le 1$) as follows:

$$v = [0 \quad 40 \quad -1 \quad 1]$$
$$\text{axis(v)}$$

or combine two program lines into one as follows:

$$\text{axis([0} \quad 40 \quad -1 \quad 1])$$

Now adding a semicolon at the end of line

$$y = \text{filter(num, den, x)};$$

and entering

$$\text{plot(y, 'o')}$$

will plot the response $y(k)$ versus $k + 1$. Note that MATLAB plot begins from $k = 1$ and ends at $k = N$. (Later we shall show how to move the plot by one sampling period so that the plot will begin from $k = 0$.)

To obtain the response $y(k)$ versus $k + 1$, together with the grid, the title of the plot, xlabel, and ylabel, we enter MATLAB Program 4-2. The resulting plot is shown in Figure 4-1.

If we wish to plot the response $y(k)$ versus $k + 1$ using a continuous curve, then we replace the command

$$\text{plot(y, 'o')}$$

by

$$\text{plot(y, '--')}$$

The result is shown in Figure 4-2.

MATLAB vectors run from 1 to $N + 1$ instead of from 0 to N. If we desire to plot the response $y(k)$ versus k, instead of plotting $y(k)$ versus $k + 1$, we need to add the statement

$$\text{k = 0:40;}$$

and change the plot command as follows:

$$\text{plot(k,y,'o')}$$

MATLAB Program 4–2

```
% ---------- Response to Kronecker delta input ----------

% ***** Finding the response of system Y(z)/X(z) to the
% Kronecker delta input *****

% ***** Enter the numerator and denominator of Y(z)/X(z) *****

num = [0   0.4673   -0.3393];
den = [1   -1.5327   0.6607];

% ***** Enter the Kronecker delta input x, axis(v), and filter command,
% and plot command *****

x = [1   zeros(1,40)];
v = [0   40   -1   1];
axis(v);
y = filter(num,den,x);
plot(y,'o')

% ***** Add grid, title, xlabel, and ylabel *****

grid
title('Response to Kronecker Delta Input')
xlabel('k + 1')
ylabel('y(k)')
```

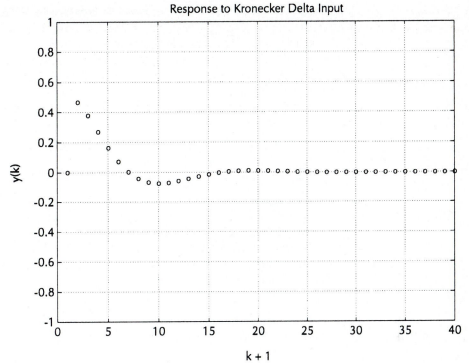

Figure 4-1

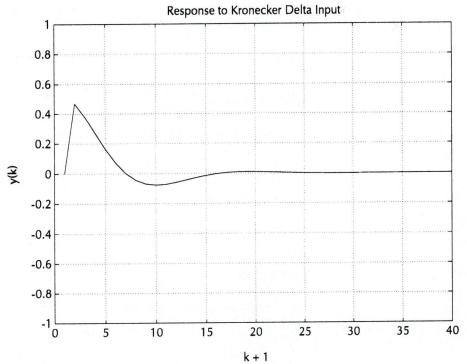

Figure 4-2

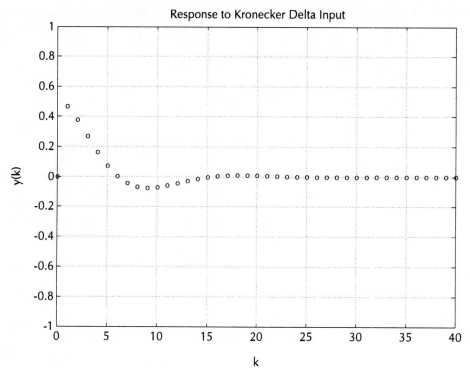

Figure 4-3

The resulting plot is shown in Figure 4-3.

It is important to note that the number of elements of row vector k(k = 0, 1, 2, . . . , 40) must agree with the dimension of the horizontal axis vector (x = 0, 1, 2, . . . , 40). The modified program is shown in MATLAB Program 4-3.

MATLAB Program 4–3

```
% ---------- Response to Kronecker delta input ----------

num = [0   0.4673   -0.3393];
den = [1   -1.5327   0.6607];
x = [1   zeros(1,40)];
v = [0   40   -1   1];
axis(v);
k = 0:40;
y = filter(num,den,x);
plot(k,y,'o')
grid
title('Response to Kronecker Delta Input')
xlabel('k')
ylabel('y(k)')
```

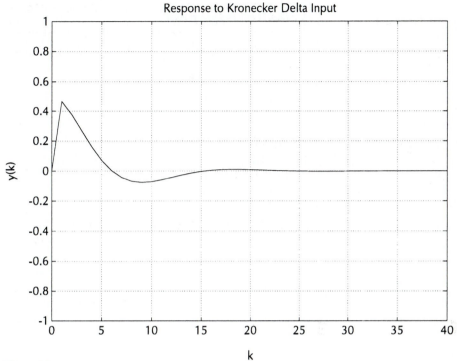

Figure 4-4

If we replace plot command

$$\text{plot(k,y,'o')}$$

by

$$\text{plot(k,y,'--')}.$$

we obtain the plot shown in Figure 4-4.

If we wish to connect consecutive points (open circles, 'o') by straight lines, we need to modify the plot command as follows:

$$\text{plot(k,y,'o',k,y,'--');}$$

A plot of $y(k)$ with open circles ('o') begins with $k = 0$ and ends at $k = 40$. Similarly, a plot of $y(k)$ using continuous lines begins at $k = 0$ and ends at $k = 40$. See MATLAB Program 4-4 and the resulting plot in Figure 4-5.

If we wish the plot to begin from $k = 5$, that is, to obtain $y(k)$ versus $k + 5$, we need to change

$$\text{k = 0:40;}$$

to

$$\text{k = 5:40;}$$

MATLAB Program 4-5 will give the desired plot, which is shown in Figure 4-6.

MATLAB Program 4–4

```
% ---------- Response to Kronecker delta input ----------

num = [0   0.4673   -0.3393];
den = [1   -1.5327   0.6607];
x = [1   zeros(1,40)];
v = [0   40   -1   1];
axis(v);
k = 0:40;
y = filter(num,den,x);
plot(k,y,'o',k,y,'-')
grid
title('Response to Kronecker Delta Input')
xlabel('k')
ylabel('y(k)')
```

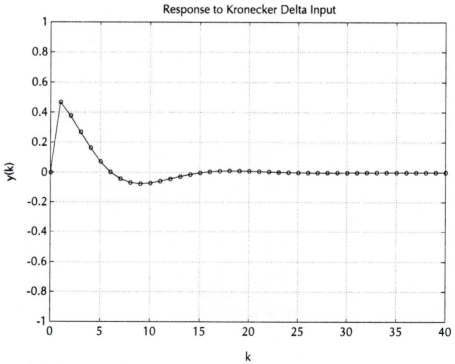

Figure 4-5

MATLAB Program 4–5

```
% ---------- Response to Kronecker delta input ----------

num = [0   0.4673   -0.3393];
den = [1   -1.5327   0.6607];
x = [1   zeros(1,40)];
v = [0   40   -1   1];
axis(v);
k = 5:40;
y = filter(num,den,x);
plot(k,y,'o',k,y,'-')
grid
title('Response to Kronecker Delta Input')
xlabel('k + 5')
ylabel('y(k)')
```

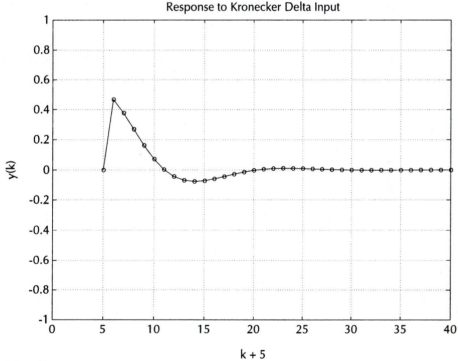

Figure 4-6

EXAMPLE 4-1

Obtain the inverse z transform of the following pulse transfer-function system.

$$\frac{Y(z)}{X(z)} = G(z) = \frac{0.01409z^3 + 0.02818z^2 + 0.01409z}{z^3 - 2.7624z^2 + 2.5811z - 0.8187}$$

The inverse z transform of $G(z)$ is the same as the response of the system to the Kronecker delta input. Let us obtain the inverse z transform of $y(k)$ up to $k = 40$.
We enter the following Kronecker delta input into the program.

$$x = [1 \quad zeros(1,40)]$$

A MATLAB program for solving this problem is given in MATLAB Program 4-6.

MATLAB Program 4–6

```
% ---------- Inverse z transform ----------

% ***** Inverse z transform can be obtained by finding the
% response of system Y(z)/X(z) to the Kronecker delta input *****

% ***** Enter the numerator and denominator of Y(z)/X(z) *****

b = [0.01409  0.02818  0.01409  0];
a = [1  -2.7624  2.5811  -0.8187];

% ***** Enter the Kronecker delta input x and filter command *****

x = [1  zeros(1,40)];
y = filter(b,a,x)
```

The output from the filter command is shown next. Note that the MATLAB output vector runs from column 1 to column 41. Column 1 corresponds to $k = 0$ and column 41 corresponds to $k = 40$.

---

y =

Columns 1 through 7

  0.0141   0.0671   0.1631   0.2888   0.4319   0.5811   0.7268

Columns 8 through 14

  0.8616   0.9798   1.0778   1.1537   1.2072   1.2394   1.2524

Columns 15 through 21

  1.2488   1.2320   1.2052   1.1718   1.1348   1.0970   1.0606

Columns 22 through 28

  1.0275   0.9989   0.9756   0.9580   0.9460   0.9392   0.9372

Columns 29 through 35

  0.9391   0.9442   0.9516   0.9604   0.9699   0.9794   0.9884

Columns 36 through 41

  0.9965   1.0034   1.0089   1.0130   1.0156   1.0170

The inverse z transform is thus given as follows:

$$y(0) = 0.0141$$
$$y(1) = 0.0671$$
$$y(2) = 0.1631$$
$$y(3) = 0.2888$$
$$\vdots$$
$$y(40) = 1.0170$$

To plot the inverse z transform $y(k)$ versus k, modify this MATLAB program as shown in MATLAB Program 4-7. The resulting plot of $y(k)$ is shown in Figure 4-7.

MATLAB Program 4–7

```
% ---------- Plot of inverse z transform y(k) versus k ----------

b = [0.01409   0.02818   0.01409   0];
a = [1   -2.7624   2.5811   -0.8187];
x = [1   zeros(1,40)];
v = [0   40   0   1.4];
axis(v);
k = 0:40;
y = filter(b,a,x);
plot(k,y,'o')
grid
title('Plot of Inverse z Transform y(k) versus k')
xlabel('k')
ylabel('y(k)')
```

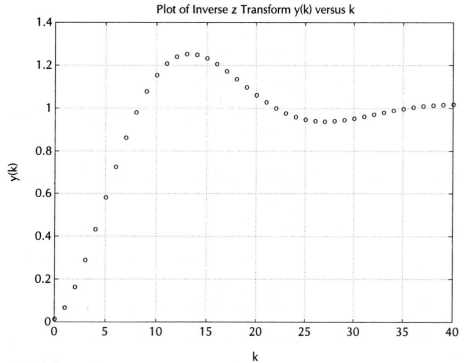

Figure 4-7

EXAMPLE 4-2

Consider the difference equation

$$x(k + 2) = x(k + 1) + x(k) \qquad\qquad (4\text{-}1)$$

where $x(0) = 0$ and $x(1) = 1$. Note that $x(2) = 1$, $x(3) = 2$, $x(4) = 3, \ldots$. The series 0, 1, 1, 2, 3, 5, 8, 13, $\ldots$ is known as the Fibonacci series. Obtain the Fibonacci series up to $k = 30$.
The z transform of Eq. (4-1) is

$$z^2 X(z) - z^2 x(0) - z x(1) = z X(z) - z x(0) + X(z)$$

Solving this equation for $X(z)$ gives

$$X(z) = \frac{z^2 x(0) + z x(1) - z x(0)}{z^2 - z - 1}$$

By substituting the initial data $x(0) = 0$ and $x(1) = 1$ into this last equation, we have

$$X(z) = \frac{z}{z^2 - z - 1}$$

The inverse z transform of $X(z)$ will give the Fibonacci series.
To get the inverse z transform of $X(z)$, obtain the response of this system to the Kronecker delta input. See MATLAB Program 4-8.

MATLAB Program 4–8

```
% ---------- Fibonacci series ----------

% ***** The Fibonacci series can be generated as the
% response of X(z) to the Kronecker delta input, where
% X(z) = z/(z^2 - z - 1) *****

% ***** Enter the numerator and denominator of X(z) *****

num = [0  1  0];
den = [1  -1  -1];

% ***** Enter the Kronecker delta input and filter command *****

u = [1  zeros(1,30)];
x = filter(num,den,u)
```

The filtered output y shown next gives the Fibonacci series.

```
x =

  Columns 1 through 6

              0           1           1           2           3           5

  Columns 7 through 12

              8          13          21          34          55          89

  Columns 13 through 18

            144         233         377         610         987        1597

  Columns 19 through 24

           2584        4181        6765       10946       17711       28657

  Columns 25 through 30

          46368       75025      121393      196418      317811      514229

  Column 31

         832040
```

Note that column 1 corresponds to $k = 0$ and column 31 corresponds to $k = 30$. The Fibonacci series is given by

$$x(0) = 0$$
$$x(1) = 1$$
$$x(2) = 1$$
$$x(3) = 2$$
$$x(4) = 3$$
$$x(5) = 5$$
$$\vdots$$
$$x(29) = 514,229$$
$$x(30) = 832,040$$

4-4 STEP RESPONSE

This section deals with responses of discrete-time systems to step inputs and arbitrary inputs. We shall begin with the step response of discrete-time systems.

Step response

Using an example system, we shall discuss methods for plotting step-response curves using MATLAB.

Consider the pulse transfer function system given by

$$\frac{Y(z)}{U(z)} = \frac{0.4673z^{-1} - 0.3393z^{-2}}{1 - 1.5327z^{-1} + 0.6607z^{-2}}$$

$$= \frac{0.4673z - 0.3393}{z^2 - 1.5327z + 0.6607}$$

where

$$U(z) = Z[\text{unit step}]$$

We shall present two methods to obtain the step response.

Method 1:   The unit step input $u(k)$ can be written as

$$u(k) = 1, \qquad \text{for } k = 0, 1, 2, \ldots$$

Let us assume that we want the response up to $k = 40$. Then the input u may be written as

$$u = \text{ones}(1, 41)$$

or

$$u = [1 \quad \text{ones}(1, 40)]$$

A MATLAB program for plotting a unit-step response curve of the system is given in MATLAB Program 4-9. The resulting plot is shown in Figure 4-8. Notice in this plot that the response curve starts from $k = 1$. (As stated earlier, MATLAB vectors run from $k = 1$ to $k = 41$ in this case. If we wish to plot the response $y(k)$ from $k = 0$ to $k = 40$, we need to make a modification in the MATLAB program. See MATLAB Program 4-10.)

MATLAB Program 4-10 enables the response curve to start from $k = 0$. See the plot of the response shown in Figure 4-9.

MATLAB Program 4–9

```
% ---------- Unit-step response ----------

num = [0   0.4673   -0.3393];
den = [1   -1.5327   0.6607];
u = ones(1,41);
v = [0   40   0   1.6];
axis(v);
y = filter(num,den,u);
plot(y,'o')
grid
title('Unit-Step Response')
xlabel('k + 1')
ylabel('y(k)')
```

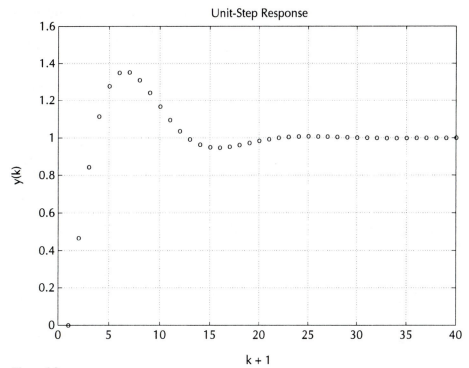

Figure 4-8

MATLAB Program 4–10

```
% ---------- Unit-step response ----------

num = [0   0.4673   -0.3393];
den = [1   -1.5327   0.6607];
u = ones(1,41);
v = [0   40   0   1.6];
axis(v);
k = 0: 40;
y = filter(num,den,u);
plot(k,y,'o')
grid
title('Unit-Step Response')
xlabel('k')
ylabel('y(k)')
```

Method 2:   In this method, we multiply $Y(z)/U(z)$ by $U(z)$, where $U(z) = z/(z - 1)$ for the unit-step input. Then we may take the inverse z transform of $Y(z)$ to get the response to the unit-step input.

Consider the same system as discussed above, or

$$\frac{Y(z)}{U(z)} = \frac{0.4673z - 0.3393}{z^2 - 1.5327z + 0.6607}$$

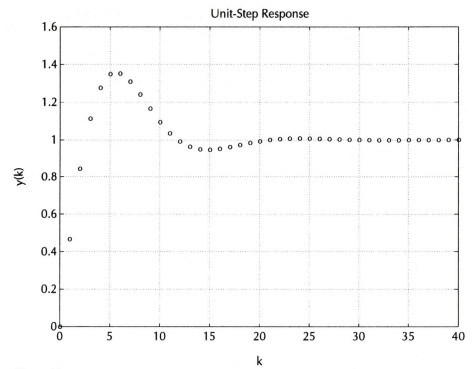

Figure 4-9

Multiplying $U(z) = z/(z - 1)$ to both sides of this last equation, we obtain

$$Y(z) = \frac{0.4673z - 0.3393}{z^2 - 1.5327z + 0.6607} U(z)$$

$$= \frac{0.4673z - 0.3393}{z^2 - 1.5327z + 0.6607} \frac{z}{z - 1}$$

$$= \frac{0.4673z^2 - 0.3393z}{z^3 - 2.5327z^2 + 2.1934z - 0.6607}$$

This last equation may be written as follows:

$$\frac{Y(z)}{X(z)} = \frac{0.4673z^2 - 0.3393z}{z^3 - 2.5327z^2 + 2.1934z - 0.6607}$$

where $X(z) = 1$. Since

$$X(z) = \sum_{k=0}^{\infty} x(k)z^{-k} = x(0) + x(1)z^{-1} + x(2)z^{-2} + \cdots$$

$$= 1$$

we have

$$x(0) = 1$$
$$x(k) = 0, \qquad \text{for } k = 1, 2, 3, \ldots$$

If we wish to plot $y(k)$ from $k = 0$ to 40, we may write the input $x(k)$ as follows:

$$x = [1 \quad \text{zeros}(1, 40)]$$

A MATLAB Program for plotting the unit-step response using the inverse z-transform approach is given in MATLAB Program 4-11. The resulting plot is shown in Figure 4-10.

MATLAB Program 4–11

```
% ---------- Unit-step response obtained as inverse z
% transform of G(z) = [Y(z)/X(z)][z/(z - 1)] ----------

% ***** Enter the numerator and denominator of G(z) *****

num = [0   0.4673  -0.3393   0];
den = [1  -2.5327   2.1934  -0.6607];

% ***** Enter the Kronecker delta input, axis(v), k,
% filter command, and plot command *****

x = [1   zeros(1,40)];
v = [0   40   0   1.6];
axis(v);
k = 0:40;
y = filter(num,den,x);
plot(k,y,'o',k,y,'-')
grid
title('Unit-Step Response Obtained as Inverse z Transform of G(z)')
xlabel('k')
ylabel('y(k)')
```

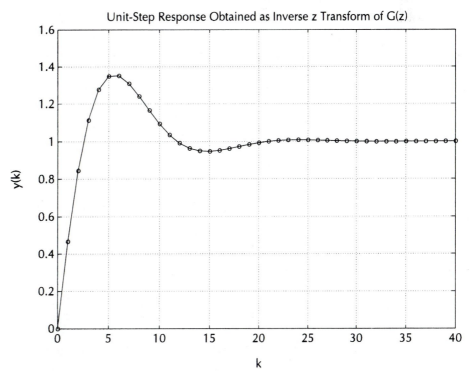

Figure 4-10

EXAMPLE 4-3

Plot the unit-step response curve of the following pulse transfer-function system:

$$\frac{Y(z)}{U(z)} = \frac{0.01409 + 0.02818z^{-1} + 0.01409z^{-2}}{1 - 1.7624z^{-1} + 0.8187z^{-2}}$$

$$= \frac{0.01409z^2 + 0.02818z + 0.01409}{z^2 - 1.7624z + 0.8187}$$

A MATLAB program for plotting the unit-step response curve is shown in MATLAB Program 4-12. The resulting plot is shown in Figure 4-11.

MATLAB Program 4–12

```
% ---------- Unit-step response ----------

b = [0.01409  0.02818  0.01409];
a = [1  -1.7624  0.8187];
u = ones(1,101);
v = [0  100  0  1.4];
axis(v);
k = 0:100;
y = filter(b,a,u);
plot(k,y,'o')
grid
title('Unit-Step Response')
xlabel('k')
ylabel('y(k)')
```

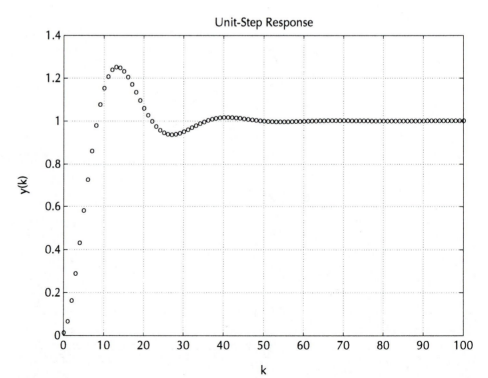

Figure 4-11

EXAMPLE 4-4

Plot the unit-step response of the following closed-loop pulse transfer-function system. The closed-loop pulse transfer function is

$$\frac{Y(z)}{U(z)} = \frac{0.3205z^{-3} - 0.1885z^{-4}}{1 - 1.3679z^{-1} + 0.3679z^{-2} + 0.3205z^{-3} - 0.1885z^{-4}}$$

$$= \frac{0.3205z - 0.1885}{z^4 - 1.3679z^3 + 0.3679z^2 + 0.3205z - 0.1885}$$

A MATLAB program for plotting the unit-step response is shown in MATLAB Program 4-13. The resulting plot is shown in Figure 4-12. Notice that the unit-step response reaches the

---

MATLAB Program 4–13

```
% ---------- Unit-step response ----------

num = [0   0   0   0.3205   -0.1885];
den = [1   -1.3679   0.3679   0.3205   -0.1885];
u = [1   ones(1,50)];
v = [0   50   0   1.6];
axis(v);
k = 0:50;
y = filter(num,den,u);
plot(k,y,'o')
grid
title('Unit-Step Response')
xlabel('k')
ylabel('y(k)')
```

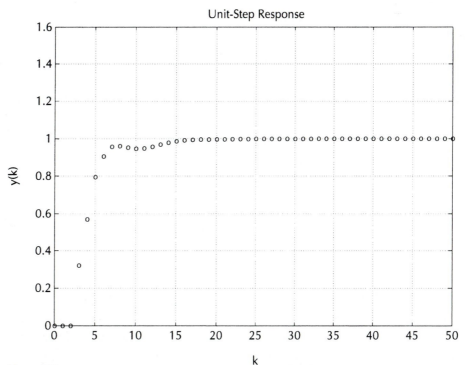

Figure 4-12

final value (unity) fairly quickly without an overshoot. Let us find the closed-loop poles for the system.

The characteristic equation for this closed-loop system is obtained from the denominator polynomial as follows:

$$den(z) = z^4 - 1.3679z^3 + 0.3679z^2 + 0.3205z - 0.1885 = 0$$

To find the characteristics roots, enter the statement

$$r = roots(den)$$

The result follows:

```
den =

    1.0000    -1.3679    0.3679    0.3205    -0.1885

r = roots(den)

r =

   0.5625 + 0.4095i
   0.5625 - 0.4095i
   0.7572
  -0.5143
```

EXAMPLE 4-5

In this example, we consider the response of a system to an arbitrary input. Suppose that the pulse transfer function of a system is given by

$$\frac{Y(z)}{U(z)} = \frac{0.3679z + 0.2642}{z^2 - 1.3679z + 0.3679}$$

The input $u(k)$ to the system is given by

$$u(0) = 1.582$$
$$u(1) = -0.582$$
$$u(k) = 0, \qquad \text{for } k = 2, 3, 4, \ldots$$

Plot the response $y(k)$ of the system to the input $u(k)$ for $k = 0, 1, 2, \ldots, 25$.

The input function $u(k)$ may be entered in the MATLAB program as

$$u = [1.582 \quad -0.582 \quad zeros(1, 24)]$$

A MATLAB program to plot the response is shown in MATLAB Program 4-14. A plot of the response is shown in Figure 4-13.

MATLAB Program 4–14

```
% ---------- Response to arbitrary input ----------

% ***** Response of system to an arbitrarily specified
% input *****

% ***** Enter the numerator and denominator of the system *****

num = [0   0.3679   0.2642];
den = [1   -1.3679   0.3679];

% ***** Enter the given input *****

u = [1.582   -0.5820   zeros(1,24)];

% ***** Enter axis(v), k, filter command, and plot command *****

v = [0   25   0   2];
axis(v);
k = 0:25;
y = filter(num,den,u);
plot(k,y,'o')

% ***** Add grid, title, xlabel, and ylabel *****

grid
title('Response of System to Arbitrarily Specified Input')
xlabel('k')
ylabel('y(k)')
```

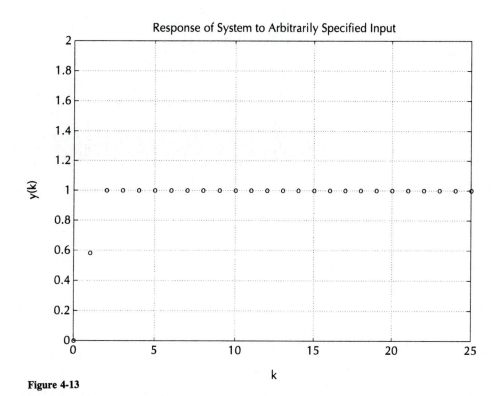

Figure 4-13

EXAMPLE 4-6

Consider the same system as in Example 4-5. Suppose that the input $u(k)$ is given by

$$u(0) = u(1) = u(2) = 1$$
$$u(3) = u(4) = u(5) = -1$$
$$u(k) = 0, \qquad \text{for } k = 6, 7, 8, \ldots, 25$$

Find the response $x(k)$ to this input and plot the response $y(k)$ versus k.

The input function may be written as

$$u = [1 \quad 1 \quad 1 \quad -1 \quad -1 \quad -1 \quad \text{zeros}(1, 20)]$$

A MATLAB program to plot the response to this input is shown in MATLAB Program 4-15. The resulting plot is shown in Figure 4-14.

MATLAB Program 4–15

```
% ---------- Response to arbitrary input ----------

% ***** Enter the numerator and denominator of the system *****

num = [0   0.3679   0.2642];
den = [1   -1.3679   0.3679];

% ***** Enter the given input *****

u = [1   1   1   -1   -1   -1   zeros(1,20)];

% ***** Enter axis(v), k, filter command, and plot command *****

v = [0   25   -3   3];
axis(v);
k = 0:25;
y = filter(num,den,u);
plot(k,y,'o')

% ***** Add grid, title, xlabel, and ylabel *****

grid
title('Response of System to Arbitrarily Specified Input')
xlabel('k')
ylabel('y(k)')
```

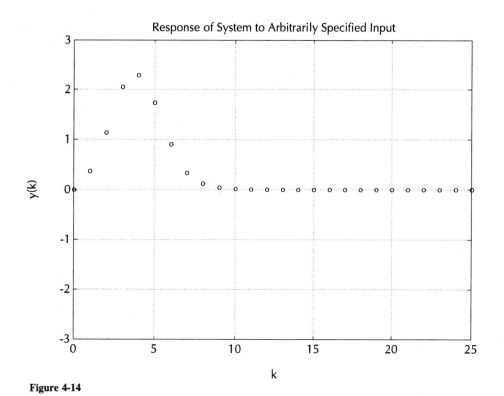

Figure 4-14

4-5 RAMP RESPONSE

In this section we shall discuss the unit-ramp response. In dealing with the ramp response, it is necessary to specify the sampling period T.

Consider the system described by

$$\frac{Y(z)}{U(z)} = \frac{0.7870z^{-1}}{1 - 0.8195z^{-1} + 0.6065z^{-2}}$$

$$= \frac{0.7870z}{z^2 - 0.8195z + 0.6065}$$

The sampling period T is 0.5 sec. Plot the unit-ramp response up to $k = 20$.

The unit-ramp response can be obtained by applying the unit-ramp input $u = kT$ $(k = 0, 1, 2, \ldots)$ to the system or by multiplying the input $U(z) = Tz/(z - 1)^2$ to the system pulse transfer function and using the Kronecker delta input. We shall consider both approaches.

Method 1: Unit-ramp response is obtained by applying the unit-ramp input to the system

The unit-ramp input u can be given by

$$u = kT, \qquad k = 0, 1, 2, \ldots$$

In the MATLAB program, this input can be given as

$$k = 0:N; \qquad u = [k * T];$$

where N is the end of the process considered.

In the ramp response, it is important to specify the sampling period T, because the slope of the ramp input plotted against k is T. (For $T = 0.5$ sec, the slope of the unit-ramp input when plotted against k is 0.5.)

A MATLAB program for plotting the unit-ramp response of the system considered is given in MATLAB Program 4-16. The resulting plot is shown in Figure 4-15.

Method 2:   Unit-ramp response is obtained as the inverse z transform of $G(z) = [Y(z)/U(z)]U(z)$

The z transform of the unit-ramp input is

$$U(z) = \frac{Tz^{-1}}{(1 - z^{-1})^2} = \frac{Tz}{(z - 1)^2}$$

By multiplying $U(z)$ to $Y(z)/U(z)$, we obtain

$$\frac{Y(z)}{U(z)} U(z) = G(z) = \frac{Y(z)}{U(z)} \frac{Tz}{(z - 1)^2}$$

For the system considered, $G(z)$ becomes

$$G(z) = Y(z) = \frac{0.7870z}{z^2 - 0.8195z + 0.6065} \frac{0.5z}{z^2 - 2z + 1}$$

$$= \frac{0.3935z^2}{z^4 - 2.8195z^3 + 3.2455z^2 - 2.0325z + 0.6065}$$

MATLAB Program 4–16

```
% ---------- Unit-ramp response ----------

% ***** Enter the numerator and denominator of the system *****

num = [0   0.7870   0];
den = [1   -0.8195   0.6065];

% ***** Enter k, unit-ramp input, filter command and plot
% command *****

k = 0:20;
u =  [0.5*k];
y = filter(num,den,u);
plot(k,y,'o',k,y,'-',k,0.5*k,'--')

% ***** Add grid, title, xlabel, and ylabel *****

grid
title('Unit-Ramp Response')
xlabel('k')
ylabel('y(k)')
```

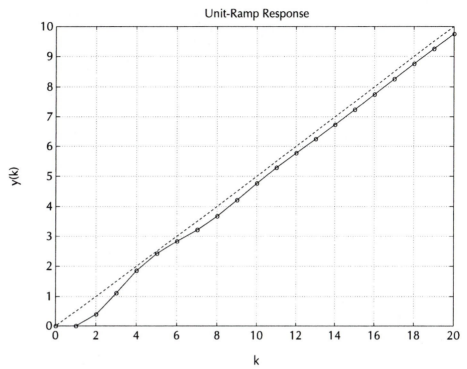

Figure 4-15

The inverse z transform of $G(z)$ will give the unit-ramp response. MATLAB Program 4-17 may be used to plot the unit-ramp response using the inverse z transform approach. The resulting plot is shown in Figure 4-16.

```
MATLAB Program 4–17

% ---------- Unit-ramp response ----------

% ***** Unit-ramp response is obatined as the inverse z
% transform of G(z) = [Y(z)/U(z)][Tz/(z - 1)^2] *****

% ***** Enter the numerator and denominator of G(z) *****

num = [0  0  0.3935  0  0];
den = [1  -2.8195  3.2455  -2.0325  0.6065];

% ***** Enter the Kronecker delta input, k, filter command,
and plot command *****

x = [1   zeros(1,20)];
k = 0:20;
y = filter(num,den,x);
plot(k,y,'o',k,y,'-',k,0.5*k,'--')

% ***** Add grid, title, xlabel, and ylabel *****

grid
title('Unit-Ramp Response Obtained as Inverse z Transform')
xlabel('k')
ylabel('y(k)')
```

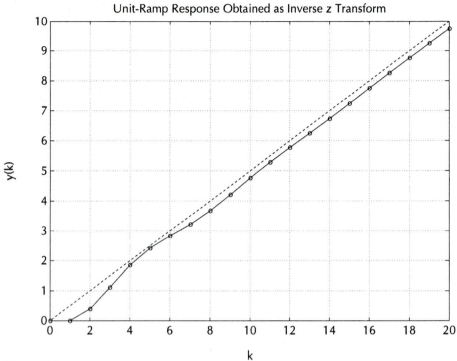

Figure 4-16

4-6 CASE STUDIES

In this section, we shall first investigate the transient-response characteristics of the PID-controlled digital control system shown in Figure 4-17. (This system has been designed to exhibit zero steady-state error in ramp response.) Then we shall discuss the response of deadbeat systems.

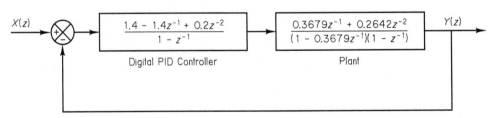

Figure 4-17

EXAMPLE 4-7

Consider the digital control system shown in Figure 4-17. The sampling period T is 1 sec. The closed-loop pulse transfer function for the system is

$$\frac{Y(z)}{X(z)} = \frac{0.5151z^{-1} - 0.1452z^{-2} - 0.2963z^{-3} + 0.0528z^{-4}}{1 - 1.8528z^{-1} + 1.5906z^{-2} - 0.6642z^{-3} + 0.0528z^{-4}}$$

or

$$\frac{Y(z)}{X(z)} = \frac{0.5151z^3 - 0.1452z^2 - 0.2963z + 0.0528}{z^4 - 1.8528z^3 + 1.5906z^2 - 0.6642z + 0.0528}$$

We shall consider the response of this system to the following three types of input:

1. Kronecker delta input
2. Unit-step input
3. Unit-ramp input

Response to Kronecker delta input   A MATLAB program to plot the response of the system to the Kronecker delta input is shown in MATLAB Program 4-18. The resulting plot is shown in Figure 4-18.

MATLAB Program 4–18

```
% ---------- Response to Kronecker delta input ----------

num = [0   0.5151   -0.1452   -0.2963   0.0528];
den = [1   -1.8528   1.5906   -0.6642   0.0528];
x = [1   zeros(1,40)];
v = [0   40   -1   1];
axis(v);
k = 0:40;
y = filter(num,den,x);
plot(k,y,'o',k,y,'-')
grid
title('Response to Kronecker Delta Input')
xlabel('k')
ylabel('y(k)')
```

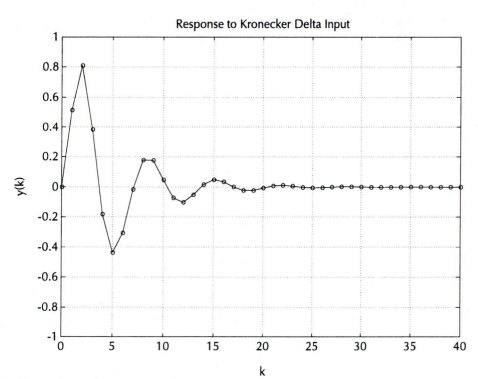

Figure 4-18

Response to unit-step input   A plot of the unit-step response of the system may be obtained by entering MATLAB Program 4-19 into the computer. The resulting plot is shown in Figure 4-19.

Response to unit-ramp input   The sampling period T is 1 sec. Hence the ramp input becomes $x = [k*T] = [k]$. A plot of the unit-ramp response may be obtained by entering MATLAB Program 4-20 into the computer. The resulting plot is shown in Figure 4-20.

MATLAB Program 4–19

```
% ---------- Unit-step response ----------

num = [0   0.5151   -0.1452   -0.2963   0.0528];
den = [1   -1.8528   1.5906   -0.6642   0.0528];
x = [1   ones(1,40)];
v = [0   40   0   2];
axis(v);
k = 0:40;
y = filter(num,den,x);
plot(k,y,'o',k,y,'-')
grid
title('Unit-Step Response')
xlabel('k')
ylabel('y(k)')
```

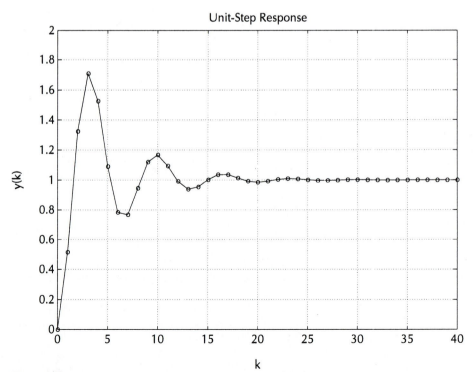

Figure 4-19

```
MATLAB Program 4–20

% ---------- Unit-ramp response ----------

num = [0   0.5151   -0.1452   -0.2963   0.0528];
den = [1   -1.8528   1.5906   -0.6642   0.0528];
v = [0   16   0   16];
axis(v);
k = 0:40;
x = [k];
y = filter(num,den,x);
plot(k,y,'o',k,y,'-',k,k,'--')
grid
title('Unit-Ramp Response')
xlabel('k')
ylabel('y(k)')
```

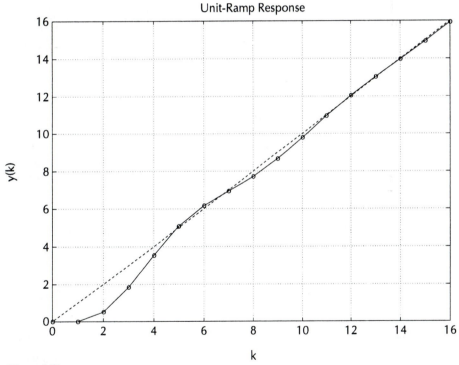

Figure 4-20

The closed-loop poles for the system can be obtained from the characteristic polynomial, which is the denominator of the closed-loop pulse transfer function.

$$\text{den}(z) = z^4 - 1.8528z^3 + 1.5906z^2 - 0.6642z + 0.0528$$

Entering the statement

$$r = \text{roots(den)}$$

we obtain the closed-loop poles for the system as follows:

```
den =

    1.0000    -1.8528    1.5906    -0.6642    0.0528

r = roots(den)

r =

    0.4763 + 0.6521i
    0.4763 - 0.6521i
    0.7989
    0.1013
```

This system has been designed to exhibit zero steady-state error in the ramp response. To verify this, let us calculate the steady-state error. The open-loop pulse transfer function for the system is

$$G(z) = \frac{(1.4z^2 - 1.4z + 0.2)(0.3679z + 0.2642)}{(z - 1)(z - 0.3679)(z - 1)z}$$

$$= \frac{0.5151(z - 0.1727)(z - 0.8273)}{z(z - 0.3679)(z - 1)^2}$$

The velocity error constant K_v of this system is

$$K_v = \lim_{z \to 1} \frac{(1 - z^{-1})G(z)}{T} = \lim_{z \to 1} \frac{(z - 1)G(z)}{T}$$

$$= \lim_{z \to 1} \frac{0.5151(z - 0.1727)(z - 0.8273)}{Tz(z - 0.3679)(z - 1)}$$

$$= \infty$$

Hence the steady-state error for the ramp response is

$$\text{steady-state error} = \frac{1}{K_v} = 0$$

EXAMPLE 4-8: Deadbeat Control System Designed for Step Inputs

If the response of a discrete-time control system to a step input exhibits the minimum possible settling time (that is, the output reaches the final value in the minimum time and stays there), no steady-state error, and no ripples between the sampling instants, then this type of response is commonly called a *deadbeat response*.

Consider the digital control system shown in Figure 4-21(a). The error signal $e(t)$, which is the difference between the input $r(t)$ and the output $c(t)$, is sampled every time interval T sec. The input to the digital controller is the error signal $e(kT)$. The output of the digital controller is the control signal $u(kT)$. The control signal $u(kT)$ is fed to the zero-order hold, and the output of the hold, $u(t)$, which is a piecewise continuous-time signal, is fed to the plant.

A discrete-time control system can be designed to exhibit the minimum possible settling time with zero steady-state error in response to a step input and, in addition, the output does not exhibit intersampling ripples after the steady state is reached.

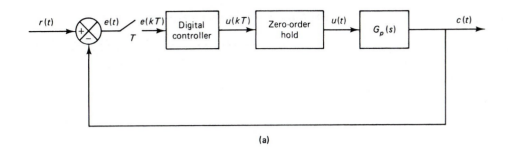

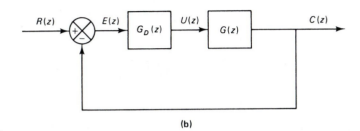

(b)

Figure 4-21

Let us define the z transform of the plant that is preceded by the zero-order hold as $G(z)$, or

$$G(z) = Z\left[\frac{1 - e^{-Ts}}{s} G_p(s)\right]$$

Then the open-loop pulse transfer function becomes $G_D(z)G(z)$, as shown in Figure 4-21(b).
Suppose that the plant transfer function $G_p(s)$ is given by

$$G_p(s) = \frac{1}{s(s + 1)}$$

A digital controller $G_D(z)$ can be designed such that the closed-loop system will exhibit a deadbeat response to a unit-step input. The sampling period T is assumed to be 1 sec.

The z transform of the plant that is preceded by the zero-order hold is

$$\begin{aligned}
G(z) &= Z\left[\frac{1 - e^{-Ts}}{s} \frac{1}{s(s + 1)}\right] \\
&= (1 - z^{-1})Z\left[\frac{1}{s^2(s + 1)}\right] \\
&= (1 - z^{-1})\left[\frac{z^{-1}}{(1 - z^{-1})^2} - \frac{1}{1 - z^{-1}} + \frac{1}{1 - 0.3679z^{-1}}\right] \\
&= \frac{0.3679(1 + 0.7181z^{-1})z^{-1}}{(1 - z^{-1})(1 - 0.3679z^{-1})}
\end{aligned}$$

Using an analytical design method, the following deadbeat controller may be designed.

$$G_D(z) = \frac{1.5820 - 0.5820z^{-1}}{1 + 0.4180z^{-1}}$$

(For details of the design technique, refer to Reference 3.)

The open-loop pulse transfer function for the system becomes

$$\begin{aligned}
G_D(z)G(z) &= \frac{1.5820 - 0.5820z^{-1}}{1 + 0.4180z^{-1}} \frac{0.3679(1 + 0.7181z^{-1})z^{-1}}{(1 - z^{-1})(1 - 0.3679z^{-1})} \\
&= \frac{0.5820(z + 0.7181)}{(z + 0.4180)(z - 1)}
\end{aligned}$$

The closed-loop pulse transfer function is

$$\frac{C(z)}{R(z)} = \frac{0.5820(z + 0.7181)}{0.5820(z + 0.7181) + (z + 0.4180)(z - 1)}$$

$$= \frac{0.5820z + 0.4180}{z^2}$$

Let us plot the unit-step response up to $k = 20$. MATLAB Program 4-21 will yield the desired result. Figure 4-22 shows the deadbeat response.

It is interesting to see the unit-ramp response of this system. This system is designed to exhibit the deadbeat response to step inputs. Such a deadbeat system will give a "best" response to the step input, but not best response to other types of inputs. (To get a "best" response to ramp inputs, the system must be designed for deadbeat response to ramp inputs. See Example 4-9.)

MATLAB Program 4–21

```
% ---------- Unit-step response ----------

num = [0   0.5820   0.4180];
den = [1   0   0];
r = ones(1,21);
k = 0:20;
v = [0   20   0   1.6];
axis(v);
c = filter(num,den,r);
plot(k,c,'o',k,c,'-')
grid
title('Unit-Step Response of Deadbeat System')
xlabel('k')
ylabel('c(k)')
```

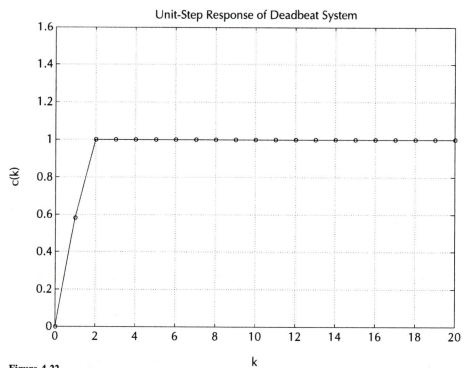

Figure 4-22

To see the unit-ramp response of this system, enter MATLAB Program 4-22 into the computer. Figure 4-23 shows the unit-ramp response.

MATLAB Program 4–22

```
% ---------- Unit-ramp response ----------

num = [0   0.5820   0.4180];
den = [1   0   0];
k = 0:20; r = [k];
v = [0   20   0   20];
axis(v);
c = filter(num,den,r);
plot(k,c,'o',k,c,'-',k,k,'--')
grid
title('Unit-Ramp Response of Deadbeat System')
xlabel('k')
ylabel('c(k)')
```

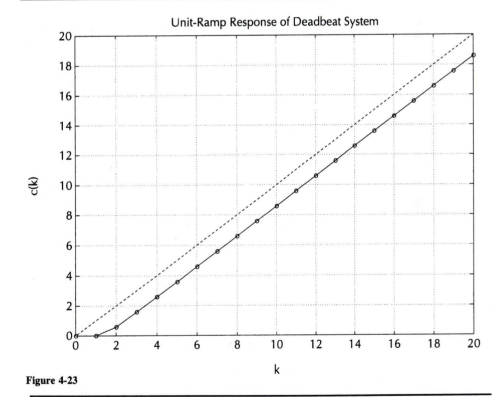

Figure 4-23

EXAMPLE 4-9: Deadbeat Control System for Ramp Inputs

Consider the system shown in Figure 4-24. The pulse transfer function $G(z)$ of the plant that is preceded by the zero-order hold is

$$G(z) = Z\left[\frac{1 - e^{-Ts}}{s}\frac{1}{s^2}\right] = (1 - z^{-1})Z\left[\frac{1}{s^3}\right]$$

$$= \frac{(1 + z^{-1})z^{-1}}{2(1 - z^{-1})^2}$$

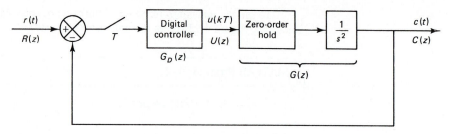

Figure 4-24

A deadbeat controller can be designed such that the system will exhibit the minimum settling time with zero steady-state error in the ramp response and will not exhibit intersampling ripples at steady state. The sampling period T is assumed to be 1 sec.

Using an analytical design method, a desired deadbeat controller can be designed. The pulse transfer function of the deadbeat controller for this system is

$$G_D(z) = \frac{2.5(1 - 0.6z^{-1})}{1 + 0.75z^{-1}}$$

(For the design of this deadbeat controller, see Reference 3.)

The open-loop pulse transfer function for the system is

$$G_D(z)G(z) = \frac{2.5(1 - 0.6z^{-1})}{1 + 0.75z^{-1}} \frac{(1 + z^{-1})z^{-1}}{2(1 - z^{-1})^2}$$

$$= \frac{2.5(z - 0.6)(z + 1)}{(z + 0.75)2(z - 1)^2}$$

The closed-loop pulse transfer function is

$$\frac{C(z)}{R(z)} = \frac{2.5(z - 0.6)(z + 1)}{2.5(z - 0.6)(z + 1) + (z + 0.75)2(z - 1)^2}$$

$$= \frac{1.25z^2 + 0.5z - 0.75}{z^3}$$

```
MATLAB Program 4–23

% ---------- Unit-ramp response ----------

num = [0  1.25  0.5  -0.75];
den = [1  0  0  0];
k = 0:20; r = [k];
v = [0  20  0  20];
axis(v);
c = filter(num,den,r);
plot(k,c,'o',k,c,'-',k,k,'--')
grid
title('Ramp Response of Deadbeat System Designed for Ramp Inputs')
xlabel('k')
ylabel('c(k)')
```

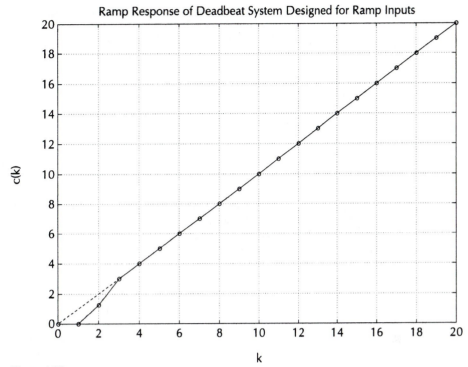

Figure 4-25

A plot of the unit-ramp response may be obtained by entering MATLAB Program 4-23 into the computer. The resulting plot is shown in Figure 4-25. Notice that for $3 \le k$ the output follows the ramp input without error. This system exhibits a "best" response to the ramp input, but will not exhibit best response to other types of inputs. For example, for a unit-step input the output will show an overshoot before reaching the steady state. MATLAB Program 4-24 will yield a plot of the unit-step response. Such a plot is shown in Figure 4-26.

```
MATLAB Program 4–24

% ---------- Unit-step response ----------

num = [0   1.25   0.5   -0.75];
den = [1   0   0   0];
r = ones(1,21);
k = 0:20;
v = [0   20   0   2];
axis(v);
c = filter(num,den,r);
plot(k,c,'o',k,c,'-')
grid
title('Step Response of Deadbeat System Designed for Ramp Inputs')
xlabel('k')
ylabel('c(k)')
```

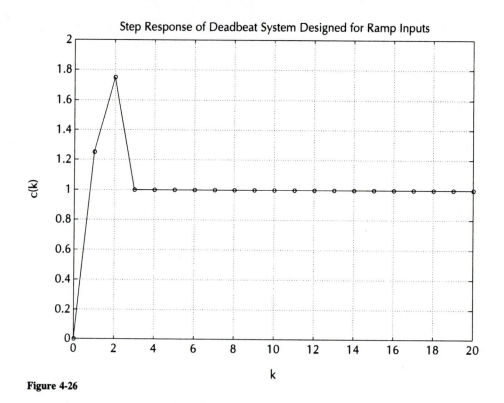

Figure 4-26

4-7 TRANSIENT RESPONSE OF DISCRETE-TIME SYSTEMS DEFINED IN STATE SPACE

In this section, we shall discuss the transient response of discrete-time systems defined in state space. Specifically, we shall find the step response of the system

$$\mathbf{x}(k + 1) = \mathbf{G}\mathbf{x}(k) + \mathbf{H}u(k)$$
$$y(k) = \mathbf{C}\mathbf{x}(k) + Du(k)$$

[The input $u(k)$ may be step input, ramp input, Kronecker delta input, and so on.] Consider, as an example, the following system:

$$\begin{bmatrix} x_1(k + 1) \\ x_2(k + 1) \end{bmatrix} = \begin{bmatrix} 0 & 1 \\ -0.16 & -1 \end{bmatrix} \begin{bmatrix} x_1(k) \\ x_2(k) \end{bmatrix} + \begin{bmatrix} 0 \\ 1 \end{bmatrix} u(k) \qquad (4\text{-}2)$$

$$y(k) = [1.16 \quad 1] \begin{bmatrix} x_1(k) \\ x_2(k) \end{bmatrix} \qquad (4\text{-}3)$$

For this system,

$$\mathbf{G} = \begin{bmatrix} 0 & 1 \\ -0.16 & -1 \end{bmatrix}, \qquad \mathbf{H} = \begin{bmatrix} 0 \\ 1 \end{bmatrix}, \qquad \mathbf{C} = [1.16 \quad 1], \qquad D = 0$$

Let us assume that the system is at rest initially and that $u(k)$ is a unit-step sequence.

First, we shall give an analytical solution to this problem. The pulse transfer function $Y(z)/U(z)$ of this system is obtained by use of the following equation:

$$\frac{Y(z)}{U(z)} = \mathbf{C}(z\mathbf{I} - \mathbf{G})^{-1}\mathbf{H} + D$$

$$= [1.16 \quad 1]\begin{bmatrix} z & -1 \\ 0.16 & z + 1 \end{bmatrix}^{-1}\begin{bmatrix} 0 \\ 1 \end{bmatrix} + 0$$

$$= \frac{z + 1.16}{z^2 + z + 0.16}$$

For a unit-step sequence input, we have

$$U(z) = \frac{z}{z - 1}$$

Hence

$$Y(z) = \frac{z + 1.16}{z^2 + z + 0.16}\frac{z}{z - 1}$$

$$= \frac{z^{-1} + 1.16z^{-2}}{1 + z^{-1} + 0.16z^{-2}}\frac{1}{1 - z^{-1}}$$

$$= \frac{z^{-1} + 1.16z^{-2}}{1 - 0.84z^{-2} - 0.16z^{-3}}$$

$$= z^{-1} + 1.16z^{-2} + 0.84z^{-3} + 1.1344z^{-4} + \cdots$$

Note that the final value $y(\infty)$ can be obtained by use of the final-value theorem as follows:

$$y(\infty) = \lim_{z \to 1}(1 - z^{-1})\frac{z^{-1} + 1.16z^{-2}}{1 + z^{-1} + 0.16z^{-2}}\frac{1}{1 - z^{-1}}$$

$$= \frac{2.16}{2.16} = 1.0000$$

Thus, y(k) can be given by

$$y(0) = 0$$
$$y(1) = 1$$
$$y(2) = 1.16$$
$$y(3) = 0.84$$
$$y(4) = 1.1344$$
$$\vdots$$
$$y(\infty) = 1.0000$$

Next, we shall find $x_2(k)$. From Eq. (4-2), we have

$$x_1(k + 1) = x_2(k)$$
$$x_2(k + 1) = -0.16x_1(k) - x_2(k) + u(k)$$

Hence, we get

$$x_2(k + 2) + x_2(k + 1) + 0.16x_2(k) = u(k + 1)$$

By taking the z transform of this equation, noting that $x_2(0) = 0$, $x_2(1) = 1$, and $u(0) = 1$, we find

$$z^2 X_2(z) - z + z X_2(z) + 0.16 X_2(z) = z U(z) - z$$

or

$$X_2(z) = \frac{z}{z^2 + z + 0.16} U(z)$$

$$= \frac{z^{-1}}{1 + z^{-1} + 0.16z^{-2}} \frac{1}{1 - z^{-1}}$$

$$= \frac{z^{-1}}{1 - 0.84z^{-2} - 0.16z^{-3}}$$

$$= z^{-1} + 0.84z^{-3} + 0.16z^{-4} + 0.7056z^{-5} + \cdots$$

The final value of $x_2(k)$ is

$$x_2(\infty) = \lim_{z \to 1} (1 - z^{-1}) \frac{z^{-1}}{1 + z^{-1} + 0.16z^{-2}} \frac{1}{1 - z^{-1}}$$

$$= \frac{1}{2.16} = 0.4630$$

Hence

$$x_2(0) = 0$$
$$x_2(1) = 1$$
$$x_2(2) = 0$$
$$x_2(3) = 0.84$$
$$x_2(4) = 0.16$$
$$x_2(5) = 0.7056$$
$$\vdots$$
$$x_2(\infty) = 0.4630$$

To find $x_1(k)$, note that $x_1(0) = 0$ and $x_1(k + 1) = x_2(k)$. Hence

$$x_1(0) = 0$$
$$x_1(1) = x_2(0) = 0$$
$$x_1(2) = x_2(1) = 1$$
$$x_1(3) = x_2(2) = 0$$
$$x_1(4) = x_2(3) = 0.84$$
$$x_1(5) = x_2(4) = 0.16$$
$$\vdots$$
$$x_1(\infty) = x_2(\infty) = 0.4630$$

Solution with MATLAB

In finding the output $y(k)$ with MATLAB, we first convert state-space equations (4-2) and (4-3) into the pulse transfer function $Y(z)/U(z)$ by use of the following command:

$$[num,den] = ss2tf(G,H,C,D)$$

we then use the filter command

$$y = filter(num,den,u)$$

where u is the unit-step sequence.

To obtain the response $x_1(k)$, use the following fictitious output equation:

$$x_1(k) = \begin{bmatrix} 1 & 0 \end{bmatrix} \begin{bmatrix} x_1(k) \\ x_2(k) \end{bmatrix} = \mathbf{F}\mathbf{x}(k) \qquad (4\text{-}4)$$

where

$$\mathbf{F} = \begin{bmatrix} 1 & 0 \end{bmatrix}$$

Then convert state-space equations (4-2) and (4-4) into the pulse transfer function $X_1(z)/U(z)$ by use of the command

$$[num1,den1] = ss2tf(G,H,F,D)$$

and then use the filter command

$$x1 = filter(num1,den1,u)$$

Similarly, to obtain the response $x_2(k)$, consider another fictitious output equation:

$$x_2(k) = \begin{bmatrix} 0 & 1 \end{bmatrix} \begin{bmatrix} x_1(k) \\ x_2(k) \end{bmatrix} = \mathbf{J}\mathbf{x} \qquad (4\text{-}5)$$

where

$$\mathbf{J} = \begin{bmatrix} 0 & 1 \end{bmatrix}$$

Convert state-space equations (4-2) and (4-5) into the pulse transfer function $X_2(z)/U(z)$ by use of the command

$$[num2,den2] = ss2tf(G,H,J,D)$$

and then use the *filter* command

$$x2 = filter(num2,den2,u)$$

Use MATLAB Program 4-25 to obtain the responses y(k) versus k, x1(k) versus k, and x2(k) versus k. Figures 4-27, 4-28, and 4-29 show, respectively, y(k) versus k, x1(k) versus k, and x2(k) versus k.

MATLAB Program 4-25

```
% ---------- Step response of discrete-time system defined in
% state space ----------

% ***** Step response of discrete-time system defined in state
% space will be obtained by first converting state-space equations
% into pulse transfer function and then by using 'filter' command
% to obtain step response *****

% ***** Enter matrices G, H, C, F, J, D *****

G = [0   1;-0.16   -1];
H = [0;1];
C = [1.16   1];
F = [1   0];
J = [0   1];
D = [0];

% ***** To obtain y(k) convert state-space equations into pulse
% transfer function Y(z)/U(z) *****

[num,den] = ss2tf(G,H,C,D);

% ***** Enter command to obtain unit-step response *****

u = ones(1,51);
axis([0   50   -0.5   2]);
k = 0:50;
y = filter(num,den,u);
plot(k,y,'o',k,y,'-')
grid
title('Unit-Step Response y(k)')
xlabel('k')
ylabel('y(k)')

% ***** To obtain x1(k) convert state-space equations into pulse
% transfer function X1(z)/U(z) *****

[num1,den1] = ss2tf(G,H,F,D);

% ***** Enter command to obtain unit-step response *****

axis([0   50   -0.5   1.5]);
x1 = filter(num1,den1,u);
plot(k,x1,'o',k,x1,'-')
grid
title('Unit-Step Response x1(k)')
xlabel('k')
ylabel('x1(k)')

% ***** To obtain x2(k) convert state-space equations into pulse
```

```
% transfer function X2(z)/U(z) *****

[num2,den2] = ss2tf(G,H,J,D);

% ***** Enter command to obtain unit-step response *****

axis([0  50  -0.5  1.5]);
x2 = filter(num2,den2,u);
plot(k,x2,'o',k,x2,'-')
grid
title('Unit-Step Response x2(k)')
xlabel('k')
ylabel('x2(k)')
```

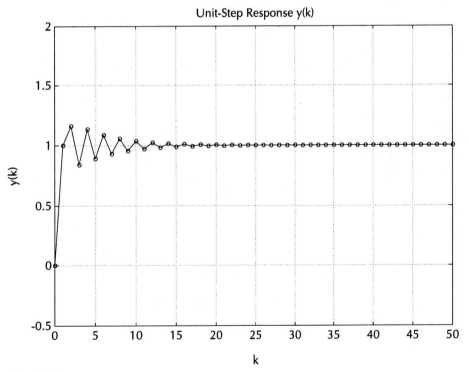

Figure 4-27

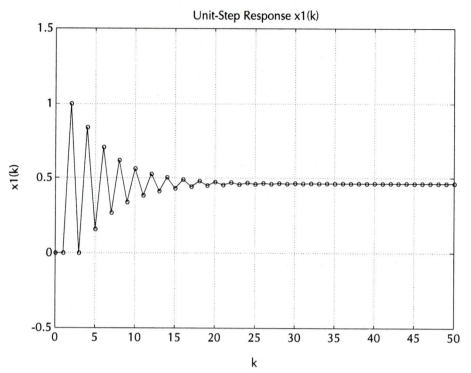

Figure 4-28

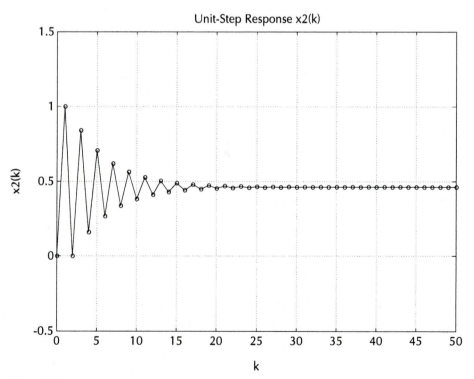

Figure 4-29

Chapter 5   Root-Locus Plots

5-1 INTRODUCTION

This chapter deals with plotting root loci of control systems. The command rlocus generates the root locus of a single-input, single-output system.

Consider the system shown in Figure 5-1. The closed-loop transfer function is

$$\frac{C(s)}{R(s)} = \frac{G(s)}{1 + G(s)H(s)} \tag{5-1}$$

The characteristic equation for this closed-loop system is obtained by setting the denominator of the right side of Eq. (5-1) equal to zero. That is,

$$1 + G(s)H(s) = 0$$

or

$$G(s)H(s) = -1 \tag{5-2}$$

Here we assume that $G(s)H(s)$ is a ratio of polynomials in s. Since $G(s)H(s)$ is a complex quantity, Eq. (5-2) can be split into two equations by equating the angles and magnitudes of both sides, respectively, to obtain

Angle condition:

$$\underline{/G(s)H(s)} = \pm180°(2k + 1), \qquad k = 0, 1, 2, \ldots \tag{5-3}$$

Magnitude condition:

$$\left|G(s)H(s)\right| = 1 \tag{5-4}$$

The values of s that fulfill the angle and magnitude conditions are the roots of the characteristic equation, or the closed-loop poles. A plot of the points of the complex plane satisfying the angle condition alone is the root locus. The roots of the characteristic equation (the closed-loop poles) corresponding to a given value of the gain can be determined from the magnitude condition.

In many cases, $G(s)H(s)$ involves a gain parameter K, and the characteristic equation may be written as

$$1 + \frac{K(s + z_1)(s + z_2)\cdots(s + z_m)}{(s + p_1)(s + p_2)\cdots(s + p_n)} = 0 \tag{5-5}$$

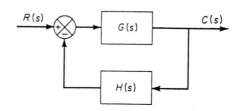

Figure 5-1

Then the root loci for the system are the loci of the closed-loop poles as the gain K is varied from zero to infinity.

In using the *rlocus* command, we rewrite Eq. (5-5) as

$$1 + K\frac{\text{num}}{\text{den}} = 0$$

where num is the numerator polynomial and den is the denominator polynomial. That is,

$$\begin{aligned}
\text{num} &= (s + z_1)(s + z_2)\cdots(s + z_m)\\
&= s^m + (z_1 + z_2 + \cdots + z_m)s^{m-1} + \cdots + z_1 z_2 \cdots z_m\\
\text{den} &= (s + p_1)(s + p_2)\cdots(s + p_n)\\
&= s^n + (p_1 + p_2 + \cdots + p_n)s^{n-1} + \cdots + p_1 p_2 \cdots p_n
\end{aligned}$$

Note that both vectors num and den must be written in descending powers of s.

A MATLAB command commonly used for plotting root loci is

rlocus(num,den)

Using this command, the root-locus plot is drawn on the screen. The gain vector K is automatically determined. The command rlocus works for both continuous- and discrete-time systems.

For the systems defined in state space, rlocus(A,B,C,D) plots the root locus of the system with the gain vector automatically determined.

Note that commands

rlocus(num,den,K)   and   rlocus(A,B,C,D,K)

use the user-supplied gain vector K. (The vector K contains the gain for which the closed-loop poles are to be computed.)

If invoked with left-hand arguments

[r,K] = rlocus(num,den)
[r,K] = rlocus(num,den,K)
[r,K] = rlocus(A,B,C,D)
[r,K] = rlocus(A,B,C,D,K)

the screen will show the matrix r and the gain vector K. (r has length K rows and length den − 1 columns containing the complex root locations. Each row of the matrix corresponds to a gain from vector K.) The plot command

plot(r,' ')

plots the root loci.

If it is desired to plot the root loci with marks 'o' or '×', it is necessary to use the following command:

$$r = \text{rlocus(num,den)}$$
$$\text{plot}(r,\text{'o'}) \quad \text{or} \quad \text{plot}(r,\text{'x'})$$

Plotting root loci using marks 'o' or '×' is instructive, since each calculated closed-loop pole is graphically shown; in some portion of the root loci those marks are densely placed and in another portion of the root loci they are sparsely placed. MATLAB supplies its own set of gain values used to calculate a root-locus plot. It does so by an internal adaptive step-size routine. Also, MATLAB uses the automatic axis-scaling feature of the *plot* command.

Finally, note that, since the gain vector is automatically determined, root-locus plots of

$$G(s)H(s) = \frac{K(s + 1)}{s(s + 2)(s + 3)}$$

$$G(s)H(s) = \frac{10K(s + 1)}{s(s + 2)(s + 3)}$$

$$G(s)H(s) = \frac{200K(s + 1)}{s(s + 2)(s + 3)}$$

are all the same. The num and den set of the system is the same for all three systems. The num and den are

$$\text{num} = \begin{bmatrix} 0 & 0 & 1 & 1 \end{bmatrix}$$
$$\text{den} = \begin{bmatrix} 1 & 5 & 6 & 0 \end{bmatrix}$$

Outline of the chapter

Section 5-1 has presented introductory material for the root-locus commands and associated subjects. Section 5-2 discusses details of plotting root loci of various systems. A number of sample root-locus plots are provided in this section. Section 5-3 deals with special cases, where root-locus plots show some strange asymmetrical shapes. Section 5-4 presents methods to plot two (or more) root loci (such as the root loci of the system and their asymptotes) on one graph. Finally, Section 5-5 treats root-locus plots in the z plane (for discrete-time systems).

5-2 OBTAINING ROOT-LOCUS PLOTS

In this section, we shall give detailed discussions of how to obtain root-locus plots using several example systems. A number of typical root-locus plots, together with MATLAB programs, are presented.

EXAMPLE 5-1

Consider the control system shown in Figure 5-2. The open-loop transfer function is

$$G(s) = \frac{K(s^2 + 1)}{s(s + 2)} = \frac{K(s^2 + 1)}{s^2 + 2s}$$

The system has open-loop zeros at $s = j$ and $s = -j$. Open-loop poles are at $s = 0$ and $s = -2$. To obtain a root-locus plot for this system, MATLAB Program 5-1 may be entered

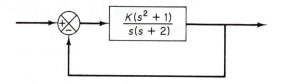

Figure 5-2

into the computer. In writing the numerator vector (num), the numerator coefficients should not be multiplied by gain K. That is, instead of

$$\text{num} = [K \quad 0 \quad K]$$

num should be

$$\text{num} = [1 \quad 0 \quad 1]$$

The root-locus plot obtained from the computer output is shown in Figure 5-3.

MATLAB Program 5–1

```
% ---------- Root-locus plot ----------

num = [1   0   1];
den = [1   2   0];
rlocus(num,den);
grid
title('Root-Locus Plot of G(s) = K(s^2+1)/[s(s+2)]')
```

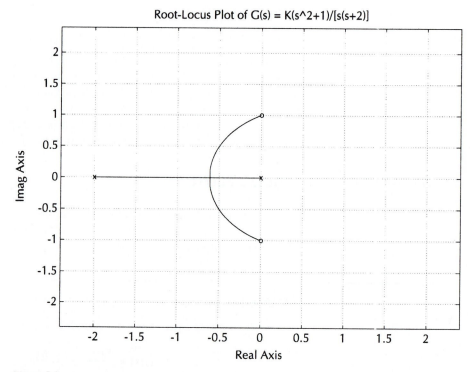

Figure 5-3

EXAMPLE 5-2

Consider the control system shown in Figure 5-4. The open-loop transfer function is

$$G(s) = \frac{K(s + 2)}{s^2 + 2s + 3}$$

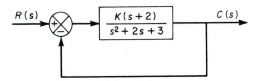

Figure 5-4

The open-loop zero and open-loop poles are located as follows:

Open-loop zero: $s = -2$
Open-loop poles: $s = -1 + j\sqrt{2}, \qquad s = -1 - j\sqrt{2}$

A MATLAB program for plotting the root loci for this system is shown in MATLAB Program 5-2. The computer-generated root-locus plot is shown in Figure 5-5. Notice that the root loci are drawn at the extreme left side of the diagram. If it is desired to draw the root loci near the center of the diagram, it is necessary to override the automatic axis scaling feature of the plot command and manually select the plotting limits. If it is desired to select the x axis from -5 to 1 and the y axis from -2.5 to 2.5, enter the following command:

$$v = [-5 \quad 1 \quad -2.5 \quad 2.5]$$
$$axis(v)$$

MATLAB Program 5–2

```
% ---------- Root-locus plot ----------

num = [0   1   2];
den = [1   2   3];
rlocus(num,den);
grid
title('Root-Locus Plot of G(s) = K(s+2)/(s^2+2s+3)')
```

The computer-generated root-locus plot based on MATLAB Program 5-3 is shown in Figure 5-6.

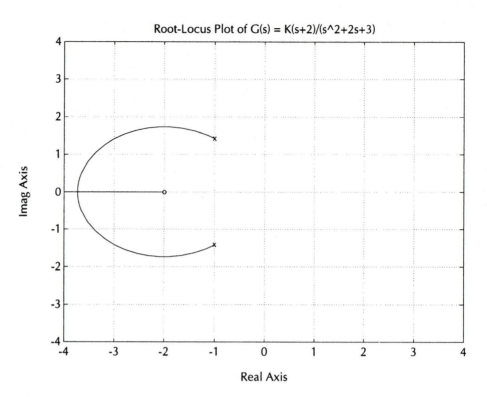

Figure 5-5

MATLAB Program 5–3

```
% ---------- Root-locus plot ----------

num = [0   1   2];
den = [1   2   3];
v = [-5   1   -2.5   2.5];
axis(v);
rlocus(num,den);

Axis scales auto-ranged

Axis scales frozen

grid
title('Root-Locus Plot of G(s) = K(s+2)/(s^2+2s+3)')
```

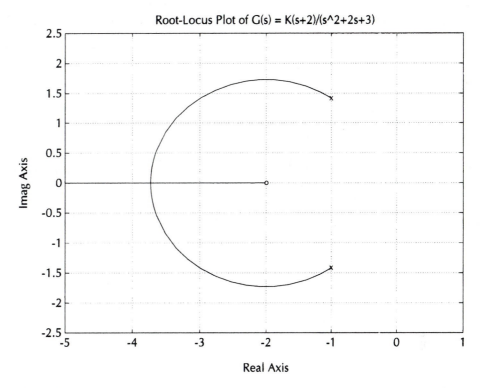

Figure 5-6

EXAMPLE 5-3

Consider the control system shown in Figure 5-7. Notice that the adjustable variable k does not appear as a multiplying factor. The characteristic equation for the system is

$$1 + \frac{20(1 + ks)}{s(s + 1)(s + 4)} = 0 \tag{5-6}$$

or

$$s^3 + 5s^2 + 4s + 20 + 20ks = 0 \tag{5-7}$$

By defining

$$20k = K$$

and dividing both sides of Eq. (5-7) by the sum of the terms that do not contain k, we get

$$1 + \frac{Ks}{s^3 + 5s^2 + 4s + 20} = 0$$

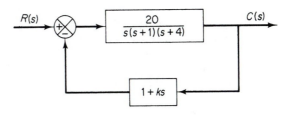

Figure 5-7

or

$$1 + \frac{Ks}{(s + j2)(s - j2)(s + 5)} = 0 \qquad (5\text{-}8)$$

Equation (5-8) is now of the form of Eq. (5-5). The num and den of this system are

$$\text{num} = [0 \quad 0 \quad 1 \quad 0]$$
$$\text{den} = [1 \quad 5 \quad 4 \quad 20]$$

A root-locus plot of this system may be obtained by entering MATLAB Program 5-4 into the computer. The resulting root-locus plot is shown in Figure 5-8.

```
MATLAB Program 5–4

% ---------- Root-locus plot ----------

num = [0  0  1  0];
den = [1  5  4  20];
rlocus(num,den);
grid
title('Root-Locus Plot of G(s) = Ks/[(s+5)(s^2+4)]')
```

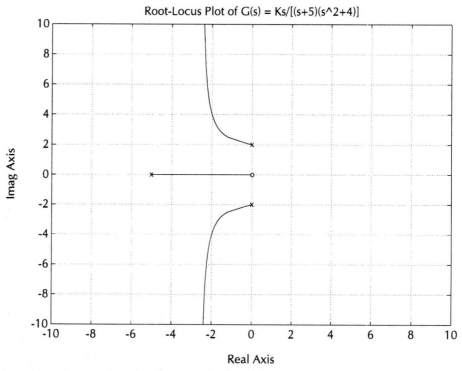

Figure 5-8

EXAMPLE 5-4

A root-locus plot may be drawn by use of the following command:

$$r = \text{rlocus(num,den)}$$
$$\text{plot}(r,'\ ')$$

If we use this command, the open-loop zeros and open-loop poles will not be shown on the plot. It is then necessary to add small circles (○) and small crosses (×) at open-loop zeros and open-loop poles, respectively. This can be easily done manually.

Consider the system shown in Figure 5-9, where

$$G(s) = \frac{K(s+1)}{s^2(s+3.6)}, \qquad H(s) = 1$$

MATLAB Program 5-5 will generate the root-locus plot for this system shown in Figure 5-10. Notice that open-loop zero and poles are not shown in the plot.

Figure 5-11 shows the same root-locus plot as that shown in Figure 5-10, but with open-loop zero and poles shown by 'o' and '×', respectively. (Note that 'o' and '×' are manually drawn in the plot.)

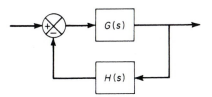

Figure 5-9

MATLAB Program 5–5

```
% ---------- Root-locus plot ----------

num = [0  0  1  1];
den = [1  3.6  0  0];
v = [-6  4  -6  6];
axis(v);
r = rlocus(num,den);
plot(r,'-')
grid
title('Root-Locus Plot of G(s) = K(s+1)/[s^2 (s+3.6)]')
xlabel('Real Axis')
ylabel('Imag Axis')

% ***** Notice that if we plot the root loci by use of
% the command "r = rlocus(num,den), plot(r,'-')", then
% the open-loop zero and poles are not shown.  It is
% necessary to add small circle (o) and small crosses (x)
% at open-loop zero and open-loop poles, respectively.
% This can be easily done manually. *****
```

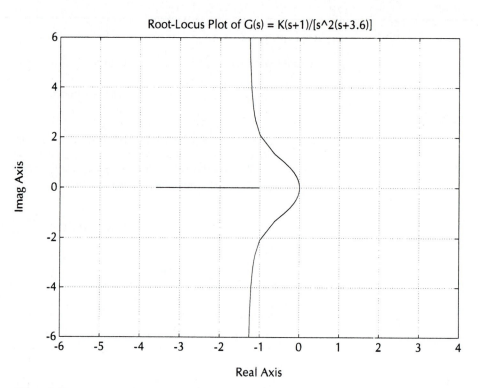

Figure 5-10

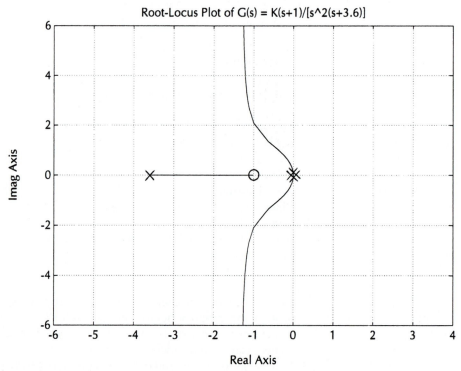

Figure 5-11

EXAMPLE 5-5

Consider the control system shown in Figure 5-12. To plot the root-locus diagram with MATLAB, it is necessary to find the numerator polynomial and denominator polynomial.

For this problem, the numerator is already given as a polynomial in s. However, the denominator is given as a product of first- and second-order terms, with the result that we must multiply these terms to get a polynomial in s. The multiplication of these terms can be done easily by use of the *convolution* command, as shown next.

Define

$$a = s(s + 4) = s^2 + 4s \quad : \quad a = [1 \quad 4 \quad 0]$$
$$b = s + 6 \qquad\qquad\quad : \quad b = [1 \quad 6]$$
$$c = s^2 + 1.4s + 1 \quad\;\; : \quad c = [1 \quad 1.4 \quad 1]$$

Then use the following command:

$$d = \text{conv}(a,b); \quad e = \text{conv}(c,d)$$

[Note that conv(a,b) gives the product of two polynomials a and b.] See the following computer output:

```
a = [1   4   0];
b = [1   6];
c = [1   1.4   1];
d = conv(a,b)

d =

    1    10    24    0

e = conv(c,d)

e =

    1.0000   11.4000   39.0000   43.6000   24.0000   0
```

The denominator polynomial is thus found to be

$$\text{den} = [1 \quad 11.4 \quad 39 \quad 43.6 \quad 24 \quad 0]$$

To find the open-loop zeros of the given transfer function, we may use the following *roots* command:

$$p = [1 \quad 2 \quad 4]$$
$$r = \text{roots}(p)$$

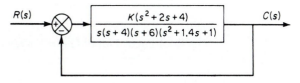

Figure 5-12

The command and the computer output are shown next.

```
p = [1   2   4];
 r = roots(p)


 r =


    -1.0000 + 1.7321i
    -1.0000 - 1.7321i
```

Similarly, to find the complex-conjugate open-loop poles (the roots of $s^2 + 1.4s + 1 = 0$), we may enter the *roots* command as follows:

```
q = roots(c)


q =


   -0.7000 + 0.7141i
   -0.7000 - 0.7141i
```

Thus the system has the following open-loop zeros and open-loop poles;

open-loop zeros:	$s = -1 + j1.7321,$	$s = -1 - j1.7321$
open-loop poles:	$s = -0.7 + j0.7141,$	$s = -0.7 - j0.7141$
	$s = 0, \qquad s = -4, \qquad s = -6$	

MATLAB Program 5-6 will plot the root-locus diagram for this system. The plot is shown in Figure 5-13.

MATLAB Program 5–6

```
% ---------- Root-locus plot ----------

num = [0   0   0   1   2   4];
den = [1   11.4   39   43.6   24   0];
v = [-10   10   -10   10];
axis(v);
rlocus(num,den);

Axis scales auto-ranged

Axis scales frozen

grid
title('Root-Locus Plot of G(s) = K(s^2+2s+4)/[s(s+4)(s+6)(s^2+1.4s+1)]')
```

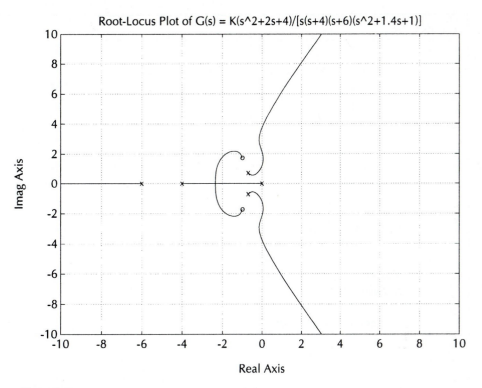

Figure 5-13

Examples of root-locus plots of typical closed-loop systems

In what follows, we shall present root-locus plots of various typical closed-loop systems. For each closed-loop system considered, a MATLAB program is given. Also, open-loop zero(s) and open-loop poles for each system are noted. The root-locus plots of these systems are shown in Examples 5-6 through 5-19.

EXAMPLE 5-6

System	$G(s) = \dfrac{K(s + 2)}{s^2}$

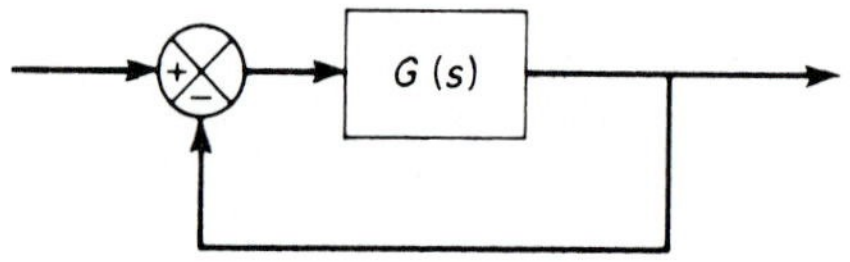

MATLAB Program

```
num = [0   1   2];
den = [1   0   0];
v = [-8   2   -5   5];
axis(v);
rlocus(num,den);
```

Axis scales auto-ranged

Axis scales frozen

```
grid
title('Root-Locus Plot of G(s) = K(s+2)/(s^2)')
```

Plot of Root Loci

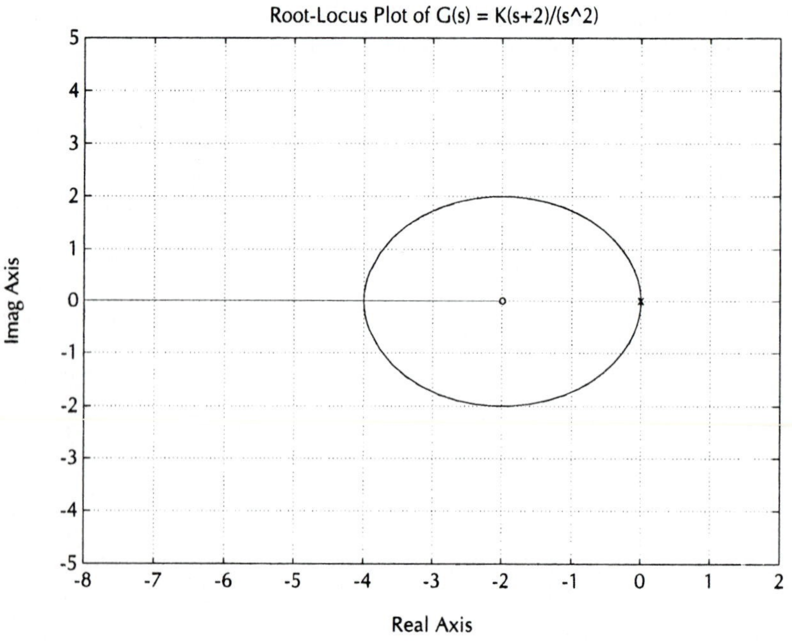

Open-loop zero(s)

$s = -2$

Open-loop poles

$s = 0$

$s = 0$

EXAMPLE 5-7

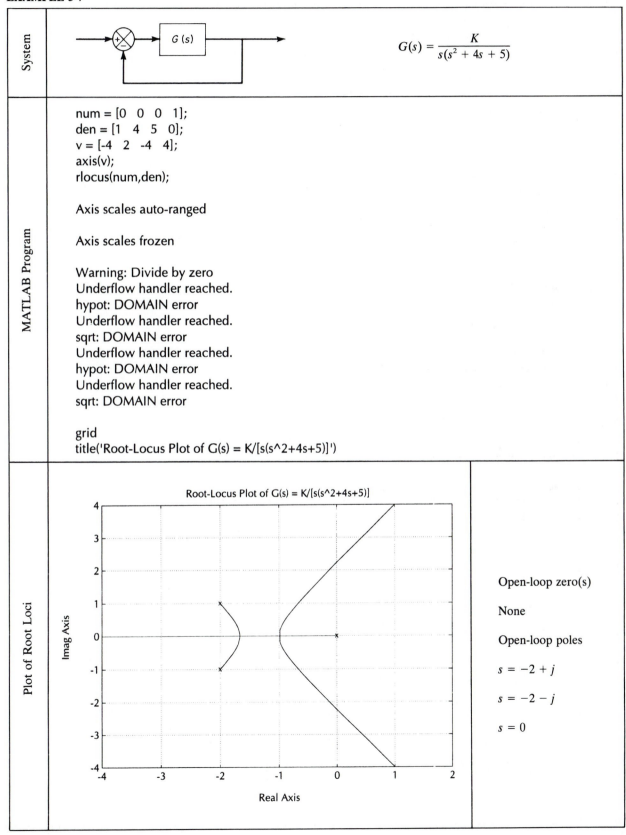

System	$G(s) = \dfrac{K}{s(s^2 + 4s + 5)}$

MATLAB Program

```
num = [0  0  0  1];
den = [1  4  5  0];
v = [-4  2  -4  4];
axis(v);
rlocus(num,den);
```

Axis scales auto-ranged

Axis scales frozen

```
Warning: Divide by zero
Underflow handler reached.
hypot: DOMAIN error
Underflow handler reached.
sqrt: DOMAIN error
Underflow handler reached.
hypot: DOMAIN error
Underflow handler reached.
sqrt: DOMAIN error
```

```
grid
title('Root-Locus Plot of G(s) = K/[s(s^2+4s+5)]')
```

Plot of Root Loci

Open-loop zero(s)

None

Open-loop poles

$s = -2 + j$

$s = -2 - j$

$s = 0$

EXAMPLE 5-8

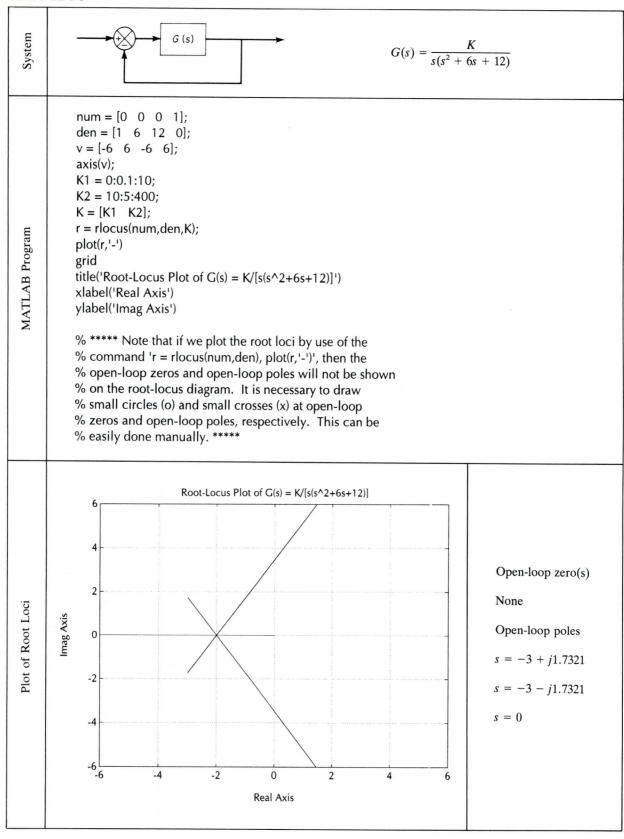

System	$G(s) = \dfrac{K}{s(s^2 + 6s + 12)}$

MATLAB Program

```
num = [0   0   0   1];
den = [1   6   12   0];
v = [-6   6   -6   6];
axis(v);
K1 = 0:0.1:10;
K2 = 10:5:400;
K = [K1   K2];
r = rlocus(num,den,K);
plot(r,'-')
grid
title('Root-Locus Plot of G(s) = K/[s(s^2+6s+12)]')
xlabel('Real Axis')
ylabel('Imag Axis')

% ***** Note that if we plot the root loci by use of the
% command 'r = rlocus(num,den), plot(r,'-')', then the
% open-loop zeros and open-loop poles will not be shown
% on the root-locus diagram.  It is necessary to draw
% small circles (o) and small crosses (x) at open-loop
% zeros and open-loop poles, respectively.  This can be
% easily done manually. *****
```

Plot of Root Loci

Root-Locus Plot of G(s) = K/[s(s^2+6s+12)]

Open-loop zero(s)

None

Open-loop poles

$s = -3 + j1.7321$

$s = -3 - j1.7321$

$s = 0$

EXAMPLE 5-9

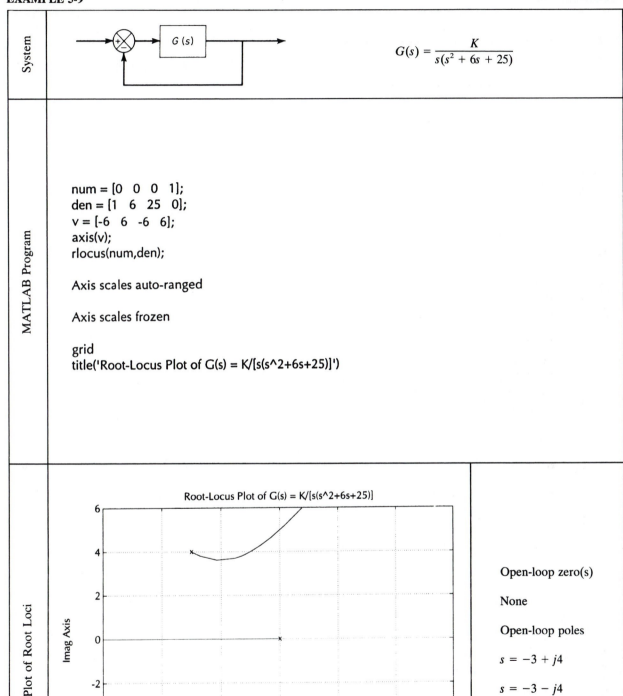

System

$$G(s) = \frac{K}{s(s^2 + 6s + 25)}$$

MATLAB Program

```
num = [0  0  0  1];
den = [1  6  25  0];
v = [-6  6  -6  6];
axis(v);
rlocus(num,den);
```

Axis scales auto-ranged

Axis scales frozen

```
grid
title('Root-Locus Plot of G(s) = K/[s(s^2+6s+25)]')
```

Plot of Root Loci

Open-loop zero(s)

None

Open-loop poles

$s = -3 + j4$

$s = -3 - j4$

$s = 0$

EXAMPLE 5-10

System	 $$G(s) = \frac{K(0.2s + 1)}{s(s + 1)(s + 2)}$$

MATLAB Program

```
num = [0  0  0.2  1];
den = [1  3  2  0];
rlocus(num,den);
grid
title('Root-Locus Plot of G(s) = K(0.2s+1)/[s(s+1)(s+2)]')
```

Plot of Root Loci

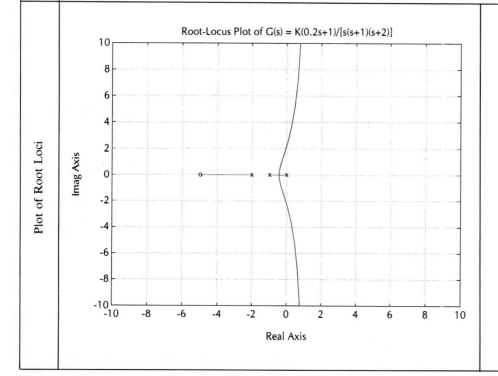

Open-loop zero(s)

$s = -5$

Open-loop poles

$s = 0$

$s = -1$

$s = -2$

EXAMPLE 5-11

System	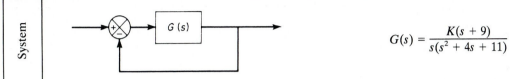 $$G(s) = \frac{K(s + 9)}{s(s^2 + 4s + 11)}$$

MATLAB Program	num = [0 0 1 9];
	den = [1 4 11 0];
	rlocus(num,den);
	grid
	title('Root-Locus Plot of G(s) = K(s+9)/[s(s^2+4s+11)]')

Plot of Root Loci	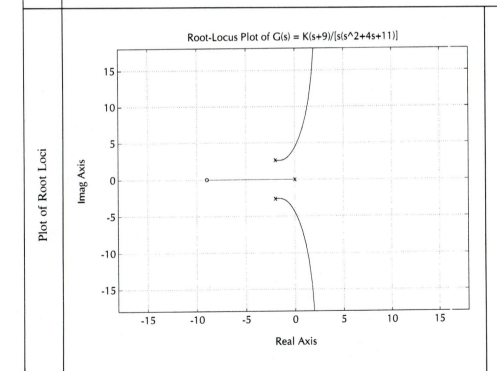

Open-loop zero(s)

$s = -9$

Open-loop poles

$s = -2 + j2.6458$

$s = -2 - j2.6458$

$s = 0$

EXAMPLE 5-12

System	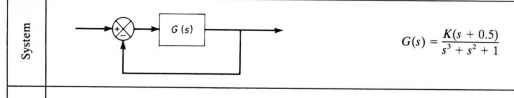 $G(s) = \dfrac{K(s + 0.5)}{s^3 + s^2 + 1}$

MATLAB Program	num = [0 0 1 0.5];
	den = [1 1 0 1];
	rlocus(num,den);
	grid
	title('Root-Locus Plot of G(s) = K(s+0.5)/(s^3+s^2+1)')

Plot of Root Loci	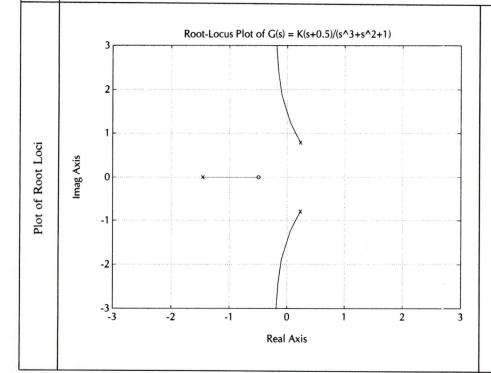 Open-loop zero(s) $s = -0.5$ Open-loop poles $s = 0.2328 + j0.7926$ $s = 0.2328 - j0.7926$ $s = -1.4656$

EXAMPLE 5-13

System

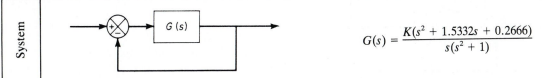

$$G(s) = \frac{K(s^2 + 1.5332s + 0.2666)}{s(s^2 + 1)}$$

MATLAB Program

```
num = [0  1  1.5332  0.2666];
den = [1  0  1  0];
v = [-5  1  -3  3];
axis(v);
rlocus(num,den);

Axis scales auto-ranged

Axis scales frozen

grid
title('Root-Locus Plot of G(s) = K(s+0.2)(s+1.3332)/[s(s^2+1)]')
```

Plot of Root Loci

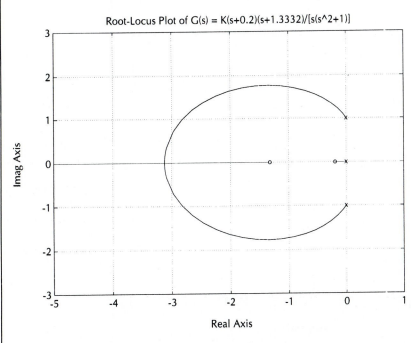

Open-loop zero(s)

$s = -0.2$

$s = -1.3332$

Open-loop poles

$s = 0$

$s = j$

$s = -j$

EXAMPLE 5-14

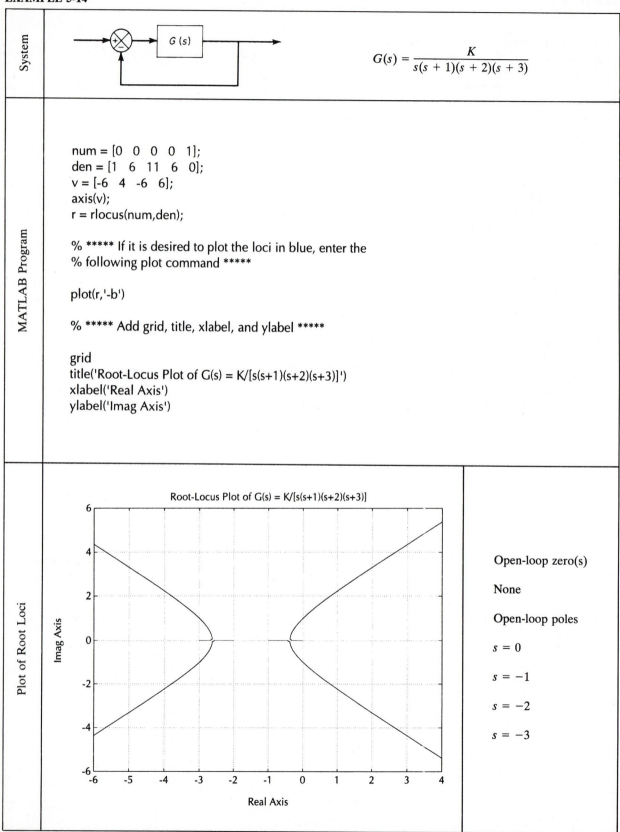

| System | $G(s) = \dfrac{K}{s(s+1)(s+2)(s+3)}$ |

MATLAB Program

```
num = [0  0  0  0  1];
den = [1  6  11  6  0];
v = [-6  4  -6  6];
axis(v);
r = rlocus(num,den);

% ***** If it is desired to plot the loci in blue, enter the
% following plot command *****

plot(r,'-b')

% ***** Add grid, title, xlabel, and ylabel *****

grid
title('Root-Locus Plot of G(s) = K/[s(s+1)(s+2)(s+3)]')
xlabel('Real Axis')
ylabel('Imag Axis')
```

Plot of Root Loci

Root-Locus Plot of G(s) = K/[s(s+1)(s+2)(s+3)]

Open-loop zero(s)

None

Open-loop poles

$s = 0$

$s = -1$

$s = -2$

$s = -3$

EXAMPLE 5-15

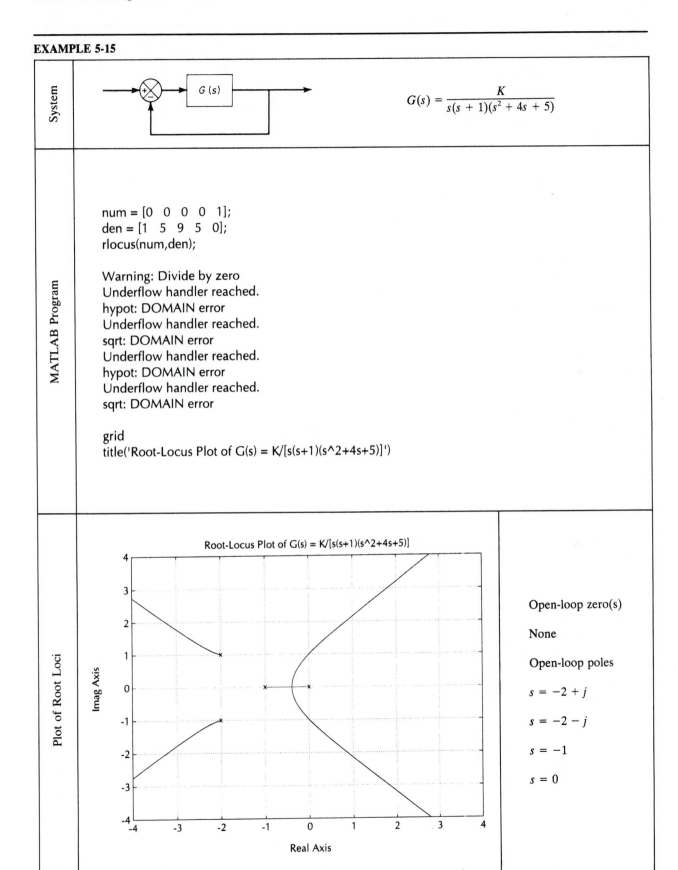

System

$$G(s) = \frac{K}{s(s + 1)(s^2 + 4s + 5)}$$

MATLAB Program

```
num = [0  0  0  0  1];
den = [1  5  9  5  0];
rlocus(num,den);

Warning: Divide by zero
Underflow handler reached.
hypot: DOMAIN error
Underflow handler reached.
sqrt: DOMAIN error
Underflow handler reached.
hypot: DOMAIN error
Underflow handler reached.
sqrt: DOMAIN error

grid
title('Root-Locus Plot of G(s) = K/[s(s+1)(s^2+4s+5)]')
```

Plot of Root Loci

Root-Locus Plot of G(s) = K/[s(s+1)(s^2+4s+5)]

Open-loop zero(s)

None

Open-loop poles

$s = -2 + j$

$s = -2 - j$

$s = -1$

$s = 0$

EXAMPLE 5-16

System	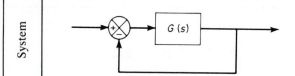 $$G(s) = \frac{K}{s(s+1)(s^2 + 4s + 13)}$$

MATLAB Program	num = [0 0 0 0 1];
	den = [1 5 17 13 0];
	rlocus(num,den);
	grid
	title('Root-Locus Plot of G(s) = K/[s(s+1)(s^2+4s+13)]')

Plot of Root Loci	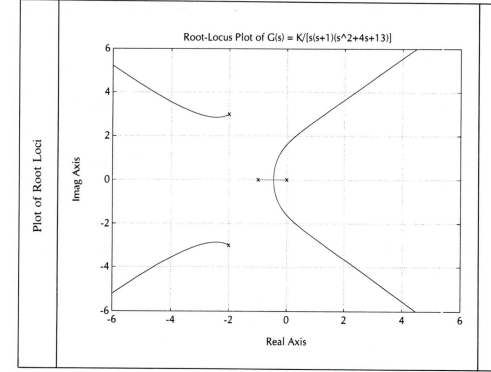

Open-loop zero(s)

None

Open-loop poles

$s = -2 + j3$

$s = -2 - j3$

$s = 0$

$s = -1$

EXAMPLE 5-17

System	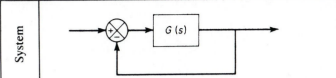 $G(s) = \dfrac{K(s + 1)}{s^2(s + 2)(s + 5)}$

MATLAB Program

```
num = [0  0  0  1  1];
den = [1  7  10  0  0];
rlocus(num,den);
grid
title('Root-Locus Plot of G(s) = K(s+1)/[s^2(s+2)(s+5)]')
```

Plot of Root Loci

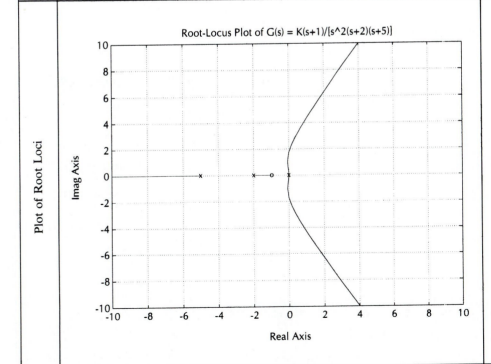

Open-loop zero(s)

$s = -1$

Open-loop poles

$s = 0$

$s = 0$

$s = -2$

$s = -5$

EXAMPLE 5-18

System	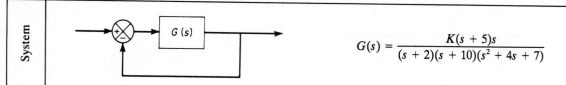 $$G(s) = \frac{K(s + 5)s}{(s + 2)(s + 10)(s^2 + 4s + 7)}$$

MATLAB Program	num = [0 0 1 5 0];
	den = [1 16 75 164 140];
	rlocus(num,den);
	grid
	title('Root-Locus Plot of G(s) = K(s+5)s/[(s+2)(s+10)(s^2+4s+7)]')

Plot of Root Loci	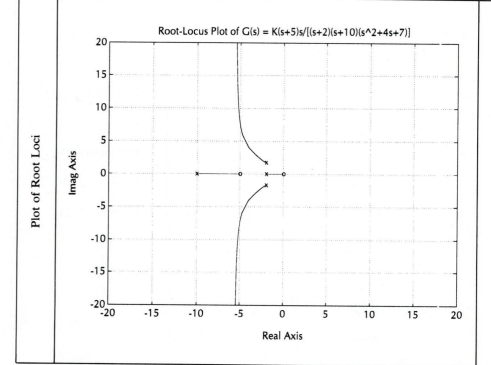 Open-loop zero(s) $s = 0$ $s = -5$ Open-loop poles $s = -2 + j1.7321$ $s = -2 - j1.7321$ $s = -2$ $s = -10$

EXAMPLE 5-19

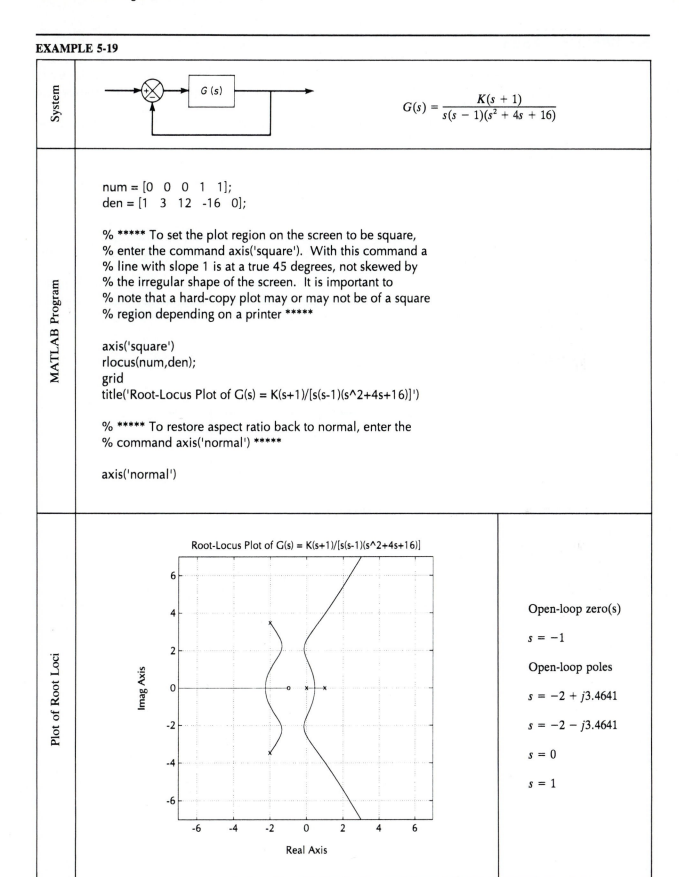

System

$$G(s) = \frac{K(s + 1)}{s(s - 1)(s^2 + 4s + 16)}$$

MATLAB Program

```
num = [0  0  0  1  1];
den = [1  3  12  -16  0];

% ***** To set the plot region on the screen to be square,
% enter the command axis('square').  With this command a
% line with slope 1 is at a true 45 degrees, not skewed by
% the irregular shape of the screen.  It is important to
% note that a hard-copy plot may or may not be of a square
% region depending on a printer *****

axis('square')
rlocus(num,den);
grid
title('Root-Locus Plot of G(s) = K(s+1)/[s(s-1)(s^2+4s+16)]')

% ***** To restore aspect ratio back to normal, enter the
% command axis('normal') *****

axis('normal')
```

Plot of Root Loci

Root-Locus Plot of G(s) = K(s+1)/[s(s-1)(s^2+4s+16)]

Open-loop zero(s)

$s = -1$

Open-loop poles

$s = -2 + j3.4641$

$s = -2 - j3.4641$

$s = 0$

$s = 1$

5-3 SPECIAL CASES

In plotting a root-locus diagram, MATLAB calculates the closed-loop poles using only a reasonably small number of gain values. It then connects the poles with a straight line.

Consider the closed-loop system shown in Figure 5-14. Assume that the transfer functions $G(s)$ and $H(s)$ are given, respectively, as

$$G(s) = \frac{K(s + 9)}{s(s^2 + 4s + 11)}, \qquad H(s) = 1$$

MATLAB Program 5-7 will generate a root-locus plot as shown in Figure 5-15. Notice that automatic step-size root-locus algorithms take larger steps where the solution is more slowly changing.

In Figure 5-15 the marks 'o' drawn show the points where the computer has computed. If these points are connected by straight lines, we get a usual root-locus diagram consisting of continuous lines or curves, as shown in Figure 5-16.

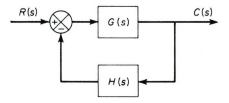

Figure 5-14

MATLAB Program 5–7

```
num = [0   0   1   9];
den = [1   4   11   0];
v = [-15   10   -15   15];
axis(v);
r = rlocus(num,den);
plot(r,'o')
grid
title('Root-Locus Plot of G(s) = K(s+9)/[s(s^2+4s+11)]')
xlabel('Real Axis')
ylabel('Imag Axis')
```

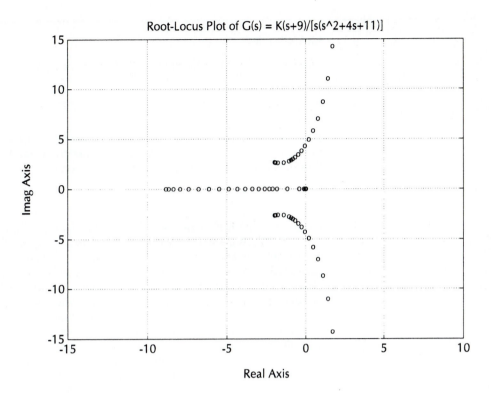

Figure 5-15

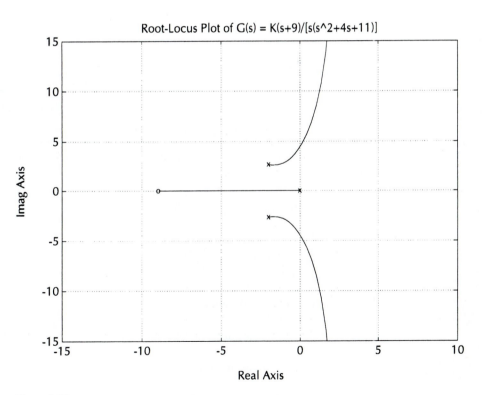

Figure 5-16

EXAMPLE 5-20

Consider the system shown in Figure 5-17. The open-loop transfer function is

$$G(s) = \frac{K(s + 0.4)}{s^2(s + 3.6)}$$

Let us plot the root loci using MATLAB Program 5-8, which generates a root-locus plot as shown in Figure 5-18. The root loci must be symmetric about the real axis. However, Figure 5-18 shows otherwise. If we zoom in the x–y region to

$$[-2 \quad 1 \quad -1.5 \quad 1.5]$$

and use MATLAB Program 5-9, we obtain the plot shown in Figure 5-19.

MATLAB supplies its own set of gain values that are used to calculate a root-locus plot. It does so by an internal adaptive step-size routine. However, in certain systems, very small changes in the gain cause drastic changes in root locations within a certain range of gains. Thus, MATLAB takes too big a jump in its gain values when calculating the roots, and root locations change by a relatively large amount. When plotting, MATLAB connects these points and causes a strange looking graph at the location of sensitive gains. Such erroneous root-locus plots typically occur when the loci approach a double pole (or triple or higher pole), since the locus is very sensitive to small gain changes.

To fix these erroneous figures, we need to specify the values of gain K spaced very close together in the area where the roots change rapidly. For example, if the range is ill-conditioned around $K = 8$, use a very small step size around $K = 8$. We may define K as

$$K1 = [0: 0.1:7.5];$$
$$K2 = [7.5:0.005:8.5];$$
$$K3 = [8.5:1:100];$$
$$K = [K1 \quad K2 \quad K3]$$

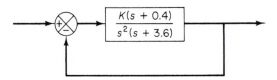

Figure 5-17

MATLAB Program 5–8

```
num = [0   0   1   0.4];
den = [1   3.6   0   0];
v = [-5   5   -5   5];
axis(v);
rlocus(num,den);

Axis scales auto-ranged

Axis scales frozen

grid
title('Root-Locus Plot of G(s) = K(s+0.4)/[s^2(s+3.6)]')
```

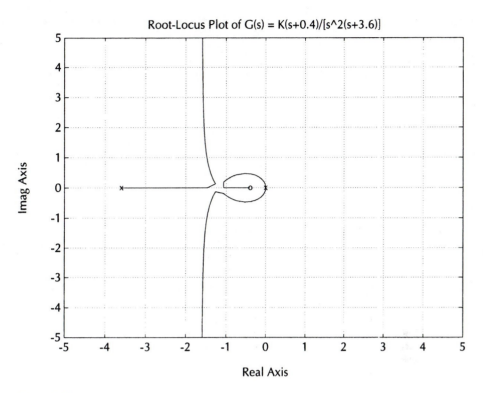

Figure 5-18

MATLAB Program 5–9

```
num = [0   0   1   0.4];
den = [1   3.6   0   0];
v = [-2   1   -1.5   1.5];
axis(v);
r = rlocus(num,den);
plot(r,'o')
grid
title('Root-Locus Plot of G(s) = K(s+0.4)/[s^2(s+3.6)]')
xlabel('Real Axis')
ylabel('Imag Axis')
```

---

and use the following command:

$$r = rlocus(num,den,K)$$

Figure 5-20 is the same root-locus plot as Figure 5-19, but the former is plotted using 'o' marks. Notice that there are no computed points near point (−1.25, 0). In investigating such a case, it is advisable to plot the root loci using 'o' or '×' marks.

In general, to find the region of gain K where the problem occurs, use a trial and error approach. For example, we may set gain K as

$$K = 0:0.5:2$$

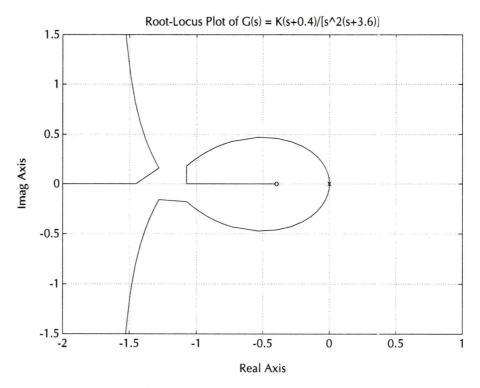

Figure 5-19

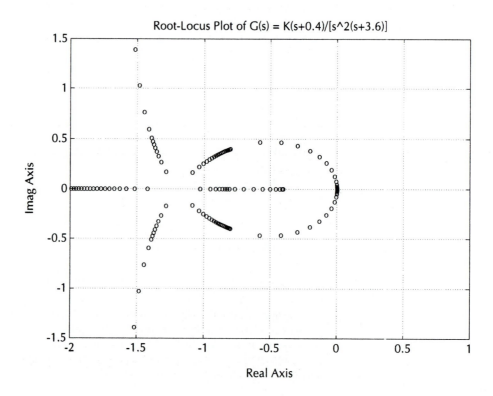

Figure 5-20

and see where the roots corresponding to $K = 2$ are located. Then change gain K to

$$K = 2{:}0.5{:}4$$

Locating the roots for $K = 2$, $K = 4$, and so on, find the range of gain K where we need a small step size.

In the example considered here, the critical region of gain K is between 3 and 5. Thus we need to set the step size small enough in this region. For regions $0 \le K \le 3$ and $5 \le K \le \infty$, the step size may be fairly large. Thus we may divide the regions for K as follows:

$$
\begin{aligned}
K1 &= [0{:}0.2{:}3]; \\
K2 &= [3{:}0.01{:}5]; \\
K3 &= [5{:}0.2{:}10]; \\
K4 &= [10{:}5{:}200]; \\
K &= [K1 \quad K2 \quad K3 \quad K4]
\end{aligned}
$$

Let us enter MATLAB Program 5-10 into the computer. The plot obtained from this program is shown in Figure 5-21. The root-locus plot looks satisfactory.

Figure 5-22 shows the root loci in the region

$$[-2 \quad 1 \quad -1.5 \quad 1.5]$$

The small circles ('○') show computed points. The program used to obtain this plot is shown in MATLAB Program 5-11.

By changing the gain steps, as shown in MATLAB Program 5-12, we obtain a slightly different plot of the root loci, as shown in Figure 5-23. The plots in Figures 5-22 and 5-23 seem satisfactory.

A change in the x–y region, as given in MATLAB Program 5-13, yields the plot shown in Figure 5-24. Using '-' marks, we get a smooth looking root-locus plot. (See MATLAB Program 5-14 and Figure 5-25.) Figure 5-25 is practically the same as Figure 5-21 obtained earlier.

MATLAB Program 5–10

```
num = [0   0   1   0.4];
den = [1   3.6   0   0];
v = [-5   5   -5   5];
axis(v);
K1 = [0:0.2:3];
K2 = [3:0.01:5];
K3 = [5:0.2:10];
K4 = [10:5:200];
K = [K1   K2   K3   K4];
r = rlocus(num,den,K);
plot(r)
grid
title('Root-Locus Plot of G(s) = K(s+0.4)/[s^2(s+3.6)]')
xlabel('Real Axis')
ylabel('Imag Axis')
```

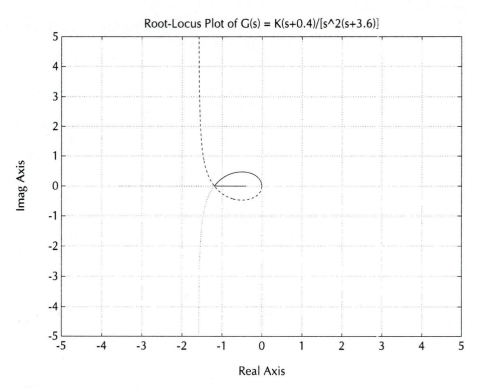

Figure 5-21

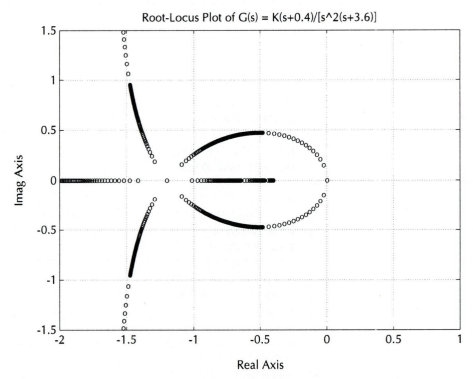

Figure 5-22

```
MATLAB Program 5–11

num = [0   0   1   0.4];
den = [1   3.6   0   0];
v = [-2   1   -1.5   1.5];
axis(v);
K1 = [0:0.2:3];
K2 = [3:0.01:5];
K3 = [5:0.2:10];
K4 = [10:5:200];
K = [K1   K2   K3   K4];
r = rlocus(num,den,K);
plot(r,'o')
grid
title('Root-Locus Plot of G(s) = K(s+0.4)/[s^2(s+3.6)]')
xlabel('Real Axis')
ylabel('Imag Axis')
```

```
MATLAB Program 5–12

num = [0   0   1   0.4];
den = [1   3.6   0   0];
v = [-2   1   -1.5   1.5];
axis(v);
K1 = [0:0.2:4.2];
K2 = [4.2:0.002:4.4];
K3 = [4.4:0.2:10];
K4 = [10:5:200];
K = [K1   K2   K3   K4];
r = rlocus(num,den,K);
plot(r,'o')
grid
title('Root-Locus Plot of G(s) = K(s+0.4)/[s^2(s+3.6)]')
xlabel('Real Axis')
ylabel('Imag Axis')
```

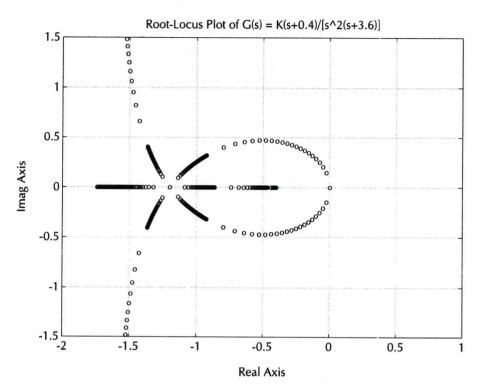

Figure 5-23

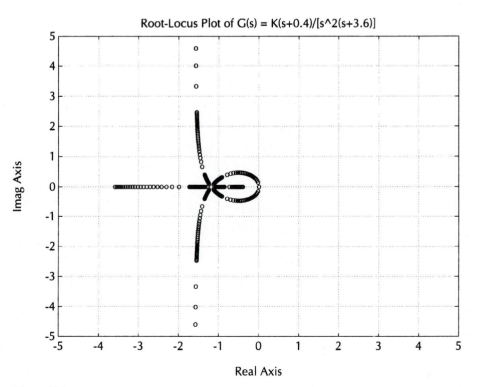

Figure 5-24

MATLAB Program 5–13

```
num = [0   0   1   0.4];
den = [1   3.6   0   0];
v = [-5   5   -5   5];
axis(v);
K1 = [0:0.2:4.2];
K2 = [4.2:0.002:4.4];
K3 = [4.4:0.2:10];
K4 = [10:5:200];
K = [K1   K2   K3   K4];
r = rlocus(num,den,K);
plot(r,'o')
grid
title('Root-Locus Plot of G(s) = K(s+0.4)/[s^2(s+3.6)]')
xlabel('Real Axis')
ylabel('Imag Axis')
```

MATLAB Program 5–14

```
num = [0   0   1   0.4];
den = [1   3.6   0   0];
v = [-5   5   -5   5];
axis(v);
K1 = [0:0.2:4.2];
K2 = [4.2:0.002:4.4];
K3 = [4.4:0.2:10];
K4 = [10:5:200];
K = [K1   K2   K3   K4];
r = rlocus(num,den,K);
plot(r,'-')
grid
title('Root-Locus Plot of G(s) = K(s+0.4)/[s^2(s+3.6)]')
xlabel('Real Axis')
ylabel('Imag Axis')
```

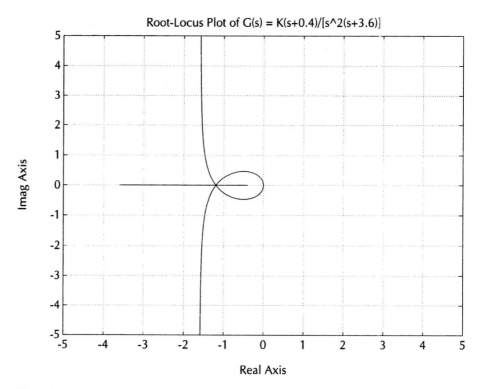

Figure 5-25

EXAMPLE 5-21

Consider the system shown in Figure 5-26. The open-loop transfer function is

$$G(s) = \frac{K}{(s-1)(s^2 + 4s + 7)}$$

$$= \frac{K}{s^3 + 3s^2 + 3s - 7}$$

There are no open-loop zeros. Open-loop poles are located at $s = -2 + j1.7321$, $s = -2 - j1.7321$, and $s = 1$. MATLAB Program 5-15 will generate the root-locus plot shown in Figure 5-27. [Note that depending on the version of MATLAB (such as Student version or Professional version 4.0) we may get a slightly different root-locus plot.]

In this plot, notice the abrupt changes in the direction of root-locus branches. Such changes suggest that there is a problem in the root-locus plot. To investigate the problem, we may plot the root loci using marks 'o' or '×'. Using MATLAB Program 5-16, we obtain the root-locus plot shown in Figure 5-28. It can be seen that there are no points computed near point $(-1, 0)$, and this is the cause of the problem.

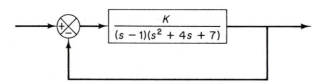

Figure 5-26

```
MATLAB Program 5–15

num = [0   0   0   1];
den = [1   3   3   -7];
rlocus(num,den);
grid
title('Root-Locus Plot of G(s) = K/[(s-1)(s^2+4s+7)]')
```

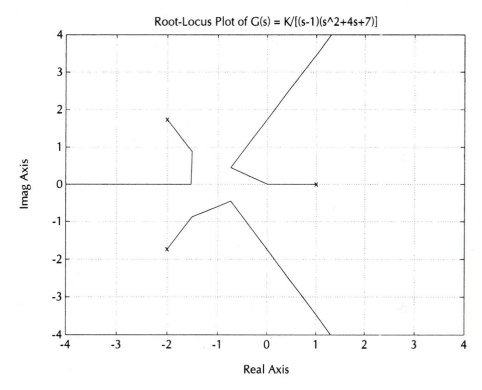

Figure 5-27

```
MATLAB Program 5–16

num = [0   0   0   1];
den = [1   3   3   -7];
v = [-4   4   -4   4];
axis(v);
r = rlocus(num,den);
plot(r,'o')
grid
title('Root-Locus Plot of G(s) = K/[(s-1)(s^2+4s+7)]')
xlabel('Real Axis')
ylabel('Imag Axis')
```

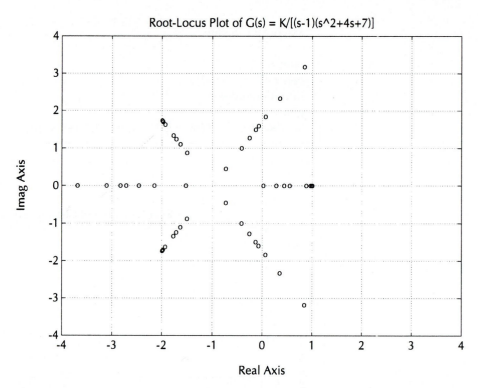

Figure 5-28

Using a trial and error approach by changing the gain K to be $0 \le K \le 2$, $2 \le K \le 4$, and so on, we can find the critical region [including point $(-1, 0)$] to be $7.5 \le K \le 8.5$. Hence, by making the step size smaller in this critical region as shown in MATLAB Program 5-17, we obtain the root-locus plot given by Figure 5-29.

If we change the plot command from plot(y,'○') to plot(y,'−'), as shown in MATLAB Program 5-18, we obtain the usual root-locus plot, as shown in Figure 5-30, which is correct. (The root loci for this system consist of three straight lines.)

```
MATLAB Program 5–17

num = [0   0   0   1];
den = [1   3   3   -7];
v = [-4   4   -4   4];
axis(v);
K1 = 0:0.5:7.5;
K2 = 7.5:0.01:8.5;
K3 = 8.5:1:20;
K4 = 20:10:100;
K = [K1   K2   K3   K4];
r = rlocus(num,den,K);
plot(r,'o')
grid
title('Root-Locus Plot of G(s) = K/[(s-1)(s^2+4s+7)]')
xlabel('Real Axis')
ylabel('Imag Axis')
```

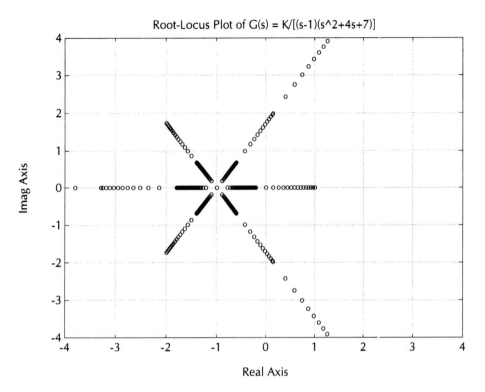

Figure 5-29

MATLAB Program 5–18

```
num = [0   0   0   1];
den = [1   3   3   -7];
v = [-4   4   -4   4];
axis(v);
K1 = 0:0.5:7.5;
K2 = 7.5:0.01:8.5;
K3 = 8.5:1:20;
K4 = 20:10:100;
K = [K1   K2   K3   K4];
r = rlocus(num,den,K);
plot(r,'-')
grid
title('Root-Locus Plot of G(s) = K/[(s-1)(s^2+4s+7)]')
xlabel('Real Axis')
ylabel('Imag Axis')
```

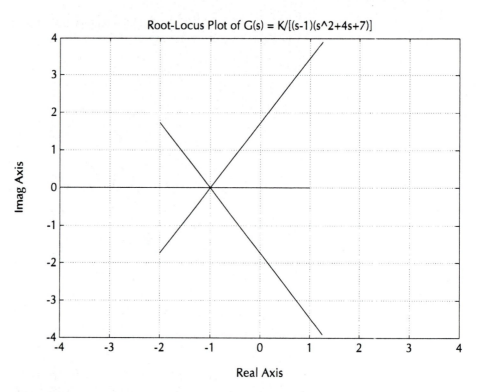

Root-Locus Plot of G(s) = K/[(s-1)(s^2+4s+7)]

Figure 5-30

EXAMPLE 5-22

Consider a system whose open-loop transfer function $G(s)H(s)$ is given by

$$G(s)H(s) = \frac{K}{(s^2 + 2s + 2)(s^2 + 2s + 5)}$$

$$= \frac{K}{s^4 + 4s^3 + 11s^2 + 14s + 10}$$

There are no open-loop zeros. Open-loop poles are at $s = -1 + j$, $s = -1 - j$, $s = -1 + 2j$, and $s = -1 - 2j$.

MATLAB Program 5-19 will generate the root-locus plot shown in Figure 5-31. In this root-locus plot, it is seen that two branches in the upper half-plane (and also in the lower half-plane) approach each other but do not touch. Careful inspection of this diagram shows that there are two short straight-line segments in the upper (and lower) half-plane. Such short straight lines may be caused by insufficient computation points. To check, we may enter

---

MATLAB Program 5–19

```
num = [0  0  0  0  1];
den = [1  4  11  14  10];
rlocus(num,den);
grid
title('Root-Locus Plot of G(s) = K/[(s^2+2s+2)(s^2+2s+5)]')
```

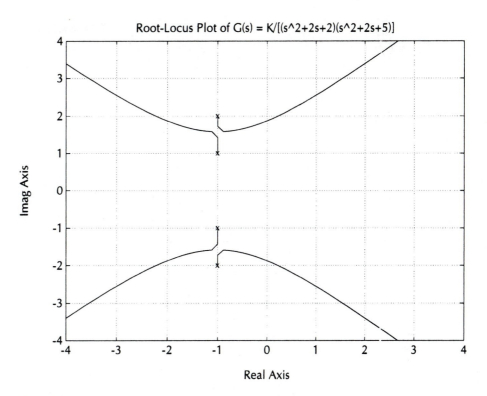

Figure 5-31

MATLAB Program 5-20, and draw a root-locus plot using marks 'o'. The plot is shown in Figure 5-32.

To zoom up the region where root-locus branches might cross each other, let us choose the x axis and y axis as follows:

$$-2 \leq x \leq 0, \qquad -3 \leq y \leq 3$$

Using MATLAB Program 5-21, we obtain the plot of root loci as shown in Figure 5-33. Notice that there are no computed points near $(-1, 1.6)$ and $(-1, -1.6)$. The regions near these

```
MATLAB Program 5–20

num = [0  0  0  0  1];
den = [1  4  11  14  10];
v = [-4  4  -4  4];
axis(v);
r = rlocus(num,den);
plot(r,'og')
grid
title('Root-Locus Plot of G(s) = K/[(s^2+2s+2)(s^2+2s+5)]')
xlabel('Real Axis')
ylabel('Imag Axis')

% ***** Note that the command 'plot(r,'og')' gives small
% circles in the screen plot in green color *****
```

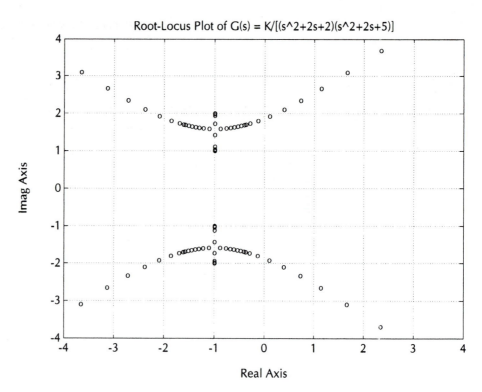

Figure 5-32

MATLAB Program 5–21

```
num = [0  0  0  0  1];
den = [1  4  11  14  10];
v = [-2  0  -3  3];
axis(v);
r = rlocus(num,den);
plot(r,'or')
grid
title('Root-Locus Plot of G(s) = K/[(s^2+2s+2)(s^2+2s+5)]')
xlabel('Real Axis')
ylabel('Imag Axis')

% ***** Note that the command 'plot(r,'or')' gives small
% circles in the screen plot in red color *****
```

---

points need to be carefully investigated. By a trial and error approach, the gain values near these points are found to be $2.0 \leq K \leq 2.5$.

By using a small gain size in the region $2.0 \leq K \leq 2.5$, we may get a better root-locus plot. Using MATLAB Program 5-22, we obtain the root-locus plot shown in Figure 5-34. Clearly, the two branches in the upper (and lower) half-plane cross each other. Extending the region of K to 800 and using continuous lines and curves, as given in MATLAB Program 5-23, we obtain the plot shown in Figure 5-35. This plot is correct and satisfactory.

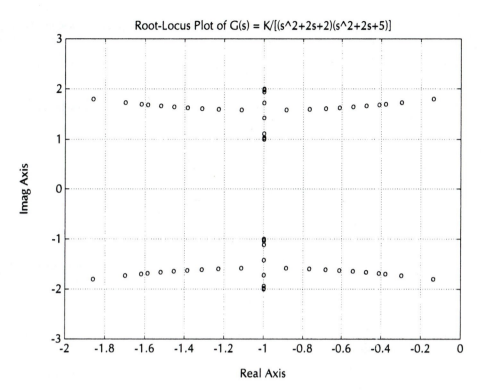

Figure 5-33

MATLAB Program 5–22

```
num = [0   0   0   0   1];
den = [1   4   11   14   10];
v = [-2   0   -3   3];
axis(v);
K1 = 0:0.5:2;
K2 = 2:0.01:2.5;
K3 = 2.5:0.5:10;
K4 = 10:10:200;
K = [K1   K2   K3   K4];
r = rlocus(num,den,K);
plot(r,'og')
grid
title('Root-Locus Plot of G(s) = K/[(s^2+2s+2)(s^2+2s+5)]')
xlabel('Real Axis')
ylabel('Imag Axis')

% ***** Note that the command 'plot(r,'og')' gives small
% circles in the screen plot in green color *****
```

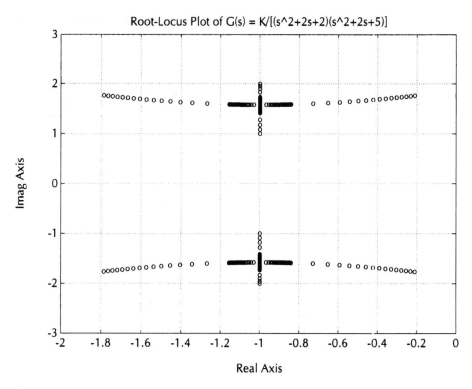

Figure 5-34

MATLAB Program 5–23

```
num = [0  0  0  0  1];
den = [1  4  11  14  10];
v = [-2  0  -3  3];
axis(v);
K1 = 0:0.5:2;
K2 = 2:0.01:2.5;
K3 = 2.5:0.5:10;
K4 = 10:10:50;
K5 = 50:50:800;
K = [K1  K2  K3  K4  K5];
r = rlocus(num,den,K);
plot(r,'-g')
grid
title('Root-Locus Plot of G(s) = K/[(s^2+2s+2)(s^2+2s+5)]')
xlabel('Real Axis')
ylabel('Imag Axis')

% ***** Note that the command 'plot(r,'-g')' gives continuous
% lines and curves in the screen plot in green color *****
```

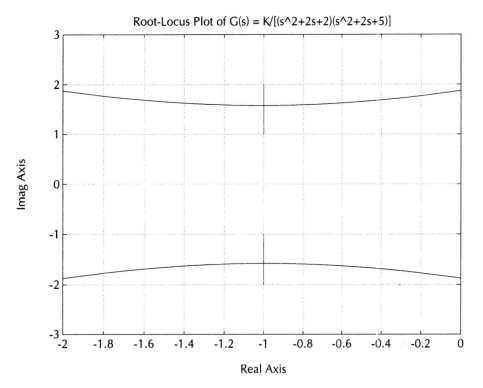

Figure 5-35

EXAMPLE 5-23

Consider the system whose open-loop transfer function $G(s)H(s)$ is

$$G(s)H(s) = \frac{K}{s(s + 0.5)(s^2 + 0.6s + 10)}$$

$$= \frac{K}{s^4 + 1.1s^3 + 10.3s^2 + 5s}$$

There are no open-loop zeros. Open-loop poles are located at $s = -0.3 + j3.1480$, $s = -0.3 - j3.1480$, $s = -0.5$, and $s = 0$.

Entering MATLAB Program 5-24 into the computer, we obtain the root-locus plot shown in Figure 5-36.

Notice that in the regions near $x = -0.3$, $y = 2.3$ and $x = -0.3$, $y = -2.3$ two loci approach each other. We may wonder if these two branches should touch or not. To explore this situation, we may plot the root loci using the command

```
r = rlocus(num,den)
plot(r,'o')
```

as shown in MATLAB Program 5-25. Figure 5-37 shows the resulting plot.

Since there are no computed points near $(-0.3, 2.3)$ and $(-0.3, -2.3)$, it is necessary to adjust steps in gain K. By a trial and error approach, we find the particular region of interest to be $20 \le K \le 30$. By entering MATLAB Program 5-26, we obtain the root-locus plot shown in Figure 5-38. From this plot, it is clear that the two branches that approach in the upper half-plane (or in the lower half-plane) do not touch.

MATLAB Program 5–24

```
num = [0  0  0  0  1];
den = [1  1.1  10.3  5  0];
rlocus(num,den);

Warning: Divide by zero
Underflow handler reached.
hypot: DOMAIN error
Underflow handler reached.
sqrt: DOMAIN error
Underflow handler reached.
hypot: DOMAIN error
Underflow handler reached.
sqrt: DOMAIN error

grid
title('Root-Locus Plot of G(s) = K/[s(s+0.5)(s^2+0.6s+10)]')
```

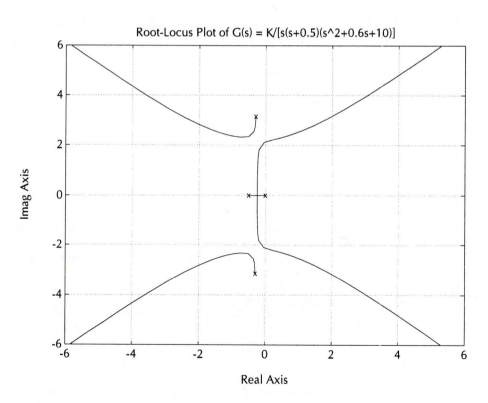

Figure 5-36

```
MATLAB Program 5–25

num = [0   0   0   0   1];
den = [1   1.1   10.3   5   0];
v = [-6   6   -6   6];
axis(v);
r = rlocus(num,den);

Warning: Divide by zero
Underflow handler reached.
hypot: DOMAIN error
Underflow handler reached.
sqrt: DOMAIN error
Underflow handler reached.
hypot: DOMAIN error
Underflow handler reached.
sqrt: DOMAIN error

plot(r,'or')
grid
title('Root-Locus Plot of G(s) = K/[s(s+0.5)(s^2+0.6s+10)]')
xlabel('Real Axis')
ylabel('Imag Axis')

% ***** Note that the command 'plot(r,'or')' gives small circles
% in the screen plot in red color *****
```

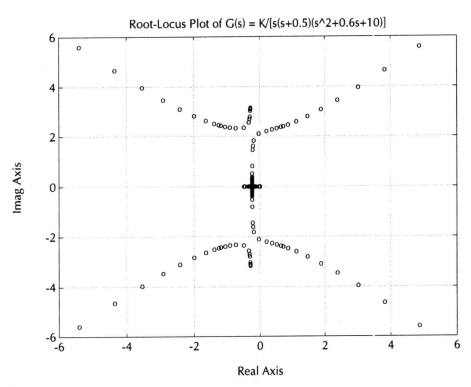

Figure 5-37

```
MATLAB Program 5–26

num = [0  0  0  0  1];
den = [1  1.1  10.3  5  0];
v = [-2  2  -4  4];
axis(v);
K1 = 0:0.2:20;
K2 = 20:0.1:30;
K3 = 30:5:100;
K = [K1  K2  K3];
r = rlocus(num,den,K);
plot(r,'ob')
grid
title('Root-Locus Plot of G(s) = K/[s(s+0.5)(s^2+0.6s+10)]')
xlabel('Real Axis')
ylabel('Imag Axis')

% ***** Note that the command 'plot(r,'ob')' gives small circles
% in the screen plot in blue color *****
```

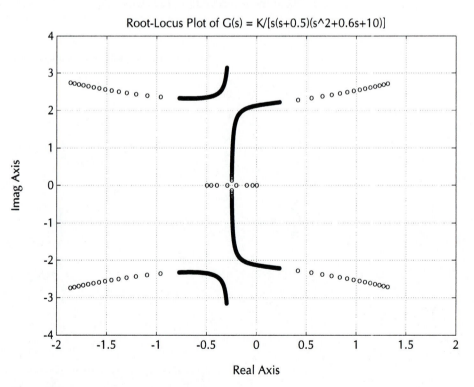

Figure 5-38

EXAMPLE 5-24

Consider the system whose open-loop transfer function $G(s)H(s)$ is

$$G(s)H(s) = \frac{K(s + 0.2)}{s^2(s + 3.6)}$$

The open-loop zero is at $s = -0.2$, and open-loop poles are located at $s = 0$, $s = 0$, and $s = -3.6$.

Entering MATLAB Program 5-27 into the computer, we obtain the root-locus plot shown in Figure 5-39. The computer-generated root-locus plot looks fine.

MATLAB Program 5–27

```
num = [0  0  1  0.2];
den = [1  3.6  0  0];
v = [-4  2  -4  4];
axis(v);
rlocus(num,den);

Axis scales auto-ranged

Axis scales frozen

grid
title('Root-Locus Plot of G(s) = K(s+0.2)/[s^2(s+3.6)]')
```

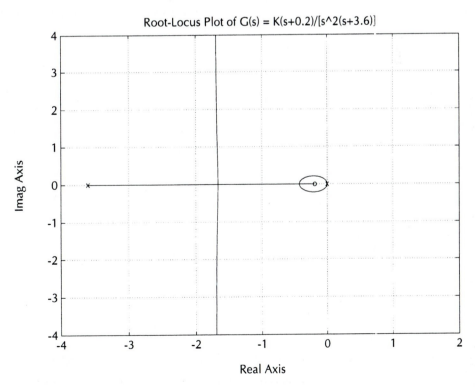

Figure 5-39

In Examples 5-20 through 5-23, we discussed how to cure problems of root-locus plots caused by an improper incremental size of the gain K. Conversely, by using an improper incremental size of the gain K, it is possible to "fool" MATLAB and generate an erroneous, funny looking root-locus plot.

In what follows, we shall generate a strange looking root-locus plot by using a constant increment of gain K. (We compute closed-loop poles of this system for $K = 0, 1, 2, \ldots, 200$ and connect the computed points.) MATLAB Program 5-28 will yield the root-locus plot shown in Figure 5-40. Obviously, it is an erroneous root-locus plot.

MATLAB Program 5–28

```
num = [0   0   1   0.2];
den = [1   3.6   0   0];
v = [-4   2   -4   4];
axis(v);
K = 0:1:200;
r = rlocus(num,den,K);
plot(r)
grid
title('Erroneous Root-Locus Plot of G(s) = K(s+0.2)/[s^2(s+3.6)]')
xlabel('Real Axis')
ylabel('Imag Axis')
```

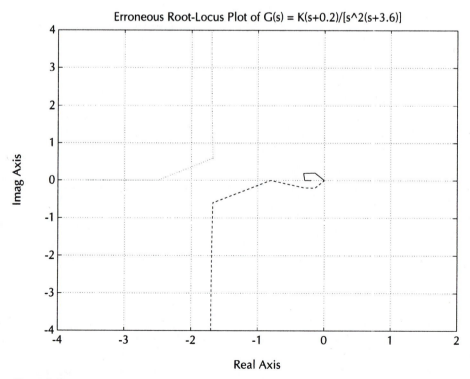

Figure 5-40

EXAMPLE 5-25

Consider a system whose open-loop transfer function is

$$G(s)H(s) = \frac{K(s + 0.5)(s + 3)}{(s + 1)(s + 2)}$$

If we enter MATLAB Program 5-29 into the computer, we get the root-locus plot shown in Figure 5-41. This plot is a correct root-locus plot.

If, however, we use the command

$$r = rlocus(num,den)$$

and enter MATLAB Program 5-30 into the computer, an erroneous root-locus plot will be generated, as shown in Figure 5-42.

If we specify the $x-y$ region as

$$\begin{bmatrix} -5 & 15 & -6 & 6 \end{bmatrix}$$

MATLAB Program 5–29

```
num = [1   3.5   1.5];
den = [1   3   2];
rlocus(num,den);
grid
title('Root-Locus Plot of G(s) = K(s+0.5)(s+3)/[(s+1)(s+2)]')
```

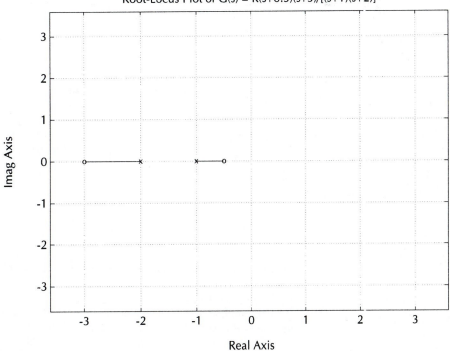

Figure 5-41

```
MATLAB Program 5-30

num = [1   3.5   1.5];
den = [1   3   2];
r = rlocus(num,den);
plot(r,'o')
grid
title('Erroneous Root-Locus Plot')
xlabel('Real Axis')
ylabel('Imag Axis')
```

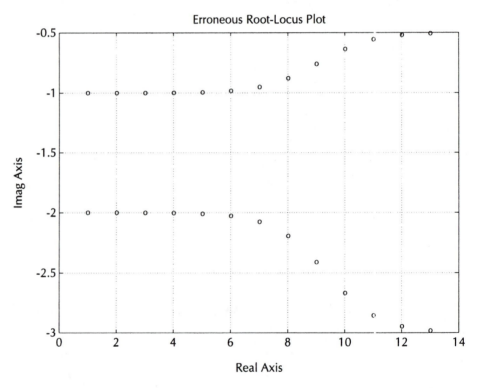

Figure 5-42

and enter MATLAB Program 5-31, we again get an erroneous root-locus plot, as shown in Figure 5-43. Such a plot may occur when the root loci do not enter the complex region, but stay only on the real axis.

To examine such an erroneous root-locus plot, we need to check the values of r. To get the values of r, enter MATLAB Program 5-32 into the computer.

From the values of r obtained, we see that they are real and stay between -1 and -0.5070 or between -2 and -2.9815. The plot shown in Figure 5-43 is actually a plot of r versus k, where k = 1, 2, 3, . . . , 13. (It is an incorrect plot for the root loci.)

MATLAB Program 5–31

```
num = [1   3.5   1.5];
den = [1   3   2];
v = [-5   15   -6   6];
axis(v);
r = rlocus(num,den);
plot(r,'o')
grid
title('Erroneous Root-Locus Plot')
xlabel('Real Axis')
ylabel('Imag Axis')
```

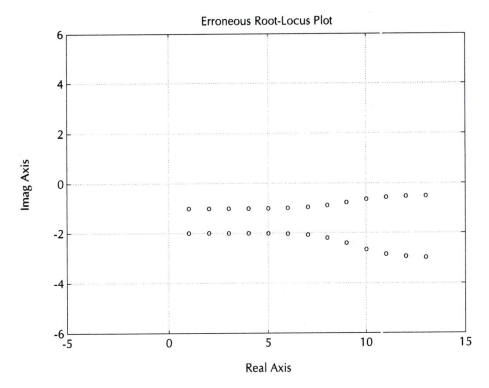

Figure 5-43

To correct this situation, we first check the size of matrix r as follows:

```
size(r)

ans =

    13    2
```

Then we enter the following plot command:

$$\text{plot(r, zeros(13,1))}$$

```
MATLAB Program 5–32

num = [1   3.5   1.5];
den = [1   3   2];
v = [-5   15   -6   6];
axis(v);
r = rlocus(num,den)

r =

    -2.0000    -1.0000
    -2.0000    -1.0000
    -2.0007    -0.9995
    -2.0027    -0.9982
    -2.0088    -0.9942
    -2.0265    -0.9825
    -2.0755    -0.9509
    -2.1932    -0.8790
    -2.4086    -0.7603
    -2.6668    -0.6363
    -2.8551    -0.5564
    -2.9463    -0.5204
    -2.9815    -0.5070
```

where zeros(13,1) is a column vector consisting of 13 zeros as follows:

```
zeros(13,1)

ans =

    0
    0
    0
    0
    0
    0
    0
    0
    0
    0
    0
    0
    0
```

This means that, instead of plotting the values of r versus k (k = 1, 2, 3, ..., 13), we let MATLAB plot the zeros versus the values of r.

MATLAB Program 5-33 gives a correct root-locus plot, which is shown in Figure 5-44.

MATLAB Program 5-34 will also give a correct root-locus plot. The plot generated from this program is shown in Figure 5-45.

MATLAB Program 5–33

```
num = [1   3.5   1.5];
den = [1   3   2];
v = [-6   6   -6   6];
axis(v);
r = rlocus(num,den);
plot(r,zeros(13,1))
grid
title('Root-Locus Plot of G(s) = K(s+0.5)(s+3)/[(s+1)(s+2)]')
xlabel('Real Axis')
ylabel('Imag Axis')
```

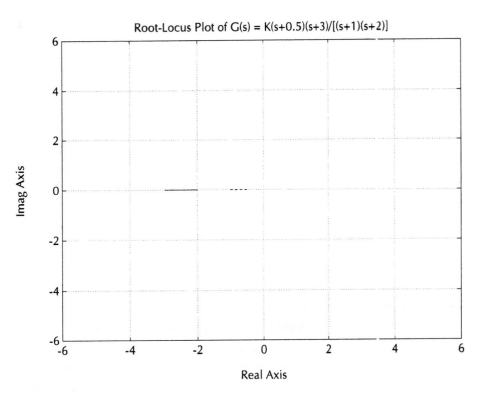

Figure 5-44

```
MATLAB Program 5–34

num = [1   3.5   1.5];
den = [1   3   2];
v = [-6   6   -6   6];
axis(v);
rlocus(num,den);

Axis scales auto-ranged

Axis scales frozen

grid
title('Root-Locus Plot of G(s) = K(s+0.5)(s+3)/[(s+1)(s+2)]')
```

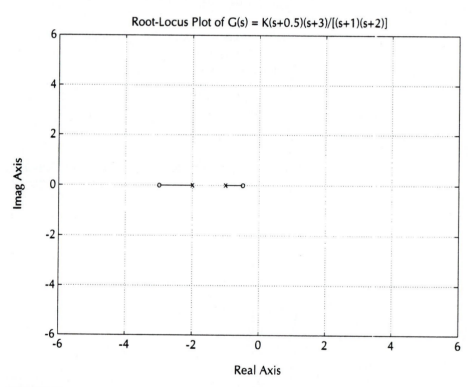

Figure 5-45

EXAMPLE 5-26: Positive Feedback System

Consider the positive feedback system shown in Figure 5-46. For this positive feedback system, the open-loop transfer function $G(s)H(s)$ can be given as

$$G(s)H(s) = -\frac{K(s + 0.5)(s + 3)}{(s + 1)(s + 2)}$$

$$= -\frac{K(s^2 + 3.5s + 1.5)}{s^2 + 3s + 2}$$

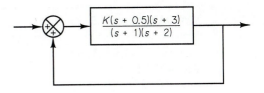

Figure 5-46

Hence

$$\text{num} = \begin{bmatrix} -1 & -3.5 & -1.5 \end{bmatrix}$$
$$\text{den} = \begin{bmatrix} 1 & 3 & 2 \end{bmatrix}$$

A root-locus plot for this system may be obtained by entering MATLAB Program 5-35. The resulting root-locus plot is shown in Figure 5-47.

To change the region of the plot, we enter MATLAB Program 5-36. The resulting root-locus plot is shown in Figure 5-48. (Note that arrows are added manually to indicate the

---

MATLAB Program 5–35

```
num = [-1  -3.5  -1.5];
den = [1  3  2];
rlocus(num,den);
grid
title('Root-Locus Plot of Positive Feedback System')
```

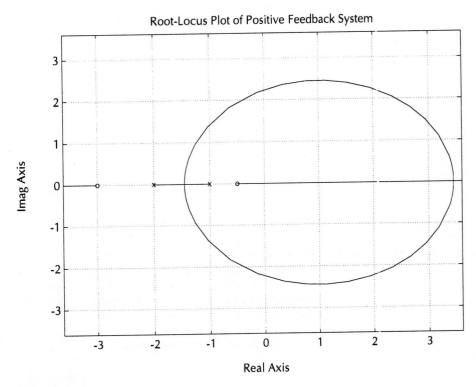

Figure 5-47

```
MATLAB Program 5–36

num = [-1   -3.5   -1.5];
den = [1   3   2];
v = [-10   10   -10   10];
axis(v);
rlocus(num,den);

Axis scales auto-ranged

Axis scales frozen

grid
title('Root-Locus Plot of Positive Feedback System')
```

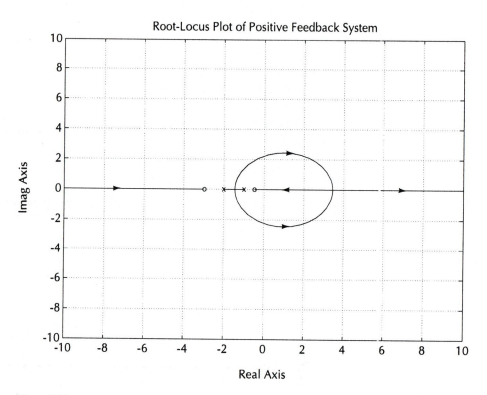

Figure 5-48

direction of increasing gain K on each branch.) The locus has a breakaway point at $s = -1.4495$ and a break-in point at $s = 3.4495$. When the locus breaks in at $s = 3.4495$, one path goes directly to $s = -0.5$, corresponding to one open-loop zero; the other path goes to $+\infty$, where it changes sign to $-\infty$ and then moves to $s = -3$, corresponding to the second open-loop zero.

Note that the use of the command

$$r = \text{rlocus(num,den)}$$
$$\text{plot(r,'-')}$$

may cause a problem. (See MATLAB Program 5-37 and the resulting plot shown in Figure 5-49.) In this example, this command gives an erroneous root-locus plot. The entire real axis is shown as a root-locus branch. This is in error.

However, if we change the command to

$$r = rlocus(num,den)$$
$$plot(r,'o')$$

as given in MATLAB Program 5-38, the root-locus plot is correct, provided that we carefully interpret the root-locus branches on the real axis. (See Figure 5-50.)

```
MATLAB Program 5–37

num = [-1   -3.5   -1.5];
den = [1   3   2];
v = [-10   10   -10   10];
axis(v);
r = rlocus(num,den);
plot(r,'-')
grid
title('Erroneous Root-Locus Plot')
xlabel('Real Axis')
ylabel('Imag Axis')
```

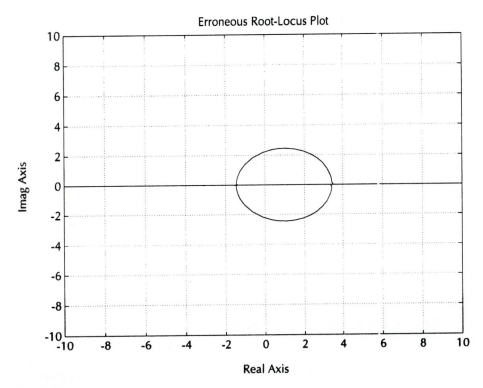

Figure 5-49

MATLAB Program 5–38

```
num = [-1  -3.5  -1.5];
den = [1  3  2];
v = [-10  10  -10  10];
axis(v);
r = rlocus(num,den);
plot(r,'o')
grid
title('Root-Locus Plot of Positive Feedback System')
xlabel('Real Axis')
ylabel('Imag Axis')
```

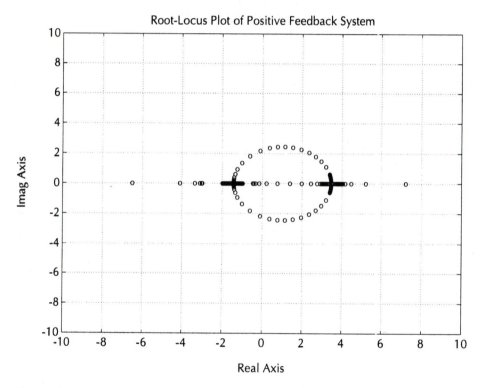

Figure 5-50

5-4 PLOTTING TWO OR MORE ROOT-LOCUS DIAGRAMS ON ONE GRAPH

In this section, we consider plotting two or more root-locus diagrams on one graph. Such a case occurs typically when we want to plot the root loci and their asymptotes on one diagram.

EXAMPLE 5-27

Consider the system whose open-loop transfer function $G(s)H(s)$ is given by

$$G(s)H(s) = \frac{K}{s(s + 1)(s + 2)}$$

A root-locus plot of this system can be obtained by entering MATLAB Program 5-39 into the computer. The resulting plot is shown in Figure 5-51.

MATLAB Program 5–39

```
num = [0  0  0  1];
den = [1  3  2  0];
rlocus(num,den);
grid
title('Root-Locus Plot of G(s) = K/[s(s+1)(s+2)]')
```

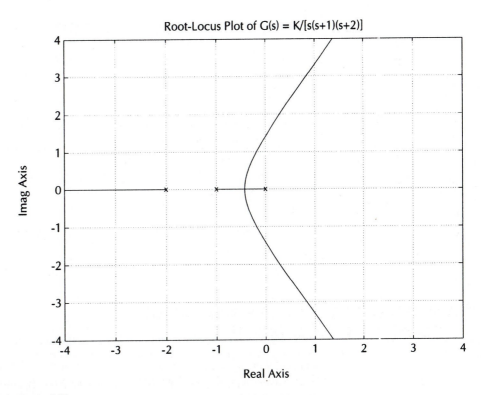

Figure 5-51

Next, let us plot root loci and asymptotes on one diagram. Since the open-loop transfer function is given by

$$G(s)H(s) = \frac{K}{s(s+1)(s+2)}$$

$$= \frac{K}{s^3 + 3s^2 + 2s}$$

the equation for the asymptotes may be obtained as follows: Noting that

$$\lim_{s\to\infty} \frac{K}{s^3+3s^2+2s} \doteq \lim_{s\to\infty} \frac{K}{s^3+3s^2+3s+1}$$

the equation for the asymptotes may be given by

$$G_a(s)H_a(s) = \frac{K}{(s+1)^3}$$

Hence, for the system we have

$$num = [0 \quad 0 \quad 0 \quad 1]$$
$$den = [1 \quad 3 \quad 2 \quad 0]$$

and for the asymptotes,

$$numa = [0 \quad 0 \quad 0 \quad 1]$$
$$dena = [1 \quad 3 \quad 3 \quad 1]$$

In using the following *root-locus* and *plot* commands

```
r = rlocus(num,den)
a = rlocus(numa, dena)
plot([r  a])
```

the number of rows of r and that of a must be the same. To ensure this, we include the gain constant K in the commands. For example,

```
K1 = 0:0.1:0.3;
K2 = 0.3:0.005:0.5:
K3 = 0.5:0.5:10;
K4 = 10:5:100;
 K = [K1  K2  K3  K4]
  r = rlocus(num,den,K)
  a = rlocus(numa,dena,K)
  y = [r  a]
plot(y,' ')
```

Including gain K in the *rlocus* command ensures that the r matrix and a matrix have the same number of rows. MATLAB Program 5-40 will generate a plot of root loci and their asymptotes. See Figure 5-52.

MATLAB Program 5-41 uses the *hold* command. The resulting root-locus plot is shown in Figure 5-53.

MATLAB Program 5–40

```
num = [0   0   0   1];
den = [1   3   2   0];
numa = [0   0   0   1];
dena = [1   3   3   1];
v = [-4   4   -4   4];
axis(v);
K1 = 0:0.1:0.3;
K2 = 0.3:0.005:0.5;
K3 = 0.5:0.5:10;
K4 = 10:5:100;
K = [K1   K2   K3   K4];
r = rlocus(num,den,K);
a = rlocus(numa,dena,K);
y = [r   a];
plot(y,'-g')
grid
title('Root-Locus Plot of G(s) = K/[s(s+1)(s+2)] and Asymptotes')
xlabel('Real Axis')
ylabel('Imag Axis')

% ***** Note that the command "plot(y,'-g')" gives continuous
% lines and curves in screen plot in green color *****

% ***** Manually draw open-loop poles in the hard copy *****
```

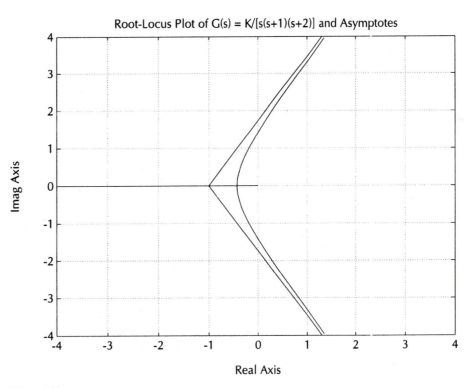

Figure 5-52

MATLAB Program 5–41

```
num = [0   0   0   1];
den = [1   3   2   0];
numa = [0   0   0   1];
dena = [1   3   3   1];
v = [-4   4   -4   4];
axis(v);
K1 = 0:0.1:0.3;
K2 = 0.3:0.005:0.5;
K3 = 0.5:0.5:10;
K4 = 10:5:100;
K = [K1   K2   K3   K4];
r = rlocus(num,den,K);
a = rlocus(numa,dena,K);
plot(r,'o')
hold
```

Current plot held

```
plot(a,'-')
grid
title('Root-Locus Plot of G(s) = K/[s(s+1)(s+2)] and Asymptotes')
xlabel('Real Axis')
ylabel('Imag Axis')
```

% ***** Manually draw open-loop poles on the hard copy *****

% ***** Remove hold on graphics *****

```
hold
```

Current plot released

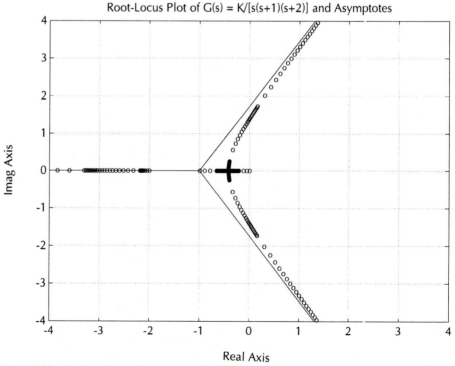

Figure 5-53

EXAMPLE 5-28

Consider a system whose open-loop transfer function is given by

$$G(s)H(s) = \frac{K(s - 0.6667)}{s^2(s + 1.670 + j2.060)(s + 1.670 - j2.060)}$$

$$= \frac{K(s - 0.6667)}{s^4 + 3.340s^3 + 7.0325s^2}$$

The system has one open-loop zero at $s = 0.6667$ and four open-loop poles at $s = -1.670 + j2.060$, $s = -1.670 - j2.060$, $s = 0$, and $s = 0$.

The equation for the asymptotes may be obtained as

$$G_a(s)H_a(s) = \frac{K}{s^3 + (3.340 + 0.6667)s^2 + \cdots}$$

$$\doteq \frac{K}{\left(s + \dfrac{3.340 + 0.6667}{3}\right)^3}$$

$$= \frac{K}{(s + 1.3356)^3}$$

$$= \frac{K}{s^3 + 4.0068s^2 + 5.3515s + 2.3825}$$

Hence, we enter the following numerators and denominators in the program. For the system,

$$\text{num} = [0 \quad 0 \quad 0 \quad 1 \quad -0.6667]$$
$$\text{den} = [1 \quad 3.340 \quad 7.0325 \quad 0 \quad 0]$$

For the asymptotes,

$$\text{numa} = [0 \quad 0 \quad 0 \quad 1]$$
$$\text{dena} = [1 \quad 4.0068 \quad 5.3515 \quad 2.3825]$$

Using the same approach as discussed in Example 5-27, include gain K in the *rlocus* command as follows:

```
K1 = 0:1:50
K2 = 50:5:200
K = [K1   K2]
 r = rlocus(num,den,K)
 a = rlocus(numa,dena,K)
 y = [r   a]
plot(y,' ')
```

See MATLAB Program 5-42 and the resulting plot shown in Figure 5-54.

MATLAB Program 5-43 uses the *hold* command. In this case, it is not necessary to include gain K in the *rlocus* command, since the plots of r and a are done independently on the same graph. The plot using this program is shown in Figure 5-55.

```
MATLAB Program 5–42

num = [0   0   0   1   -0.6667];
den = [1   3.34   7.0325   0   0];
numa = [0   0   0   1];
dena = [1   4.0068   5.3515   2.3825];
v = [-4   3   -5   5];
axis(v);
K1 = 0:1:50;
K2 = 50:5:200;
K = [K1   K2];
r = rlocus(num,den,K);
a = rlocus(numa,dena,K);
y = [r   a];
plot(y,'-g')
grid
title('Root-Locus Plot of G(s) and Asymptotes')
xlabel('Real Axis')
ylabel('Imag Axis')

% ***** Note that the command "plot(y,'-g')" gives continuous
% lines and curves in screen plot in green color *****

% ***** Manually draw open-loop zero and open-loop poles
% on the hard copy *****
```

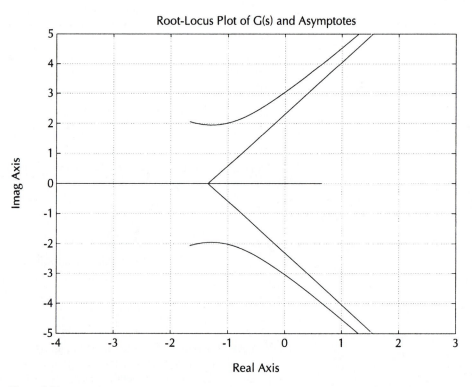

Figure 5-54

```
num = [0   0   0   1   -0.6667];
den = [1   3.340   7.0325   0   0];
numa = [0   0   0   1];
dena = [1   4.0068   5.3515   2.3825];
v = [-4   3   -5   5];
axis(v);
r = rlocus(num,den);
plot(r,'o')
hold

Current plot held

a = rlocus(numa,dena);
plot(a,'-')
grid
title('Root-Locus Plot of G(s) and Asymptotes')
xlabel('Real Axis')
ylabel('Imag Axis')

% ***** Manually draw open-loop zero and open-loop poles
% on the hard copy *****

% ***** Remove hold on graphics *****

hold

Current plot released
```

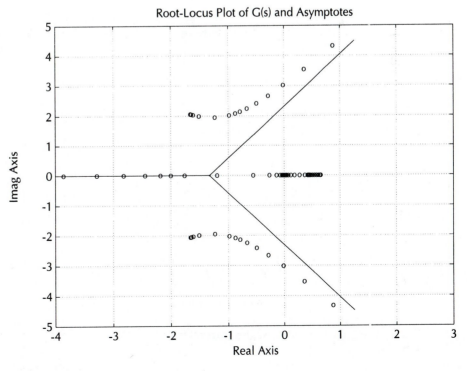

Figure 5-55

5-5 ROOT-LOCUS PLOTS IN THE z PLANE

The construction of root-locus plots in the z plane is exactly the same as that for root-locus plots in the s plane. The only difference in the plots in these two planes is the interpretation of the stability region. In the s plane, the closed-loop poles in the right half-plane are unstable poles, while in the z plane the closed-loop poles outside the unit circle centered at the origin are unstable poles.

EXAMPLE 5-29

Plot the root loci of the system shown in Figure 5-56. Assume that the open-loop pulse transfer function $G_D(z)G(z)$ is given by

$$G_D(z)G(z) = \frac{0.0176K(z + 0.8760)}{(z - 0.2543)(z - 1)}$$

To plot the root loci for this system, we lump gain K and constant 0.0176 as K', and let K' vary from zero to a large number. This means that $G_D(z)G(z)$ may be written as

$$G_D(z)G(z) = \frac{K'(z + 0.8760)}{(z - 0.2543)(z - 1)}$$

where K' is the overall gain. In writing the numerator polynomial, it is not multiplied by the new gain K', and the num and den become

$$\text{num} = [0 \quad 1 \quad 0.8760]$$
$$\text{den} = [1 \quad -1.2543 \quad 0.2543]$$

MATLAB Program 5-44 will yield a plot of the root loci. The plot is shown in Figure 5-57.

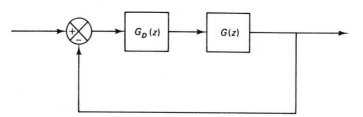

Figure 5-56

MATLAB Program 5–44

```
num = [0  1  0.8760];
den = [1  -1.2543  0.2543];
v = [-4  4  -4  4];
axis(v);
rlocus(num,den);

Axis scales auto-ranged

Axis scales frozen

grid
title('Root-Locus Plot of G(z) = K(z+0.8760)/[(z-0.2543)(z-1)]')
```

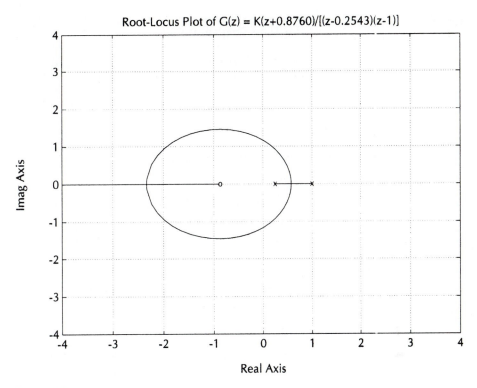

Figure 5-57

EXAMPLE 5-30

Consider the system shown in Figure 5-58. Plot the root-locus diagram. The open-loop pulse transfer function becomes

$$G_D(z)G(z) = \frac{(1.4 - 1.4z^{-1} + 0.2z^{-2})(0.3679z^{-1} + 0.2642z^{-2})}{(1 - z^{-1})(1 - 0.3679z^{-1})(1 - z^{-1})}$$

$$= \frac{0.5151z^3 - 0.1452z^2 - 0.2963z + 0.05284}{z^4 - 2.3679z^3 + 1.7358z^2 - 0.3679z}$$

MATLAB Program 5-45 may be used to generate a root-locus plot. The plot obtained by the use of this program is shown in Figure 5-59.

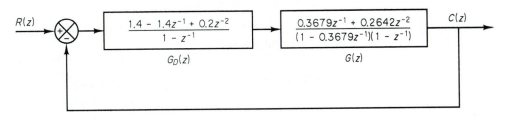

Figure 5-58

MATLAB Program 5–45

```
num = [0.5151  -0.1452  -0.2963  0.05284];
den = [1  -2.3679  1.7358  -0.3679  0];
v = [-3  2  -2  2];
axis(v);
rlocus(num,den);

Axis scales auto-ranged

Axis scales frozen

grid
title('Root-Locus Plot of Digital Control System')
```

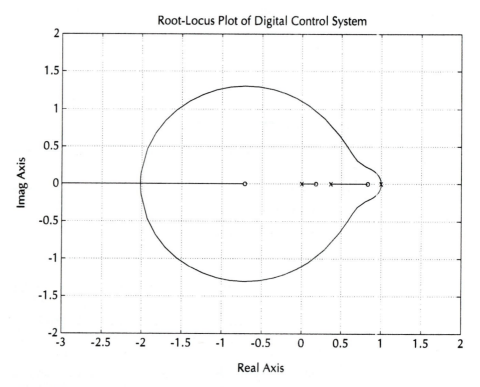

Figure 5-59

EXAMPLE 5-31: Unit Circle

In plotting the root-locus diagram in the z plane, it is frequently desired to superimpose the unit circle on the diagram.

The unit circle, centered at the origin, can be easily drawn by using the following command:

$$p = 0:0.01:2*pi;$$
$$x = \sin(p); \; y = \cos(p);$$
$$\text{plot}(x,y)$$

See MATLAB Program 5-46 and the resulting unit circle shown in Figure 5-60.

```
MATLAB Program 5–46

p = 0:0.01:2*pi;
x = sin(p);
y = cos(p);
v = [-2  2  -2  2];
axis(v)
plot(x,y)
grid
title('Unit Circle')
xlabel('Real Axis')
ylabel('Imag Axis')
```

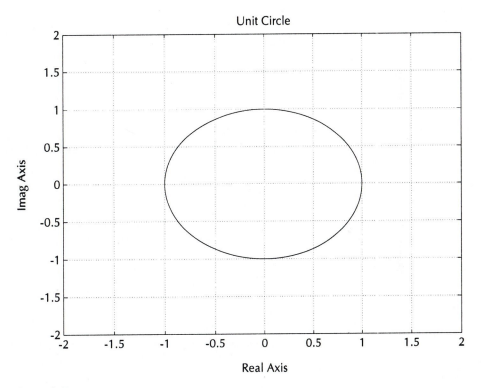

Figure 5-60

EXAMPLE 5-32

Consider the system shown in Figure 5-61. Obtain a root-locus plot for the system.

Entering MATLAB Program 5-47 into the computer, we obtain the root-locus plot shown in Figure 5-62.

Suppose that we wish to superimpose the unit circle on the diagram. This can be easily done by using the *hold* command and the command for plotting a unit circle, as presented in Example 5-31. See MATLAB Program 5-48 and the resulting plot shown in Figure 5-63.

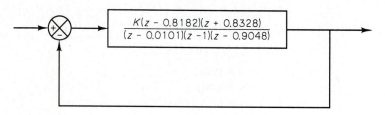

Figure 5-61

MATLAB Program 5–47

```
num = [0   1   0.0146   -0.6814];
den = [1   -1.9149   0.9240   -0.0091];
v = [-4   2   -2   2];
axis(v);
rlocus(num,den);

Axis scales auto-ranged

Axis scales frozen

grid
title('R L Plot of G(z) = K(z-0.8182)(z+0.8328)/[(z-0.0101)(z-1)(z-0.9048)]')
```

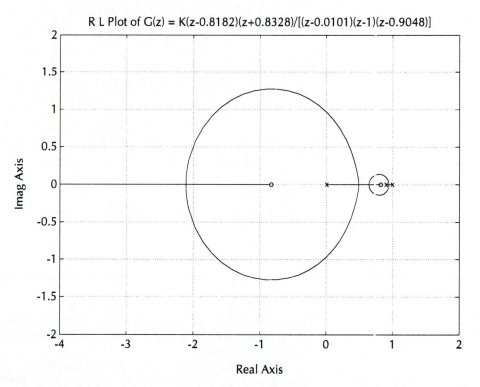

Figure 5-62

```
% ---------- Plot of root loci and unit circle ----------

num = [0   1   0.0146   -0.6814];
den = [1   -1.9149   0.9240   -0.0091];
v = [-4   2   -2   2];
axis(v);
rlocus(num,den);

Axis scales auto-ranged

Axis scales frozen

grid

% ***** To superimpose a unit circle on the root-locus plot,
% enter hold command and a command for generating a unit circle *****

hold

Current plot held

p = 0:0.01:2*pi; x = sin(p); y = cos(p); plot(x,y,'--')
title('Plot of Root Loci and Unit Circle')
text(0.8,-0.8,'Unit circle')

% ***** Remove hold on graphics *****

hold

Current plot released
```

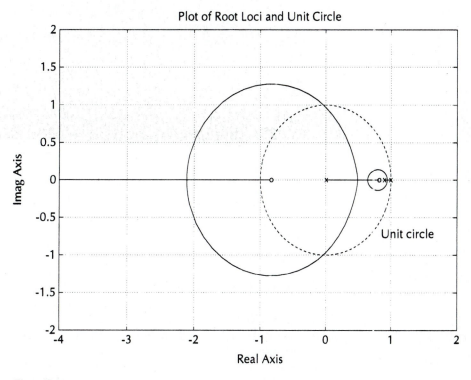

Figure 5-63

EXAMPLE 5-33: Deadbeat Control System

Consider the control system shown in Figure 5-64. The sampling period T is 1 sec. The pulse transfer function for the digital controller and that for the plant are given, respectively, by

$$G_D(z) = \frac{2.5(1 - 0.6z^{-1})}{1 + 0.75z^{-1}} = \frac{2.5(z - 0.6)}{z + 0.75}$$

$$G(z) = \frac{(1 + z^{-1})z^{-1}}{2(1 - z^{-1})^2} = \frac{z + 1}{2(z - 1)^2}$$

Thus

$$G_D(z)G(z) = \frac{1.25(z^2 + 0.4z - 0.6)}{z^3 - 1.25z^2 - 0.5z + 0.75}$$

$$= \frac{K(z^2 + 0.4z - 0.6)}{z^3 - 1.25z^2 - 0.5z + 0.75}, \qquad K = 1.25$$

This system is designed to exhibit a deadbeat response to the ramp inputs. (The transient-response characteristics of this system were investigated in Example 4-9.) Note that such a deadbeat response system has all closed-loop poles at the origin. For this system, there are three closed-loop poles at the origin, as follows:

$$\frac{C(z)}{R(z)} = \frac{2.5(z^2 + 0.4z - 0.6)}{(2z + 1.5)(z^2 - 2z + 1) + 2.5(z^2 + 0.4z - 0.6)}$$

$$= \frac{1.25(z^2 + 0.4z - 0.6)}{z^3}$$

To obtain a root-locus plot for the system, enter MATLAB Program 5-49 into the computer.

Looking at the root-locus plot shown in Figure 5-65, obtained by use of MATLAB Program 5-49, we notice that near the origin the plot shows a peculiar shape. This is caused by an insufficient number of computed points near the origin. To investigate the cause of these

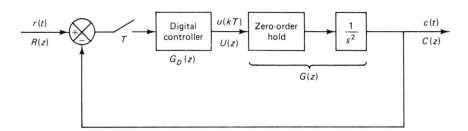

Figure 5-64

MATLAB Program 5–49

num = [0 1 0.4 -0.6];
den = [1 -1.25 -0.5 0.75];
rlocus(num,den);
grid
title('Deadbeat Response System Designed for Ramp Inputs')

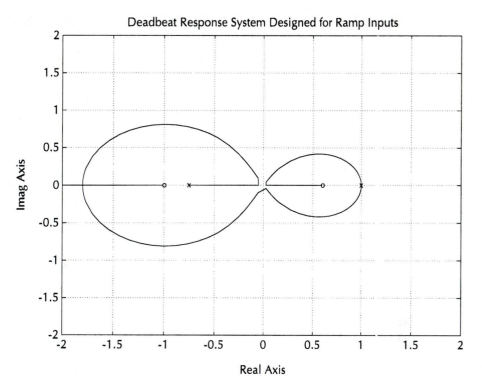

Figure 5-65

root loci, let us plot the root loci using marks 'o'. MATLAB Program 5-50 generates the plot shown in Figure 5-66.

In the plot of Figure 5-66, notice that there are no computed points in the vicinity of the origin. To get some computed points near the origin, we specify the values of gain *K* spaced very close together in the area near the origin. For example, we may specify gain *K* as follows:

$$K1 = 0{:}0.01{:}1.5;$$
$$K2 = 1.5{:}0.1{:}4.26;$$
$$K3 = 4.26{:}0.001{:}4.32;$$
$$K4 = 4.32{:}1{:}10;$$
$$K5 = 10{:}5{:}100;$$
$$K = [K1 \quad K2 \quad K3 \quad K4 \quad K5]$$

Using MATLAB Program 5-51, we obtain the root-locus plot shown in Figure 5-67.

MATLAB Program 5–50

```
num = [0  1  0.4  -0.6];
den = [1  -1.25  -0.5  0.75];
v = [-2  2  -2  2];
axis(v);
r = rlocus(num,den);
plot(r,'o')
grid
title('Deadbeat Response System Designed for Ramp Inputs')
xlabel('Real Axis')
ylabel('Imag Axis')
```

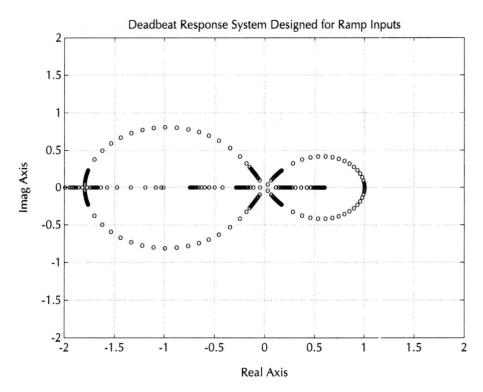

Figure 5-66

MATLAB Program 5–51

```
num = [0   1   0.4   -0.6];
den = [1   -1.25   -0.5   0.75];
v = [-2   2   -2   2];
axis(v);
K1 = 0:0.01:1.5;
K2 = 1.5:0.1:4.26;
K3 = 4.26:0.001:4.32;
K4 = 4.32:1:10;
K5 = 10:5:100;
K = [K1   K2   K3   K4   K5];
r = rlocus(num,den,K);
plot(r,'o')
grid
title('Deadbeat Response System Designed for Ramp Inputs')
xlabel('Real Axis')
ylabel('Imag Axis')
```

Changing the *plot* command in MATLAB Program 5-51 from plot(r,'o') to plot(r,'-'), we obtain the root-locus plot shown in Figure 5-68, which consists of continuous lines and continuous curves. The MATLAB program that generates this plot is given as MATLAB Program 5-52.

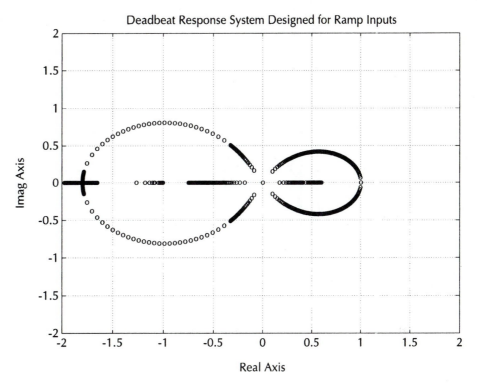

Figure 5-67

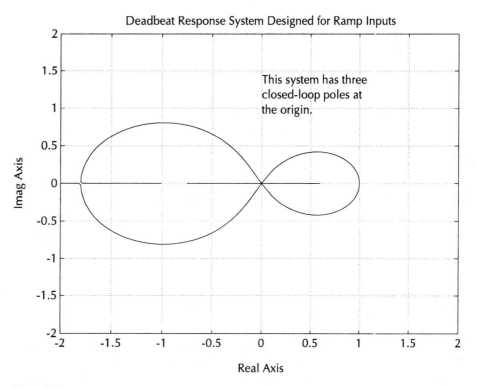

Figure 5-68

MATLAB Program 5–52

```
num = [0   1   0.4   -0.6];
den = [1   -1.25   -0.5   0.75];
v = [-2   2   -2   2];
axis(v);
K1 = 0:0.01:1.5;
K2 = 1.5:0.1:4.26;
K3 = 4.26:0.001:4.32;
K4 = 4.32:1:10;
K5 = 10:5:100;
K = [K1   K2   K3   K4   K5];
r = rlocus(num,den,K);
plot(r,'-')
grid
title('Deadbeat Response System Designed for Ramp Inputs')
xlabel('Real Axis')
ylabel('Imag Axis')
text(0,1.3,'This system has three')
text(0,1.1,'closed-loop poles at')
text(0,0.9,'the origin.')
```

EXAMPLE 5-34: Deadbeat Control System

Consider the deadbeat control system shown in Figure 5-69. (The step response and ramp response of this deadbeat control system were discussed in Example 4-8.) The open-loop pulse transfer function is

$$G_D(z)G(z) = \frac{0.5820(z + 0.7181)}{(z + 0.4180)(z - 1)}$$

Note that all closed-loop poles of the deadbeat control systems are located at the origin. For this system, there are two closed-loop poles at the origin, as follows:

$$\frac{C(z)}{R(z)} = \frac{0.5820(z + 0.7181)}{(z + 0.4180)(z - 1) + 0.5820(z + 0.7181)}$$

$$= \frac{0.5820(z + 0.7181)}{z^2}$$

MATLAB Program 5-53 generates the root-locus plot shown in Figure 5-70. A careful check reveals that the closed curve does not quite go through the origin. To check the root loci near the origin, we may enter MATLAB Program 5-54 into the computer. The resulting plot is shown in Figure 5-71.

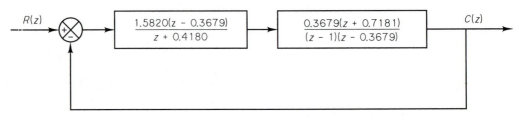

Figure 5-69

The erroneous root-locus plot near the origin and near point $(-1.4, 0)$ can be corrected by using very small step sizes in gain K in the affected regions, as shown in MATLAB Program 5-55. The resulting plot is shown in Figure 5-72, which looks good. The unit circle is added to the plot.

MATLAB Program 5–53

```
num = [0  1  0.7181];
den = [1  -0.5820  -0.4180];
rlocus(num,den);
grid
title('Root-Locus Plot for Deadbeat Control System')
```

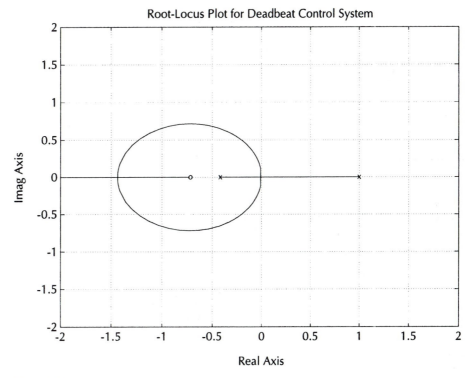

Figure 5-70

MATLAB Program 5–54

```
num = [0  1  0.7181];
den = [1  -0.5820  -0.4180];
v = [-2  2  -2  2];
axis(v);
r = rlocus(num,den);
plot(r,'-')
grid
title('Root-Locus Plot for Deadbeat Control System')
xlabel('Real Axis')
ylabel('Imag Axis')
```

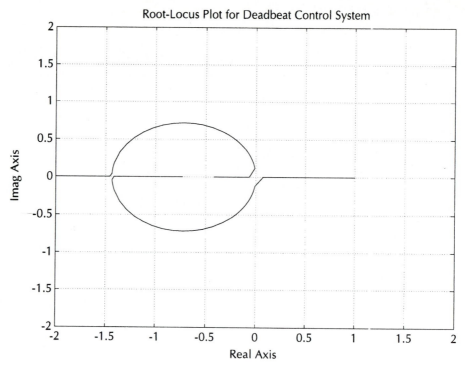

Figure 5-71

MATLAB Program 5–55

```
num = [0  1  0.7181];
den = [1  -0.5820  -0.4180];
v = [-2  2  -2  2];
axis(v);
K1 = 0:0.1:0.5;
K2 = 0.5:0.001:0.6;
K3 = 0.6:0.1:3.4;
K4 = 3.4:0.002:3.6;
K5 = 3.6:1:30.6;
K = [K1  K2  K3  K4  K5];
r = rlocus(num,den,K);
plot(r,'-')
grid
title('Root-Locus Plot for Deadbeat Control System')
xlabel('Real Axis')
ylabel('Imag Axis')
hold

Current plot held

p = 0:0.01:2*pi; x = sin(p); y = cos(p); plot(x,y,'--')
text(0.6,-1,'Unit circle')
text(0,1.5,'There are two closed-loop')
text(0,1.3,'poles at the origin.')

% ***** Remove hold on graphics *****

hold

Current plot released
```

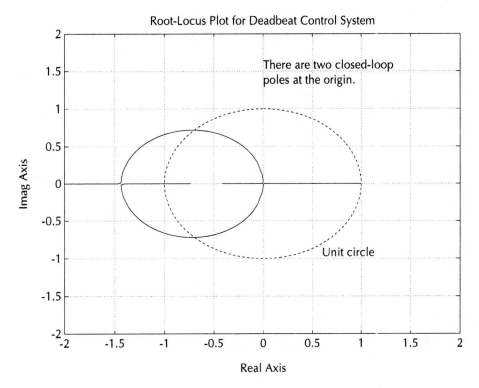

Figure 5-72

Chapter 6 | **Frequency-Response Plots**

6-1 INTRODUCTION

By the term *frequency response*, we mean the steady-state response of a system to a sinusoidal input. In frequency-response methods, we vary the frequency of the input signal over a certain range and study the resulting response.

The Nyquist stability criterion enables us to investigate both the absolute and relative stabilities of linear closed-loop systems from a knowledge of their open-loop frequency-response characteristics. An advantage of the frequency-response approach is that frequency-response tests are, in general, simple and can be made accurately by use of readily available sinusoidal signal generators and precise measurement equipment. Often the transfer functions of complicated components can be determined experimentally by frequency-response tests. In addition, the frequency-response approach has the advantages that a system may be designed so that the effects of undesirable noise are negligible and that such analysis and design can be extended to certain nonlinear control systems.

Although the frequency response of a control system presents a qualitative picture of the transient response, the correlation between frequency and transient responses is indirect, except for the case of second-order systems. In designing a closed-loop system, we adjust the frequency-response characteristic of the open-loop transfer function by using several design criteria in order to obtain acceptable transient-response characteristics for the system.

Outline of the chapter

Section 6-1 has given introductory remarks. Sections 6-2 through 6-5 deal with continuous-time control systems and Section 6-6 treats discrete-time control systems. Specifically, Section 6-2 presents background materials on the frequency-response methods. Section 6-3 discusses plotting Bode diagrams with MATLAB. We first deal with Bode diagrams of transfer-function systems and then treat Bode diagrams of systems defined in state space. Section 6-4 is concerned with Nyquist plots. Here we present Nyquist plots of transfer-function systems and of systems defined in state space. Section 6-5 gives case studies that involve the design of control systems using Bode diagrams. Finally, Section 6-6 treats the frequency response of discrete-time control systems in the w plane.

Note also that, when expressed in decibels, the reciprocal of a number differs from its value only in sign; that is, for the number K

$$20 \log K = -20 \log \frac{1}{K}$$

In the logarithmic representation, the curves are drawn on semilog paper, using the log scale for frequency and the linear scale for either magnitude (but in decibels) or phase angle (in degrees). The frequency range of interest determines the number of logarithmic cycles required on the abscissa.

In Bode diagrams, frequency ratios are expressed in terms of octaves or decades. An octave is a frequency band from ω_1 to $2\omega_1$, where ω_1 is any frequency value. A decade is a frequency band from ω_1 to $10\omega_1$ where again ω_1 is any frequency. (On the logarithmic scale of semilog paper, any given frequency ratio can be represented by the same horizontal distance. For example, the horizontal distance from $\omega = 1$ to $\omega = 10$ is equal to that from $\omega = 3$ to $\omega = 30$.)

The Bode diagram is useful in that it shows both the low- and high-frequency characteristics of the transfer function. Expanding the low-frequency range by use of a logarithmic scale for the frequency is very advantageous since the characteristics at low frequencies are most important in practical systems. (Note that, because of the logarithmic frequency scale, it is impossible to plot the curves right down to zero frequency; however, this does not create any serious problems.)

Integral and derivative factors

The logarithmic magnitude of $1/j\omega$ in decibels is

$$20 \log \left| \frac{1}{j\omega} \right| = -20 \log \omega \text{ dB}$$

The phase angle of $1/j\omega$ is constant and equal to $-90°$.

If the log magnitude $-20 \log \omega$ dB is plotted against ω on a logarithmic scale, it is a straight line. Since

$$(-20 \log 10\omega) \text{ dB} = (-20 \log \omega - 20) \text{ dB}$$

the slope of the line is -20 dB/decade.

Similarly, the log magnitude of $j\omega$ in decibels is

$$20 \log |j\omega| = 20 \log \omega \text{ dB}$$

The phase angle of $j\omega$ is constant and equal to $90°$. The log-magnitude curve is a straight line with a slope of 20 dB/decade. Figures 6-3 and 6-4 show Bode diagrams of $1/j\omega$ and $j\omega$, respectively.

First-order factor

The log magnitude of the first-order factor $1/(1 + j\omega T)$ is

$$20 \log \left| \frac{1}{1 + j\omega T} \right| = -20 \log \sqrt{1 + \omega^2 T^2} \text{ dB}$$

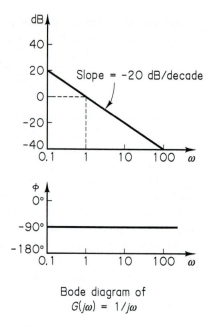

Bode diagram of
$G(j\omega) = 1/j\omega$

Figure 6-3

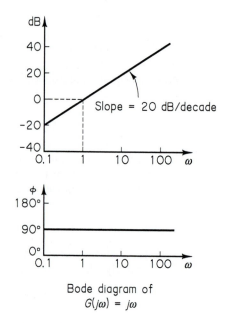

Bode diagram of
$G(j\omega) = j\omega$

Figure 6-4

For low frequencies, such that $\omega \ll 1/T$, the log magnitude may be approximated by

$$-20 \log \sqrt{1 + \omega^2 T^2} \doteqdot -20 \log 1 = 0 \text{ dB}$$

Thus, the log-magnitude curve at low frequencies is the constant 0-dB line. For high frequencies, such that $\omega \gg 1/T$,

$$-20 \log \sqrt{1 + \omega^2 T^2} \doteqdot -20 \log \omega T \text{ dB}$$

This is an approximate expression for the high-frequency range. At $\omega = 1/T$, the log magnitude equals 0 dB; at $\omega = 10/T$, the log magnitude is -20 dB. Thus the value of $-20 \log \omega T$ dB decreases by 20 dB for every decade of ω. For $\omega \gg 1/T$, the log-magnitude curve is thus a straight line with a slope of -20 dB/decade.

Our analysis shows that the Bode diagram or logarithmic representation of the frequency-response curve of the factor $1/(1 + j\omega T)$ can be approximated by two straight-line asymptotes, one a straight line at 0 dB for the frequency range $0 < \omega < 1/T$ and the other a straight line with slope -20 dB/decade for the frequency range $1/T < \omega < \infty$. The exact log-magnitude curve, the asymptotes, and the exact phase-angle curve of the factor $1/(1 + j\omega T)$ are shown in Figure 6-5.

The frequency at which the two asymptotes meet is called the *corner* frequency or *break* frequency. For the factor $1/(1 + j\omega T)$, the frequency $\omega = 1/T$ is the corner frequency, since at $\omega = 1/T$ the two asymptotes have the same value. (The low-frequency asymptotic expression at $\omega = 1/T$ is $20 \log 1$ dB $= 0$ dB, and the high-frequency asymptotic expression at $\omega = 1/T$ is also $20 \log 1$ dB $= 0$ dB.) The corner frequency divides the frequency-response curve into two regions, a curve for the low-frequency region and a curve for the high-frequency region.

The exact phase angle ϕ of the factor $1/(1 + j\omega T)$ is

$$\phi = -\tan^{-1} \omega T$$

At zero frequency, the phase angle is $0°$. At the corner frequency, the phase angle is

$$\phi = -\tan^{-1} \frac{T}{T} = -\tan^{-1} 1 = -45°$$

At infinity, the phase angle becomes $-90°$. Since the phase angle is given by an inverse-tangent function, the phase angle is skew symmetric about the inflection point at $\phi = -45°$.

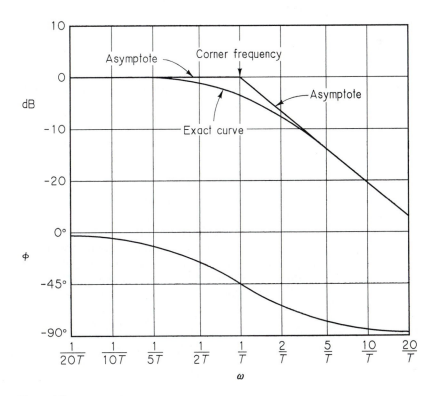

Figure 6-5

Quadratic factor

Control systems often possess quadratic factors of the form

$$\frac{1}{1 + 2\zeta\left(j\dfrac{\omega}{\omega_n}\right) + \left(j\dfrac{\omega}{\omega_n}\right)^2} \qquad (6\text{-}1)$$

If $\zeta > 1$, this quadratic factor can be expressed as a product of two first-order factors with real poles. If $0 < \zeta < 1$, this quadratic factor is the product of two complex-conjugate factors.

The asymptotic frequency-response curve may be obtained as follows: Since

$$20 \log \left| \frac{1}{1 + 2\zeta\left(j\dfrac{\omega}{\omega_n}\right) + \left(j\dfrac{\omega}{\omega_n}\right)^2} \right| = -20 \log \sqrt{\left(1 - \frac{\omega^2}{\omega_n^2}\right)^2 + \left(2\zeta\frac{\omega}{\omega_n}\right)^2}$$

for low frequencies such that $\omega \ll \omega_n$, the log magnitude becomes

$$-20 \log 1 = 0 \text{ dB}$$

The low-frequency asymptote is thus a horizontal line at 0 dB. For high frequencies such that $\omega \gg \omega_n$, the log magnitude becomes

$$-20 \log \frac{\omega^2}{\omega_n^2} = -40 \log \frac{\omega}{\omega_n} \text{ dB}$$

The equation for the high-frequency asymptote is a straight line having the slope -40 dB/decade, since

$$-40 \log \frac{10\omega}{\omega_n} = -40 - 40 \log \frac{\omega}{\omega_n}$$

The high-frequency asymptote intersects the low-frequency one at $\omega = \omega_n$, since at this frequency

$$-40 \log \frac{\omega}{\omega_n} = -40 \log 1 = 0 \text{ dB}$$

This frequency is the corner frequency for the quadratic factor considered.

The two asymptotes just derived are independent of the value of ζ. Near the frequency $\omega = \omega_n$, a resonant peak occurs, as may be expected from (6-1). The damping ratio ζ determines the magnitude of this resonant peak.

Figure 6-6 shows a Bode diagram for the quadratic factor given by (6-1). It shows the exact log-magnitude curves together with the straight-line asymptotes and the exact phase-angle curves for the quadratic factor with several values of ζ.

The phase angle of the quadratic factor $[1 + 2\zeta(j\omega/\omega_n) + (j\omega/\omega_n)^2]^{-1}$ is

$$\phi = \left/ \frac{1}{1 + 2\zeta\left(j\dfrac{\omega}{\omega_n}\right) + \left(j\dfrac{\omega}{\omega_n}\right)^2} \right. = -\tan^{-1}\left[\frac{2\zeta\dfrac{\omega}{\omega_n}}{1 - \left(\dfrac{\omega}{\omega_n}\right)^2}\right]$$

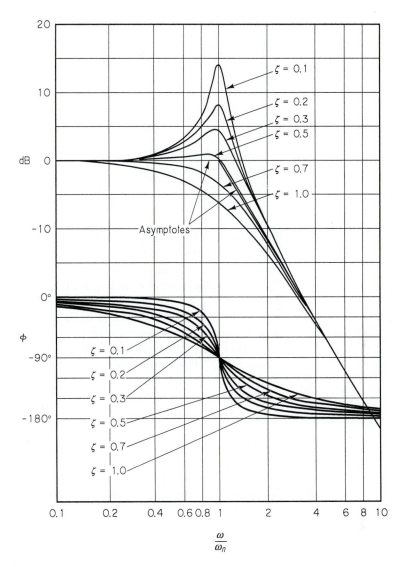

Figure 6-6

The phase angle is a function of both ω and ζ. At $\omega = 0$, the phase angle equals $0°$. At the corner frequency $\omega = \omega_n$, the phase angle is $-90°$ regardless of ζ since

$$\phi = -\tan^{-1}\left(\frac{2\zeta}{0}\right) = -\tan^{-1}\infty = -90°$$

At $\omega = \infty$, the phase angle becomes $-180°$. The phase-angle curve is skew symmetric about the inflection point, the point where $\phi = -90°$.

Relationship between system type and log-magnitude curve

Consider the system shown in Figure 6-7. The static position error constant K_p, static velocity error constant K_v, and static acceleration error constant K_a are defined as follows:

$$K_p = \lim_{s \to 0} G(s)H(s) = G(0)H(0) \tag{6-2}$$

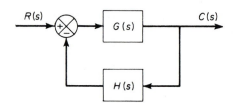

Figure 6-7

$$K_v = \lim_{s \to 0} sG(s)H(s) \tag{6-3}$$

$$K_a = \lim_{s \to 0} s^2G(s)H(s) \tag{6-4}$$

These static error constants describes the low-frequency behavior of type 0, type 1, and type 2 systems. [Remember that the number of the integrators ($1/s$) involved in $G(s)H(s)$ determines the type of the system; that is, if $G(s)H(s)$ involves 0, 1, 2, . . . integrators, then the system is called type 0, type 1, type 2, . . . , respectively. Note that, for a given system, only one of the static error constants is finite and significant. (The larger the value of the finite static error constant, the higher the loop gain is as ω approaches zero.)

The type of the system determines the slope of the log-magnitude curve at low frequencies. Thus information concerning the existence and magnitude of the steady-state error of a control system to a given input can be determined from the observation of the low-frequency region of the log-magnitude curve.

Determination of the static position error constant

Figure 6-8 shows an example of the log-magnitude plot of a type 0 system. In such a system, the magnitude of $G(j\omega)H(j\omega)$ equals K_p at low frequencies, or

$$\lim_{\omega \to 0} G(j\omega)H(j\omega) = K_p$$

It follows that the low-frequency asymptote is a horizontal line at 20 log K_p dB.

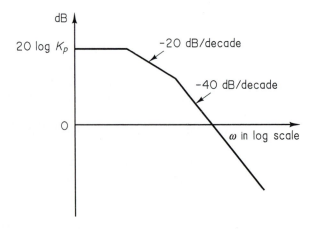

Figure 6-8

Determination of the static velocity error constant

Figure 6-9 shows an example of the log-magnitude plot of a type 1 system. The intersection of the initial -20-dB/decade segment (or its extension) with the line $\omega = 1$ has the magnitude $20 \log K_v$. This may be seen as follows: In a type 1 system,

$$G(j\omega)H(j\omega) = \frac{K_v}{j\omega}, \qquad \text{for } \omega \ll 1 \tag{6-5}$$

Thus

$$20 \log \left| \frac{K_v}{j\omega} \right|_{\omega=1} = 20 \log K_v$$

The intersection of the initial -20-dB/decade segment (or its extension) with the 0-dB line has a frequency numerically equal to K_v. To see this, define the frequency at this intersection to be ω_1; then from Eq. (6-5) we have

$$\left| \frac{K_v}{j\omega_1} \right| = 1$$

or

$$K_v = \omega_1$$

Determination of the static acceleration error constant

Figure 6-10 shows an example of the log-magnitude plot of a type 2 system. The intersection of the initial -40-dB/decade segment (or its extension) with the $\omega = 1$ line has the magnitude of $20 \log K_a$, since at low frequencies

$$G(j\omega)H(j\omega) = \frac{K_a}{(j\omega)^2}, \qquad \text{for } \omega \ll 1 \tag{6-6}$$

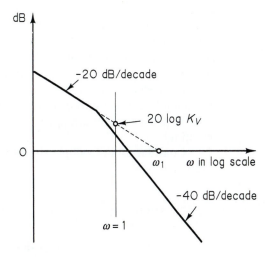

Figure 6-9

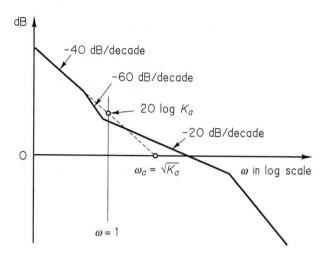

Figure 6-10

it follows that

$$20 \log \left| \frac{K_a}{(j\omega)^2} \right|_{\omega=1} = 20 \log K_a$$

The frequency ω_a at the intersection of the initial -40-dB/decade segment (or its extension) with the 0-dB line gives the square root of K_a numerically. This can be seen from the following: Define the frequency at this intersection as ω_a. Then from Eq. (6-6) we have

$$\left| \frac{K_a}{(j\omega_a)^2} \right| = 1$$

or

$$\omega_a = \sqrt{K_a}$$

Minimum phase systems and nonminimum phase systems

Transfer functions having neither poles nor zeros in the right-half s plane are minimum-phase transfer functions, whereas those having poles and/or zeros in the right-half s plane are nonminimum-phase transfer functions. Systems with minimum-phase transfer functions are called minimum-phase systems; those with nonmini-mum-phase transfer functions are called nonminimum-phase systems.

For systems with the same magnitude characteristic, the range in phase angle of the minimum-phase transfer function is minimum for all such systems, while the range in phase angle of any nonminimum-phase transfer function is greater than this minimum.

Consider as an example the two systems whose sinusoidal transfer functions are, respectively,

$$G_1(j\omega) = \frac{1 + j\omega T}{1 + j\omega T_1}, \qquad G_2(j\omega) = \frac{1 - j\omega T}{1 + j\omega T_1}, \qquad 0 < T < T_1$$

The pole-zero configurations of these systems are shown in Figure 6-11. The two sinusoidal transfer functions have the same magnitude characteristics, but they have

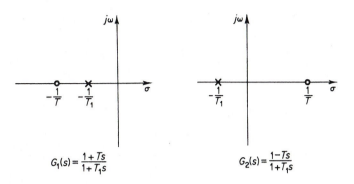

Figure 6-11

different phase-angle characteristics, as shown in Figure 6-12. These two systems differ from each other by the factor

$$G(j\omega) = \frac{1 - j\omega T}{1 + j\omega T}$$

The magnitude of the factor $(1 - j\omega T)/(1 + j\omega T)$ is always unity. But the phase angle equals $-2\tan^{-1}\omega T$ and varies from 0 to $-180°$ as ω is increased from zero to infinity.

For a minimum phase system, the magnitude and phase-angle characteristics are directly related. This means that, if the magnitude curve of a system is specified over the entire frequency range from zero to infinity, then the phase-angle curve is uniquely determined, and vice versa. This, however, does not hold for a nonminimum-phase system.

Nonminimum-phase situations may arise in two different ways. One is simply when a system includes a nonminimum-phase element or elements. The other situation may arise in the case where a minor loop is unstable.

For a minimum-phase system, the phase angle at $\omega = \infty$ becomes $-90°(q - p)$, where p and q are the degrees of the numerator and denominator polynomials of the transfer function, respectively. For a nonminimum-phase system, the phase angle at $\omega = \infty$ differs from $-90°(q - p)$. In either system, the slope of the log-magnitude curve at $\omega = \infty$ is equal to $-20(q - p)$ dB/decade. It is therefore possible to detect whether or not the system is minimum phase by examining both the slope of the high-frequency asymptote of the log-magnitude curve and the phase angle at $\omega = \infty$. If the slope of the log-magnitude curve as ω approaches infinity is $-20(q - p)$ dB/decade and the phase angle at $\omega = \infty$ is equal to $-90°(q - p)$, the system is minimum phase.

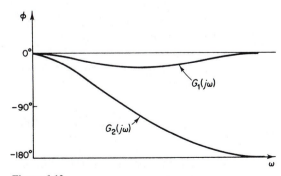

Figure 6-12

Nonminimum-phase systems are slow in response because of their faulty behavior at the start of response. In most practical control systems, excessive phase lag should be carefully avoided. In designing a system, if fast speed of response is of primary importance, we should not use nonminimum-phase components.

Nyquist plots

The Nyquist plot of a sinusoidal transfer function $G(j\omega)$ is a plot of the magnitude of $G(j\omega)$ versus the phase angle of $G(j\omega)$ on polar coordinates as ω is varied from zero to infinity. Thus the polar plot is the locus of vectors $|G(j\omega)|\underline{/G(j\omega)}$ as ω is varied from zero to infinity. Note that in polar plots a positive (negative) phase angle is measured counterclockwise (clockwise) from the positive real axis. The Nyquist plot is often called the polar plot. An example of such a plot is shown in Figure 6-13. Each point on the polar plot of $G(j\omega)$ represents the terminal point of a vector at a particular value of ω. The projections of $G(j\omega)$ on the real and imaginary axes are its real and imaginary components.

An advantage in using a Nyquist plot is that it depicts the frequency-response characteristics of a system over the entire frequency range in a single plot. One disadvantage is that the plot does not clearly indicate the contributions of each individual factor of the open-loop transfer function.

The general shapes of the low-frequency portions of the Nyquist plots of type 0, type 1, and type 2 minimum-phase systems are shown in Figure 6-14(a). It can be seen that, if the degree of the denominator polynomial of $G(j\omega)$ is greater than that of the numerator, then the $G(j\omega)$ loci converge clockwise to the origin. At $\omega = \infty$, the loci are tangent to one or the other axis, as shown in Figure 6-14(b).

For the case where the degrees of the denominator and numerator polynomials of $G(j\omega)$ are the same, the Nyquist plot starts at a finite distance on the real axis and ends at a finite point on the real axis.

Note that any complicated shapes in the Nyquist plot curves are caused by the numerator dynamics, that is, by the time constants in the numerator of the transfer function.

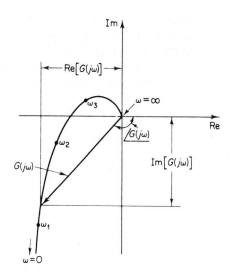

Figure 6-13

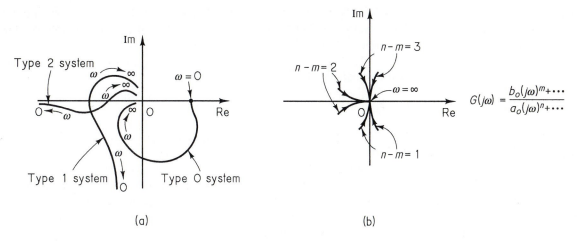

Figure 6-14

Nyquist stability criterion

Consider the system shown in Figure 6-15. The closed-loop transfer function is

$$\frac{C(s)}{R(s)} = \frac{G(s)}{1 + G(s)H(s)}$$

For stability, all roots of the characteristic equation

$$1 + G(s)H(s) = 0$$

must lie in the left-half s plane. The Nyquist stability criterion relates the open-loop frequency response $G(j\omega)H(j\omega)$ to the number of zeros and poles of $1 + G(j\omega)H(j\omega)$ that lie in the right-half s plane. This criterion, due to H. Nyquist, is useful in control engineering because the absolute stability of the closed-loop system can be determined graphically from open-loop frequency-response curves, and there is no need for actually determining the closed-loop poles. Analytically obtained open-loop frequency-response curves, as well as experimentally obtained curves, can be used for the stability analysis. This is convenient because, in designing a control system, it often happens that mathematical expressions for some of the components are not known; only their frequency-response data are available.

The Nyquist stability criterion can be stated as follows:

Nyquist stability criterion: In the system shown in Figure 6-15, if the open-loop transfer function $G(s)H(s)$ has P poles in the right-half s plane, then for stability the

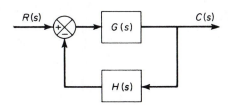

Figure 6-15

$G(s)H(s)$ locus, as a representative point s traces out the Nyquist path in the clockwise direction, must encircle the $-1 + j0$ point P times in the counterclockwise direction.

Remarks on the Nyquist stability criterion

1. This criterion can be expressed as

$$Z = N + P \qquad (6\text{-}7)$$

where Z = number of zeros of $1 + G(s)H(s)$ in the right-half s plane
$\quad\; N$ = number of clockwise encirclements of the $-1 + j0$ point
$\quad\; P$ = number of poles of $G(s)H(s)$ in the right-half s plane

If P is not zero, for a stable control system, we must have $Z = 0$, or $N = -P$, which means that we must have P counterclockwise encirclements of the $-1 + j0$ point.

If $G(s)H(s)$ does not have any poles in the right-half s plane, then, from Eq. (6-7), we must have $Z = N$ for stability. For example, consider the system with the following open-loop transfer function:

$$G(s) = \frac{K}{s(T_1 s + 1)(T_2 s + 1)}$$

Figure 6-16 shows the Nyquist path and $G(s)H(s)$ loci for a small and large value of gain K. Since the number of poles of $G(s)H(s)$ in the right-half s plane is zero, for this system to be stable, it is necessary that $N = Z = 0$ or that the $G(s)H(s)$ locus not encircle the $-1 + j0$ point.

For small values of K, there is no encirclement of the $-1 + j0$ point. Hence the system is stable for small values of K. For large values of K, the locus of $G(s)H(s)$ encircles the $-1 + j0$ point twice in the clockwise direction, indicating two closed-loop poles in the right-half s plane, and the system is unstable. (For good accuracy, K should be large. From the stability viewpoint, however, a large value of K causes poor stability or even instability. To compromise between accuracy and stability, it is necessary to insert a compensation network into the system.

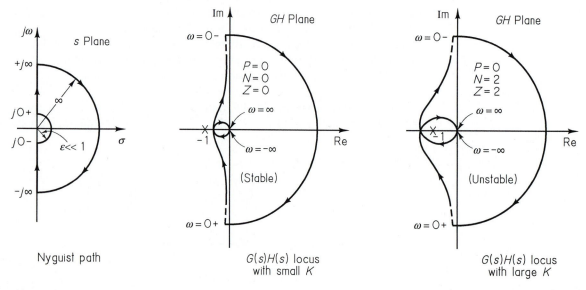

Figure 6-16

2. We must be careful when testing the stability of multiple-loop systems since they may include poles in the right-half s plane. (Note that although an inner loop may be unstable the entire closed-loop system can be made stable by proper design.) Simple inspection of the encirclements of the $-1 + j0$ point by the $G(j\omega)H(j\omega)$ locus is not sufficient to detect instability in multiple-loop systems. In such cases, however, whether or not any pole of $1 + G(s)H(s)$ is in the right-half s plane may be determined easily by applying the Routh stability criterion to the denominator of $G(s)H(s)$ or actually finding the poles of $G(s)H(s)$ by use of MATLAB.

3. If the locus of $G(j\omega)H(j\omega)$ passes through the $-1 + j0$ point, then the zeros of the characteristic equation, or closed-loop poles, are located on the $j\omega$ axis. This is not desirable for practical control systems. For a well-designed closed-loop system, none of the roots of the characteristic equation should lie on the $j\omega$ axis.

Phase and gain margins

Figure 6-17 shows Nyquist plots of $G(j\omega)$ for three different values of the open-loop gain K. For a large value of the gain K, the system is unstable. As the gain is decreased to a certain value, the $G(j\omega)$ locus passes through the $-1 + j0$ point. This means that with this gain value the system is on the verge of instability, and the system will exhibit sustained oscillations. For a small value of the gain K, the system is stable.

In general, the closer the $G(j\omega)$ locus comes to encircling the $-1 + j0$ point, the more oscillatory is the system response. The closeness of the $G(j\omega)$ locus to the $-1 + j0$ point can be used as a measure of the margin of stability. (This does not apply, however, to conditionally stable systems.) It is common practice to represent the closeness in terms of phase margin and gain margin.

Phase margin

The phase margin is that amount of additional phase lag at the gain crossover frequency required to bring the system to the verge of instability. The gain crossover frequency is the frequency at which $|G(j\omega)|$, the magnitude of the open-loop transfer

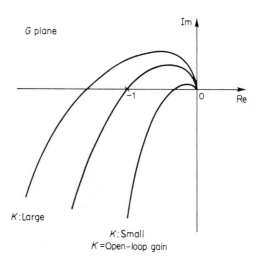

Figure 6-17

function, is unity. The phase margin γ is 180° plus the phase angle ϕ of the open-loop transfer function at the gain crossover frequency, or

$$\gamma = 180° + \phi$$

On the Nyquist plot, a line may be drawn from the origin to the point at which the unit circle crosses the $G(j\omega)$ locus. The angle from the negative real axis to this line is the phase margin. The phase margin is positive for $\gamma > 0$ and negative for $\gamma < 0$. For a minimum-phase system to be stable, the phase margin must be positive.

Figures 6-18(a) and (b) illustrate the phase margin of both a stable and unstable system in Nyquist plots and Bode diagrams. In the Bode diagrams, the critical point in the complex plane corresponds to the 0-dB line and −180° line.

Gain margin

The gain margin is the reciprocal of the magnitude $|G(j\omega)|$ at the frequency where the phase angle is −180°. Defining the phase crossover frequency ω_1 to be the frequency at which the phase angle of the open-loop transfer function equals −180° gives the gain margin K_g:

$$K_g = \frac{1}{|G(j\omega_1)|}$$

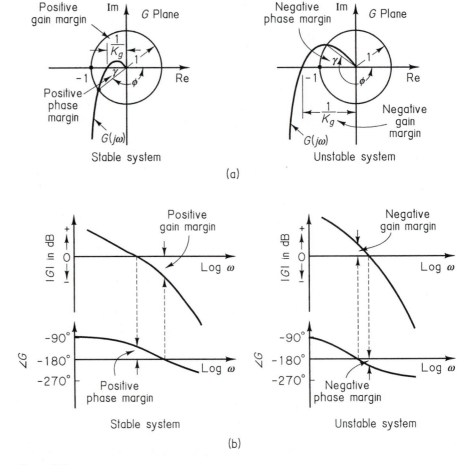

Figure 6-18

In terms of decibels,

$$K_g \text{ dB} = 20 \log K_g = -20 \log \left| G(j\omega_1) \right|$$

The gain margin expressed in decibels is positive if K_g is greater than unity and negative if K_g is smaller than unity. Thus a positive gain margin (in decibels) means that the system is stable, and a negative gain margin (in decibels) means that the system is unstable. The gain margin is shown in Figures 6-18(a) and (b).

For a stable minimum-phase system, the gain margin indicates how much the gain can be increased before the system becomes unstable. For an unstable system, the gain margin is indicative of how much the gain must be decreased to make the system stable.

The gain margins of the first- and second-order minimum-phase systems are infinite since the Nyquist plots for such systems do not cross the negative real axis. Thus such first- and second-order systems cannot be unstable.

It is important to point out that for a nonminimum-phase system the stability condition will not be satisfied unless the $G(j\omega)$ plot encircles the $-1 + j0$ point. Hence a stable nonminimum-phase system will have negative phase and gain margins.

A few comments on phase and gain margins

The phase and gain margins of a control system are a measure of the closeness of the Nyquist plot to the $-1 + j0$ point. Therefore, these margins may be used as design criteria.

It should be noted that either the gain margin alone or the phase margin alone does not give a sufficient indication of relative stability. Both should be given in the determination of relative stability.

For a minimum-phase system, both the phase and gain margins must be positive for the system to be stable. Negative margins indicate instability.

Proper phase and gain margins ensure against variations in the system components. For satisfactory performance, the phase margin should be between 30° and 60°, and the gain margin should be greater than 6 dB. With these values, a minimum-phase system has guaranteed stability, even if the open-loop gain and time constants of the components vary to a certain extent. Although the phase and gain margins give only rough estimates of the effective damping ratio of the closed-loop system, they do offer a convenient means for designing control systems or adjusting the gain constants of systems.

For minimum-phase systems, the magnitude and phase characteristics of the open-loop transfer function are definitely related. The requirement that the phase margin be between 30° and 60° means that in a Bode diagram the slope of the log-magnitude curve at the gain crossover frequency is more gradual than −40 dB/decade. In most practical cases, a slope of −20 dB/decade is desirable at the gain crossover frequency for stability. If it is −40 dB/decade, the system could be either stable or unstable. (Even if the system is stable, however, the phase margin is small.) If the slope at the gain crossover frequency is −60 dB/decade or steeper, the system will be unstable.

Conditionally stable systems

Figure 6-19 shows an example of a $G(j\omega)H(j\omega)$ locus for which the closed-loop system can be made stable or unstable by varying the open-loop gain. If the open-loop gain is increased sufficiently, the $G(j\omega)H(j\omega)$ locus encloses the $-1 + j0$ point twice, and the system becomes unstable. If the open-loop gain is decreased sufficiently, again the $G(j\omega)H(j\omega)$ locus encloses the $-1 + j0$ point twice. The system

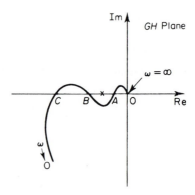

Figure 6-19

is stable only for the limited range of values of the open-loop gain for which the $-1 + j0$ point is completely outside the $G(j\omega)H(j\omega)$ locus. Such a system is conditionally stable.

Such a conditionally stable system becomes unstable when large input signals are applied since a large signal may cause saturation, which in turn reduces the open-loop gain of the system.

For stable operation of the conditionally stable system considered here, the critical point $-1 + j0$ must not be located in the regions between OA and BC shown in Figure 6-19.

6-3 PLOTTING BODE DIAGRAMS WITH MATLAB

The command bode computes magnitudes and phase angles of the frequency response of continuous-time, linear, time-invariant systems. As stated earlier, Bode diagrams are frequently used for analyzing and designing control systems. Bode diagrams indicate gain margin, phase margin, DC gain, bandwidth, and so on.

When the command bode (without left-hand arguments) is entered in the computer, MATLAB produces a Bode plot on the screen.

When invoked with left-hand arguments,

$$[\text{mag,phase,w}] = \text{bode(num,den,w)}$$

bode returns the frequency response of the system in matrices mag, phase, and w. No plot is drawn on the screen. The matrices mag and phase contain magnitudes and phase angles of the frequency response of the system evaluated at user-specified frequency points. The phase angle is returned in degrees. The magnitude can be converted to decibels with the statement

$$\text{magdB} = 20 * \log10(\text{mag})$$

To specify the frequency range, use the command logspace(d1,d2) or logspace(d1,d2,n). logspace(d1,d2) generates a vector of 50 points logarithmically equally spaced between decades 10^{d1} and 10^{d2}. That is, to generate 50 points between 0.1 rad/sec and 100 rad/sec, enter the command

$$\text{w} = \text{logspace}(-1,2)$$

logspace(d1,d2,n) generates n points logarithmically equally spaced between decades 10^{d1} and 10^{d2}. For example, to generate 100 points between 1 rad/sec and 1000 rad/sec, enter the following command:

$$\text{w} = \text{logspace}(0,3,100)$$

To incorporate these frequency points when plotting Bode diagrams, use the command bode(num,den,w) or bode(A,B,C,D,iu,w). These commands use the user-specified frequency vector w.

EXAMPLE 6-1

Consider the following transfer function:

$$\frac{Y(s)}{U(s)} = \frac{25}{s^2 + 4s + 25}$$

Plot a Bode diagram for this transfer function.

When the system is defined in the form

$$G(s) = \frac{num(s)}{den(s)}$$

use the command bode(num,den) to draw the Bode diagram. [When the numerator and denominator contain the polynomial coefficients in descending powers of s, bode(num,den) draws the Bode diagram.] MATLAB Program 6-1 shows a program to plot the Bode diagram for this system. The resulting Bode diagram is shown in Figure 6-20.

MATLAB Program 6–1

```
num = [0   0   25];
den = [1   4   25];
bode(num,den)
title('Bode Diagram of G(s) = 25/(s^2+4s+25)')
```

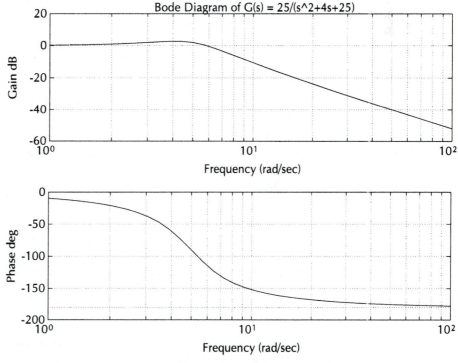

Figure 6-20

EXAMPLE 6-2

Consider the system shown in Figure 6-21. The open-loop transfer function is

$$G(s) = \frac{9(s^2 + 0.2s + 1)}{s(s^2 + 1.2s + 9)}$$

Plot a Bode diagram.

MATLAB Program 6-2 is a program to plot a Bode diagram for the system. The resulting plot is shown in Figure 6-22. The frequency range in this case is automatically determined to be from 0.1 rad/sec to 10 rad/sec.

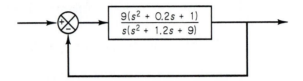

Figure 6-21

MATLAB Program 6–2

```
num = [0  9  1.8  9];
den = [1  1.2  9  0];
bode(num,den)
title('Bode Diagram of G(s) = 9(s^2+0.2s+1)/[s(s^2+1.2s+9)]')
```

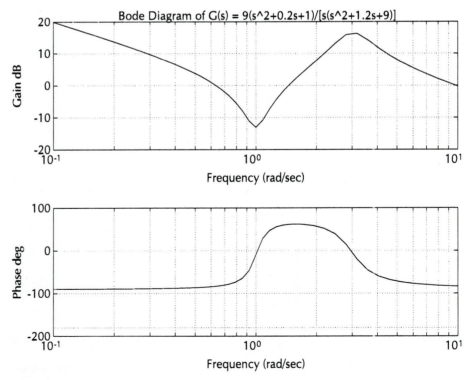

Figure 6-22

If it is desired to plot the Bode diagram from 0.01 rad/sec to 1000 rad/sec, enter the following command:

$$w = \text{logspace}(-2,3,100)$$

This command generates 100 points logarithmically equally spaced between 0.01 rad/sec and 1000 rad/sec. (Note that such a vector w specifies the frequencies in radians per second at which the frequency response will be calculated.)

If we use the command

$$\text{bode(num,den,w)}$$

then the frequency range is as user specified, but the magnitude range and phase-angle range will be automatically determined. See MATLAB Program 6-3 and the resulting plot in Figure 6-23.

To specify the magnitude range and phase-angle range, use the following command:

$$[\text{mag,phase,w}] = \text{bode(num,den,w)}$$

MATLAB Program 6–3

```
num = [0   9   1.8   9];
den = [1   1.2   9   0];
w = logspace(-2,3,100);
bode(num,den,w)
title('Bode Diagram of G(s) = 9(s^2+0.2s+1)/[s(s^2+1.2s+9)]')
```

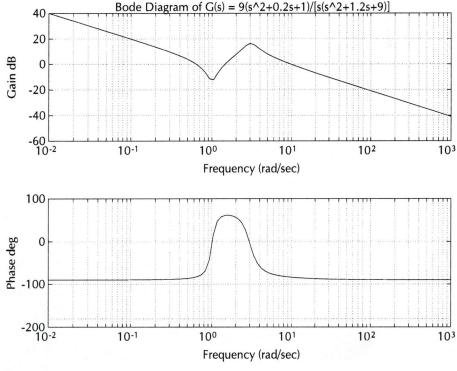

Figure 6-23

The matrices mag and phase contain the magnitudes and phase angles of the frequency response evaluated at the user-specified frequency points. The phase angle is returned in degrees. The magnitude can be converted to decibels with the statement

$$\text{magdB} = 20 * \log 10(\text{mag})$$

If we wish to specify the magnitude range to be, for example, at least between -45 dB and $+45$ dB, then enter invisible lines at -45 dB and $+45$ dB in the plot by specifying dBmax (maximum magnitude) and dBmin (minimum magnitude) as follows:

$$\text{dBmax} = 45 * \text{ones}(1,100);$$
$$\text{dBmin} = -45 * \text{ones}(1,100);$$

Then enter the following semilog plot command:

$$\text{semilogx}(w,\text{magdB},'o',w,\text{magdB},'-',w,\text{dBmax},'--i',w,\text{dBmin},':i')$$

(Note that the number of dBmax points and that of dBmin points must be equal to the number of frequency points in w. In this example, all numbers are 100.) Then the screen will show the magnitude curve magdB with 'o' marks. (Straight lines at $+45$ dB and -45 dB are invisible.)

Note that 'i' is an invisible color. For example, 'og' will show small circles in green color and 'oi' will show small circles in 'invisible' color: that is, you will not see small circles in the screen. By changing a portion of the semilogx command above from

$$w,\text{dBmax},'--i',w,\text{dBmin},':i'$$

to

$$w,\text{dBmax},'--',w,\text{dBmin},':'$$

the $+45$-dB line and -45-dB line will become visible on the screen.

The range for the magnitude is normally a multiple of 5 dB, 10 dB, 20 dB, or 50 dB. (There are exceptions.) For the present case, the range for the magnitude will be from -50 dB to $+50$ dB.

For the phase angle, if we wish to specify the range to be, for example, at least between $-145°$ and $+115°$, we enter invisible lines at $-145°$ and $+115°$ in the program by specifying pmax (maximum phase) and pmin (minimum phase) as follows:

$$\text{pmax} = 115 * \text{ones}(1,100)$$
$$\text{pmin} = -145 * \text{ones}(1,100)$$

Then enter the semilog plot command:

$$\text{semilogx}(w,\text{phase},'o',w,\text{phase},'-',w,\text{pmax},'--i',w,\text{pmin},':i')$$

(The number of pmax points and that of pmin points must be equal to the number of frequency points in w.) The screen will show the phase curve. Straight lines at $+115°$ and $-145°$ are invisible.

The range for the phase angle is normally a multiple of 5°, 10°, 50°, or 100°. (There are exceptions.) For the present case, the range for the phase angle will be from $-150°$ to $+150°$.

MATLAB Program 6-4 produces the Bode diagram for the system such that the frequency range is from 0.01 rad/sec to 1000 rad/sec, the magnitude range is from -50 dB to $+50$ dB (the magnitude range is a multiple of 50 dB), and the phase-angle range is from $-150°$ to $+150°$ (the phase-angle range is a multiple of 50°). Figure 6-24 shows the Bode diagram obtained by use of MATLAB Program 6-4.

MATLAB Program 6–4

```
% ---------- Bode diagram ----------

% ***** In this program we shall obtain Bode diagram of
% transfer-function system using user-specified frequency
% range *****

% ***** Enter the numerator and denominator of the transfer
% function *****

num = [0   9   1.8   9];
den = [1   1.2   9   0];

% ***** Specify the frequency range and enter the command
% [mag,phase,w] = bode(num,den,w) *****

w = logspace(-2,3,100);
[mag,phase,w] = bode(num,den,w);

% ***** Convert mag to decibels *****

magdB = 20*log10(mag);

% ***** Specify the range for magnitude.  For the system
% considered, the magnitude range should include -45 dB
% and +45 dB.  Enter dBmax and dBmin in the program and
% draw dBmax line and dBmin line in invisible color.  To
% plot the magdB curve and invisible lines, enter the
% following dBmax, dBmin, and semilogx command *****

dBmax = 45*ones(1,100);
dBmin = -45*ones(1,100);
semilogx(w,magdB,'o',w,magdB,'-',w,dBmax,'--i',w,dBmin,':i')

% ***** Enter grid, title, xlabel, and ylabel *****

grid
title('Bode Diagram of G(s) = 9(s^2+0.2s+1)/[s(s^2+1.2s+9)]')
xlabel('Frequency (rad/sec)')
ylabel('Gain dB')

% ***** Next, we shall plot the phase-angle curve *****

% ***** Specify the range for phase angle.  For the system
% considered, the phase-angle range should include -145 degrees
% and +115 degrees.  Enter pmax and pmin in the program and
% draw pmax line and pmin line in invisible color.  To plot
% the phase curve and ivnisible lines, enter the following
% pmax, pmin, and semilogx command *****

pmax = 115*ones(1,100);
```

```
pmin = -145*ones(1,100);
semilogx(w,phase,'o',w,phase,'-',w,pmax,'--i',w,pmin,':i')

% ***** Enter grid, xlabel, and ylabel *****

grid
xlabel('Frequency (rad/sec)')
ylabel('Phase deg')
```

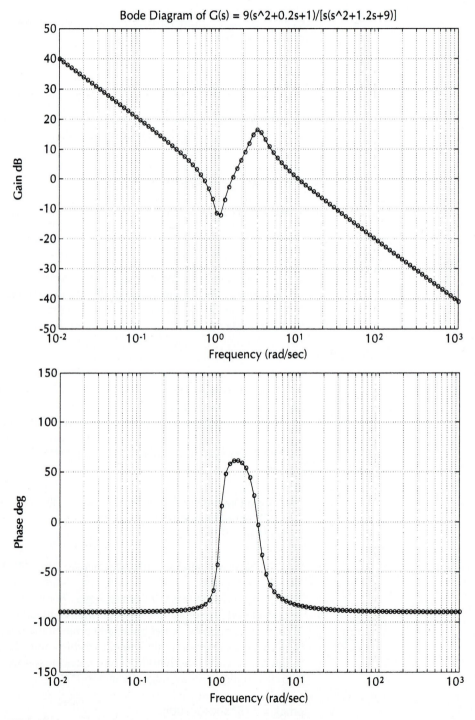

Figure 6-24

What happens to the Bode diagram if the gain becomes infinite at a certain frequency point

If there is a system pole on the $j\omega$ axis and the w vector happens to contain this frequency point, the gain becomes infinite at this frequency. In such a case, MATLAB produces warning messages. Consider the following example.

EXAMPLE 6-3

Consider a system with the following open-loop transfer function:

$$G(s) = \frac{1}{s^2 + 1}$$

This open-loop transfer function has poles on the $j\omega$ axis at $\pm j$.

MATLAB Program 6-5 may be used to plot the Bode diagram for this system. The resulting plot is shown in Figure 6-25. Theoretically, the magnitude becomes infinite at a frequency point where $\omega = 1$ rad/sec. However, this frequency point is not among the computing frequency points. In the plot the peak magnitude is shown to be approximately 50 dB. This value is computed near, but not exactly at, $\omega = 1$ rad/sec.

If, however, one of the computing frequency points coincides with the pole at $\omega = 1$, then the magnitude becomes infinite at this point. MATLAB sends out warning messages. See MATLAB Program 6-6, where computing points include the point at $\omega = 1$ rad/sec. (There are 101 computing points in this case. The computing points range from $\omega = 0.1$ to

---

MATLAB Program 6–5

num = [0   0   1];
den = [1   0   1];
bode(num,den)
title('Bode Diagram of G(s) = 1/(s^2+1)')

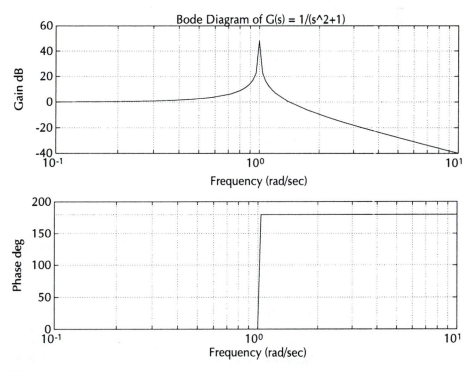

Figure 6-25

$\omega = 10$. The fifty-first point is at $\omega = 1$.) When MATLAB Program 6-6 is entered into the computer, warning messages appear, as shown. The resulting Bode diagram, shown in Figure 6-26, does not include the computed magnitude at $\omega = 1$. (Theoretically, this magnitude is infinite.) The magnitude curve shows the peak value at about 20 dB. The phase curve shows a gradual change in the phase angle from 0° to +180° near point $\omega = 1$. (Theoretically, the change in the phase angle from 0° to +180° should be abrupt at $\omega = 1$.) Obviously, the Bode diagram shown in Figure 6-26 is incorrect.

If the w vector contains such a frequency point, where the gain becomes infinite, change the number of frequency points, for example, from 101 to 100. Normally, a small change in the number of frequency points will avoid this kind of problem.

MATLAB Program 6–6

```
num = [0   0   1];
den = [1   0   1];
w = logspace(-1,1,101);
bode(num,den,w)

Warning:  Divide by zero
Underflow handler reached

Warning:  Infinity or NaN found in data and not shown on plot.

title('Incorrect Bode Diagram')
```

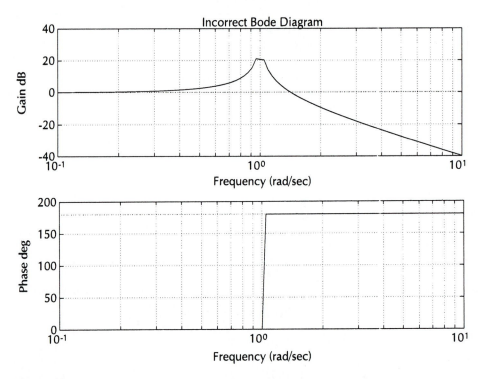

Figure 6-26

Examples of Bode diagrams

In the following, we shall give some typical Bode diagrams, including those of a nonminimum-phase system and a positive feedback system. These diagrams are presented in Examples 6-4 through 6-10.

EXAMPLE 6-4

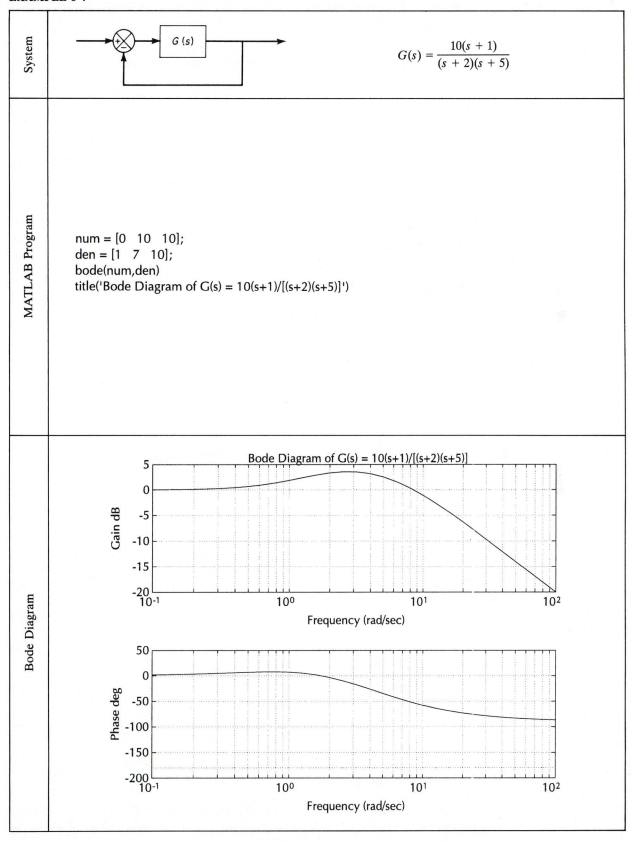

System

$$G(s) = \frac{10(s + 1)}{(s + 2)(s + 5)}$$

MATLAB Program

```
num = [0   10   10];
den = [1   7   10];
bode(num,den)
title('Bode Diagram of G(s) = 10(s+1)/[(s+2)(s+5)]')
```

Bode Diagram

EXAMPLE 6-5

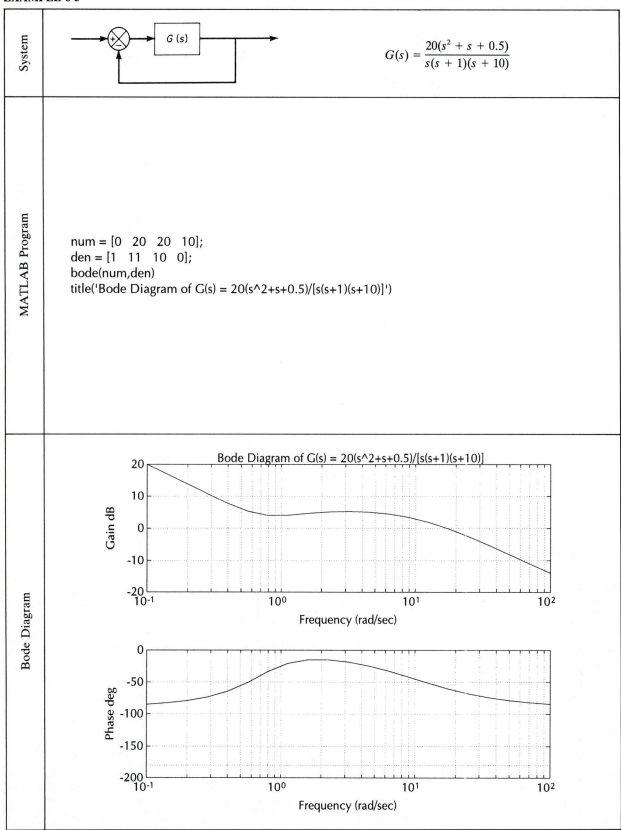

System	$G(s) = \dfrac{20(s^2 + s + 0.5)}{s(s + 1)(s + 10)}$

MATLAB Program

```
num = [0   20   20   10];
den = [1   11   10   0];
bode(num,den)
title('Bode Diagram of G(s) = 20(s^2+s+0.5)/[s(s+1)(s+10)]')
```

Bode Diagram

EXAMPLE 6-6

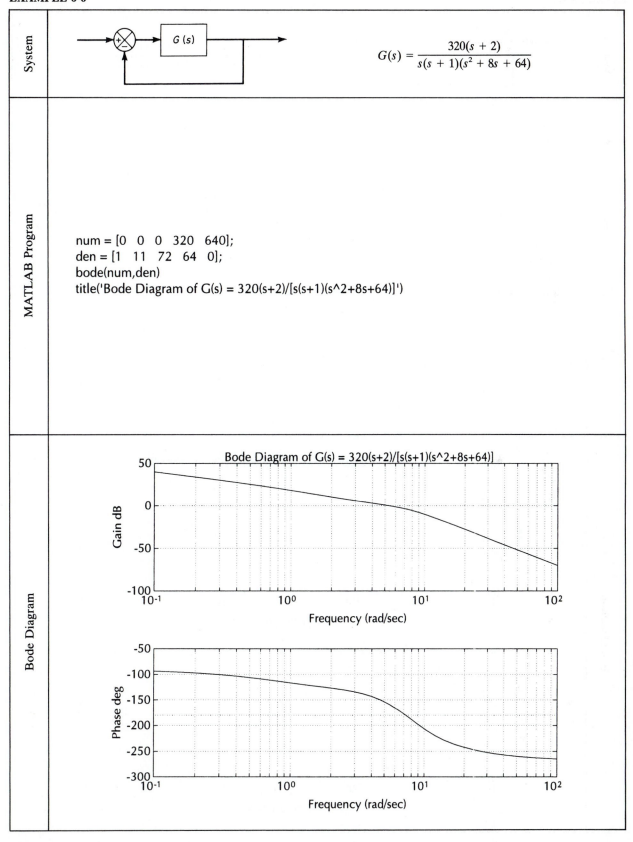

System

$$G(s) = \frac{320(s + 2)}{s(s + 1)(s^2 + 8s + 64)}$$

MATLAB Program

```
num = [0  0  0  320  640];
den = [1  11  72  64  0];
bode(num,den)
title('Bode Diagram of G(s) = 320(s+2)/[s(s+1)(s^2+8s+64)]')
```

Bode Diagram

EXAMPLE 6-7

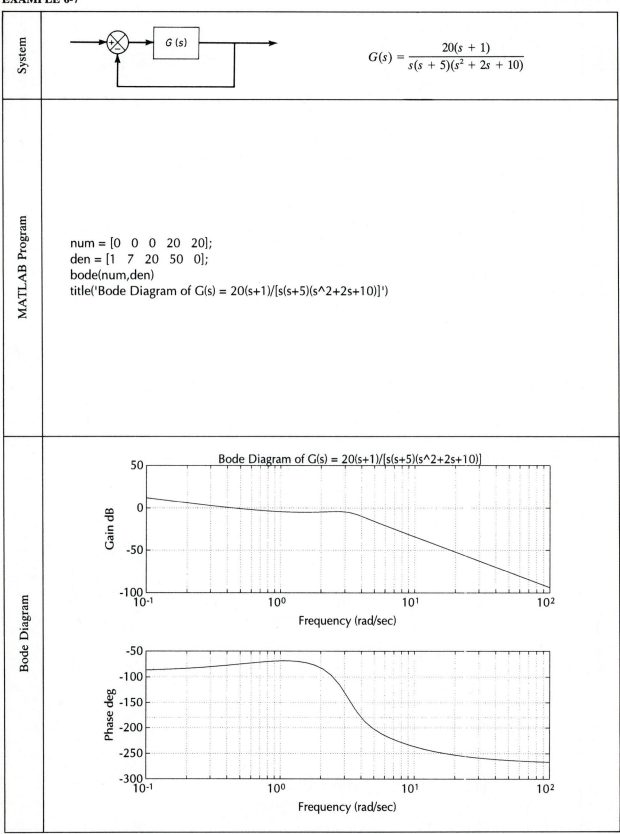

System	$G(s) = \dfrac{20(s + 1)}{s(s + 5)(s^2 + 2s + 10)}$

MATLAB Program

```
num = [0  0  0  20  20];
den = [1  7  20  50  0];
bode(num,den)
title('Bode Diagram of G(s) = 20(s+1)/[s(s+5)(s^2+2s+10)]')
```

Bode Diagram

EXAMPLE 6-8

System	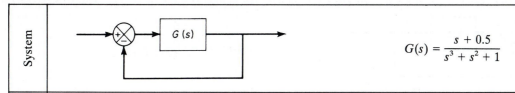 $$G(s) = \frac{s + 0.5}{s^3 + s^2 + 1}$$

MATLAB Program

This is a nonminimum-phase system. Two of the three open-loop poles are located in the right-half s plane, as follows:

$$\text{open-loop poles at } s = -1.4656$$
$$s = 0.2328 + j0.7926$$
$$s = 0.2328 - j0.7926$$

The phase angle starts from 0° and approaches +180°.

```
num = [0   0   1   0.5];
den = [1   1   0   1];
bode(num,den)
title('Bode Diagram of G(s) = (s+0.5)/(s^3+s^2+1)')
```

Bode Diagram

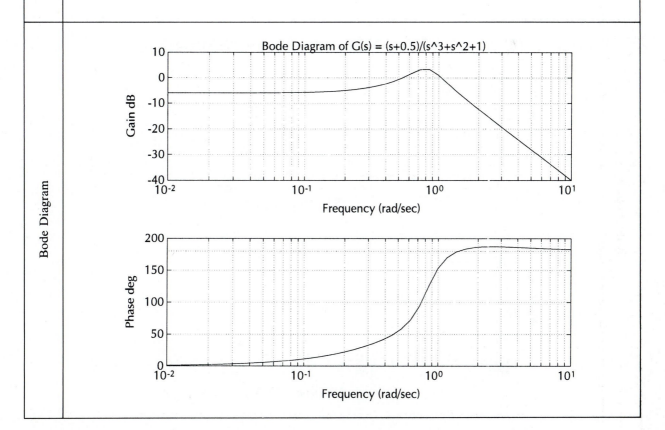

EXAMPLE 6-9

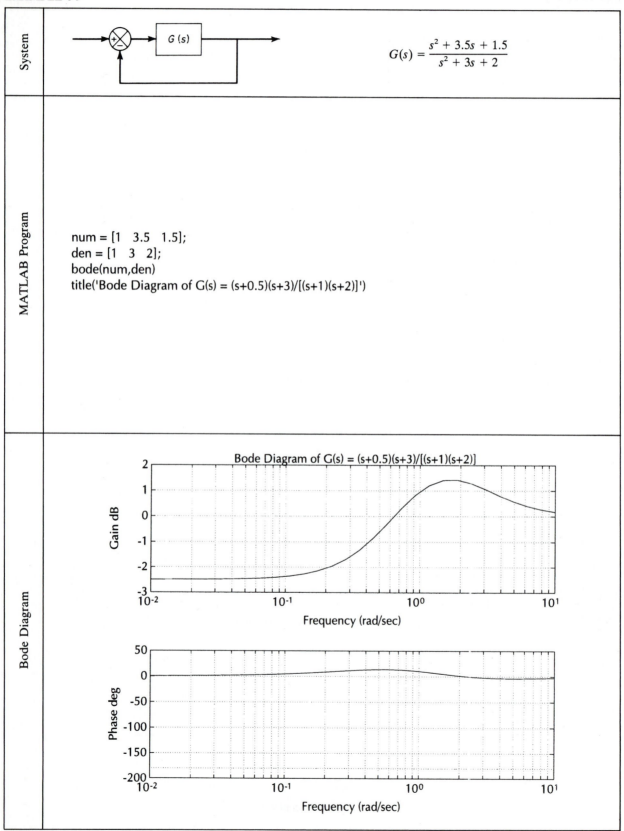

System	$G(s) = \dfrac{s^2 + 3.5s + 1.5}{s^2 + 3s + 2}$

MATLAB Program

```
num = [1   3.5   1.5];
den = [1   3   2];
bode(num,den)
title('Bode Diagram of G(s) = (s+0.5)(s+3)/[(s+1)(s+2)]')
```

EXAMPLE 6-10

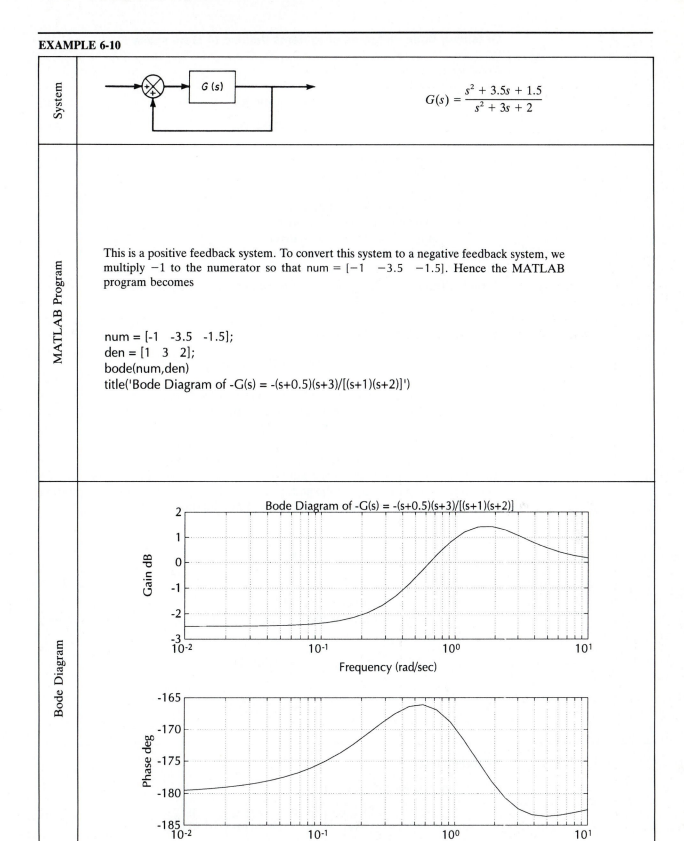

System

$$G(s) = \frac{s^2 + 3.5s + 1.5}{s^2 + 3s + 2}$$

MATLAB Program

This is a positive feedback system. To convert this system to a negative feedback system, we multiply -1 to the numerator so that num $= [-1 \quad -3.5 \quad -1.5]$. Hence the MATLAB program becomes

```
num = [-1  -3.5  -1.5];
den = [1  3  2];
bode(num,den)
title('Bode Diagram of -G(s) = -(s+0.5)(s+3)/[(s+1)(s+2)]')
```

Bode Diagram

Bode Diagram of -G(s) = -(s+0.5)(s+3)/[(s+1)(s+2)]

Obtaining Bode diagrams of systems defined in state space

Consider the system defined by

$$\dot{\mathbf{x}} = \mathbf{A}\mathbf{x} + \mathbf{B}\mathbf{u} \qquad (6\text{-}8)$$

$$\mathbf{y} = \mathbf{C}\mathbf{x} + \mathbf{D}\mathbf{u} \qquad (6\text{-}9)$$

where $\mathbf{x}$ = state vector (n-vector)
   $\mathbf{y}$ = output vector (m-vector)
   $\mathbf{u}$ = control vector (r-vector)
   $\mathbf{A}$ = state matrix ($n \times n$ matrix)
   $\mathbf{B}$ = control matrix ($n \times r$ matrix)
   $\mathbf{C}$ = output matrix ($m \times n$ matrix)
   $\mathbf{D}$ = direct transmission matrix ($m \times r$ matrix)

A Bode diagram for this system may be obtained by entering the command

bode(A,B,C,D)

or

bode(A,B,C,D,iu)

The command bode(A,B,C,D) produces a series of Bode plots, one for each input of the system, with the frequency range automatically determined. (More points are used when the response is changing rapidly.)

The command bode(A,B,C,D,iu), where iu is the ith input of the system, produces the Bode diagrams from the input iu to all the outputs ($y_1, y_2, \ldots, y_m$) of the system, with frequency range automatically determined. (The scalar iu is an index into the inputs of the system and specifies which input is to be used for plotting Bode diagrams.) If the control vector $\mathbf{u}$ has three inputs such that

$$\mathbf{u} = \begin{bmatrix} u_1 \\ u_2 \\ u_3 \end{bmatrix}$$

then iu must be set to either 1, 2, or 3.

If the system has only one input u, then either of the following commands may be used

bode(A,B,C,D)

or

bode(A,B,C,D,1)

EXAMPLE 6-11

Consider the following system:

$$\begin{bmatrix} \dot{x}_1 \\ \dot{x}_2 \end{bmatrix} = \begin{bmatrix} 0 & 1 \\ -25 & -4 \end{bmatrix} \begin{bmatrix} x_1 \\ x_2 \end{bmatrix} + \begin{bmatrix} 0 \\ 25 \end{bmatrix} u$$

$$y = \begin{bmatrix} 1 & 0 \end{bmatrix} \begin{bmatrix} x_1 \\ x_2 \end{bmatrix}$$

This system has one input u and one output y. By using the command

$$\text{bode(A,B,C,D)}$$

and entering the program as given by MATLAB Program 6-7 into the computer, we obtain the Bode diagram shown in Figure 6-27.

If we replace the command bode(A,B,C,D) in MATLAB Program 6-7 with

$$\text{bode(A,B,C,D,1)}$$

then MATLAB will produce the Bode diagram identical to that shown in Figure 6-27. Note that if we use, by mistake, the command

$$\text{bode(A,B,C,D,2)}$$

MATLAB Program 6–7

```
A = [0   1;-25   -4];
B = [0;25];
C = [1   0];
D = [0];
bode(A,B,C,D)
title('Bode Diagram')
```

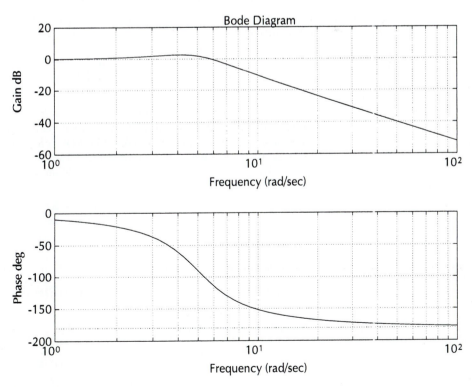

Figure 6-27

MATLAB produces an error message, because the present system has only one input and iu should be set to '1', not '2' or any other number. See the following MATLAB output:

```
A = [0  1;−25  −4];
B = [0;25];
C = [1  0];
D = [0];
bode(A,B,C,D,2)
[[[  Index exceeds matrix dimensions.

Error in MM \MATLAB\SIGSYS\freqresp.m
On line 38   MM   b = p' * b(:,iu);

Error in MM \MATLAB\SIGSYS\bode.m
On line 73   MM   g = freqresp(a,b,c,d,iu,sqrt(−1) * w);
```

To avoid such an error, for single-input, single-output systems we should use the command bode(A,B,C,D).

EXAMPLE 6-12

Consider the system defined by

$$\begin{bmatrix} \dot{x}_1 \\ \dot{x}_2 \end{bmatrix} = \begin{bmatrix} 0 & 1 \\ -25 & -4 \end{bmatrix}\begin{bmatrix} x_1 \\ x_2 \end{bmatrix} + \begin{bmatrix} 1 & 1 \\ 0 & 1 \end{bmatrix}\begin{bmatrix} u_1 \\ u_2 \end{bmatrix}$$

$$\begin{bmatrix} y_1 \\ y_2 \end{bmatrix} = \begin{bmatrix} 1 & 0 \\ 0 & 1 \end{bmatrix}\begin{bmatrix} x_1 \\ x_2 \end{bmatrix}$$

Obtain the sinusoidal transfer functions $Y_1(j\omega)/U_1(j\omega)$, $Y_2(j\omega)/U_1(j\omega)$, $Y_1(j\omega)/U_2(j\omega)$, and $Y_2(j\omega)/U_2(j\omega)$. In deriving $Y_1(j\omega)/U_1(j\omega)$ and $Y_2(j\omega)/U_1(j\omega)$, we assume that $U_2(j\omega) = 0$. Similarly, in obtaining $Y_1(j\omega)/U_2(j\omega)$ and $Y_2(j\omega)/U_2(j\omega)$, we assume that $U_1(j\omega) = 0$. Obtain also the Bode diagrams of these four transfer functions with MATLAB.

The transfer matrix expression for the system defined by

$$\dot{\mathbf{x}} = \mathbf{Ax} + \mathbf{Bu} \tag{6-10}$$
$$\mathbf{y} = \mathbf{Cx} + \mathbf{Du} \tag{6-11}$$

is given by

$$Y(s) = G(s)U(s) \tag{6-12}$$

where $G(s)$ is the transfer matrix and is given by

$$\mathbf{G}(s) = \mathbf{C}(s\mathbf{I} - \mathbf{A})^{-1}\mathbf{B} + \mathbf{D}$$

For the system considered here, the transfer matrix becomes

$$\mathbf{C}(s\mathbf{I} - \mathbf{A})^{-1}\mathbf{B} + \mathbf{D} = \begin{bmatrix} 1 & 0 \\ 0 & 1 \end{bmatrix} \begin{bmatrix} s & -1 \\ 25 & s+4 \end{bmatrix}^{-1} \begin{bmatrix} 1 & 1 \\ 0 & 1 \end{bmatrix}$$

$$= \frac{1}{s^2 + 4s + 25} \begin{bmatrix} s+4 & 1 \\ -25 & s \end{bmatrix} \begin{bmatrix} 1 & 1 \\ 0 & 1 \end{bmatrix}$$

$$= \begin{bmatrix} \dfrac{s+4}{s^2+4s+25} & \dfrac{s+5}{s^2+4s+25} \\ \dfrac{-25}{s^2+4s+25} & \dfrac{s-25}{s^2+4s+25} \end{bmatrix} \tag{6-13}$$

Thus, by substituting Eq. (6-13) into Eq. (6-12), we obtain

$$\begin{bmatrix} Y_1(s) \\ Y_2(s) \end{bmatrix} \begin{bmatrix} \dfrac{s+4}{s^2+4s+25} & \dfrac{s+5}{s^2+4s+25} \\ \dfrac{-25}{s^2+4s+25} & \dfrac{s-25}{s^2+4s+25} \end{bmatrix} \begin{bmatrix} U_1(s) \\ U_2(s) \end{bmatrix} \tag{6-14}$$

Hence, from Eq. (6-14), we have

$$Y_1(s) = \frac{s+4}{s^2+4s+25} U_1(s) + \frac{s+5}{s^2+4s+25} U_2(s)$$

$$Y_2(s) = \frac{-25}{s^2+4s+25} U_1(s) + \frac{s-25}{s^2+4s+25} U_2(s)$$

Assuming $U_2(j\omega) = 0$, we find $Y_1(j\omega)/U_1(j\omega)$ and $Y_2(j\omega)/U_1(j\omega)$ as follows:

$$\frac{Y_1(j\omega)}{U_1(j\omega)} = \frac{j\omega+4}{(j\omega)^2+4j\omega+25}$$

$$\frac{Y_2(j\omega)}{U_1(j\omega)} = \frac{-25}{(j\omega)^2+4j\omega+25}$$

Similarly, assuming $U_1(j\omega) = 0$, we find $Y_1(j\omega)/U_2(j\omega)$ and $Y_2(j\omega)/U_2(j\omega)$ as follows:

$$\frac{Y_1(j\omega)}{U_2(j\omega)} = \frac{j\omega+5}{(j\omega)^2+4j\omega+25}$$

$$\frac{Y_2(j\omega)}{U_2(j\omega)} = \frac{j\omega-25}{(j\omega)^2+4j\omega+25}$$

Notice that $Y_2(j\omega)/U_2(j\omega)$ is a nonminimum-phase transfer function.

To plot Bode diagrams for $Y_1(j\omega)/U_1(j\omega)$, $Y_2(j\omega)/U_1(j\omega)$, $Y_1(j\omega)/U_2(j\omega)$, and $Y_2(j\omega)/U_2(j\omega)$ with MATLAB, we may use the command

bode(A,B,C,D)

Then MATLAB produces Bode diagrams when u_1 is the input and when u_2 is the input. See MATLAB Program 6-8 and the resulting Bode diagrams shown in Figure 6-28.

An alternative way to plot the four individual Bode diagrams is to use the command

bode(A,B,C,D,1)

```
A = [0  1;-25  -4];
B = [1  1;0  1];
C = [1  0;0  1];
D = [0  0;0  0];
bode(A,B,C,D)
Strike any key after each screen
```

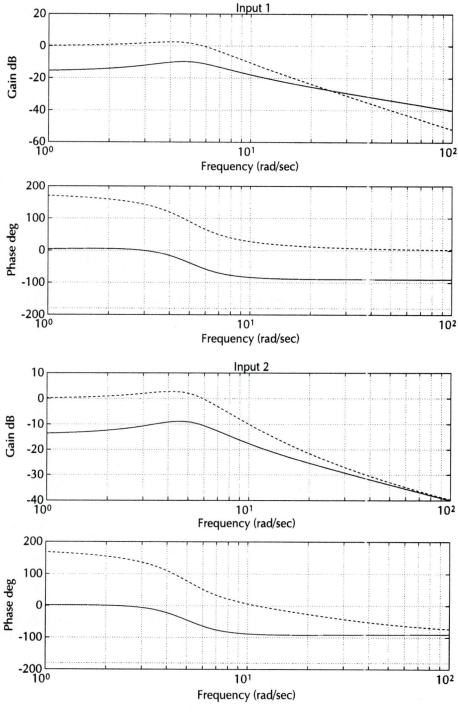

Figure 6-28

to obtain Bode diagrams for $Y_1(j\omega)/U_1(j\omega)$ and $Y_2(j\omega)/U_1(j\omega)$. To obtain Bode diagrams for $Y_1(j\omega)/U_2(j\omega)$ and $Y_2(j\omega)/U_2(j\omega)$, we use the following command:

$$bode(A,B,C,D,2)$$

See MATLAB Program 6-9. The Bode diagrams produced by this program are shown in Figures 6-29 and 6-30. In these diagrams it may not be easy to identify which curves are for $Y_1(j\omega)$ or $Y_2(j\omega)$. Ordinarily, *text* command may be used to identify curves. However, the *text* command does not apply to the present *bode* commands.

To use the *text* command, we need to use the following command:

$$[mag,phase,w] = bode(A,B,C,D,iu,w)$$

The matrices mag and phase contain the magnitudes of $Y_1(j\omega)$ and $Y_2(j\omega)$ and phase angles for $Y_1(j\omega)$ and $Y_2(j\omega)$ evaluated at each frequency point considered.

To plot the magnitude of $Y_1(j\omega)$, we first specify the range of frequency by entering, for example,

$$w = logspace(-1,2,100)$$

into the computer. (This means that the frequency range is from $w = 10^{-1} = 0.1$ to $w = 10^2 = 100$ and computes 100 points logarithmically evenly spaced.) Then use the following command:

$$Y1 = mag*[1;0]$$

MATLAB Program 6–9

```
% ---------- Bode diagram ----------

% ***** In this program we shall obtain Bode diagrams
% of system having two inputs, u1 and u2 *****

% ***** Enter state matrix A, control matrix B, output
% matrix C, and direct transmission matrix D *****

A = [0   1;-25  -4];
B = [1   1;0   1];
C = [1   0;0   1];
D = [0   0;0   0];

% ***** We shall first obtain the frequency response when
% u2 = 0; that is, we obtain Y1(jw)/U1(jw) and Y2(jw)/U1(jw) *****

% ***** Enter command bode(A,B,C,D,1) *****

bode(A,B,C,D,1)
title('Bode Diagrams : bode(A,B,C,D,1)')

% ***** Next, we shall obtain the frequency response when
% u1 = 0; that is, we obtain Y1(jw)/U2(jw) and Y2(jw)/U2(jw) *****

% ***** Enter command bode(A,B,C,D,2) *****

bode(A,B,C,D,2)
title('Bode Diagrams : bode(A,B,C,D,2)')
```

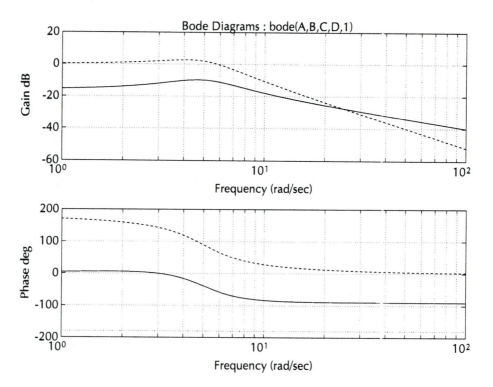

Figure 6-29

To convert the magnitude to decibels, use the statement

$$magdB = 20 * log10(mag)$$

Hence, to convert Y1 to decibels, enter the statement

$$Y1dB = 20 * log10(Y1)$$

Finally, enter the command

$$semilogx(w, Y1dB, 'o', w, Y1dB, '-')$$

or

$$semilogx(w, Y1dB, 'o')$$

Similarly, to plot the magnitude of Y2 in decibels, use the following command:

```
Y2 = mag * [0;1];
Y2db = 20 * log10(Y2);
semilogx(w,Y2db,'x',w,Y2db,'-')
```

The *text* command can be used to write text in the figure.
    Similarly, to plot the phase angles for $Y_1(j\omega)$ and $Y_2(j\omega)$, we use the commands

```
Y1p = phase * [1;0];
semilogx(w,Y1p,'o',w,Y1p,'-')
```

and

```
Y2p = phase * [0;1];
semilogx(w,Y2p,'x',w,Y2p,'-')
```

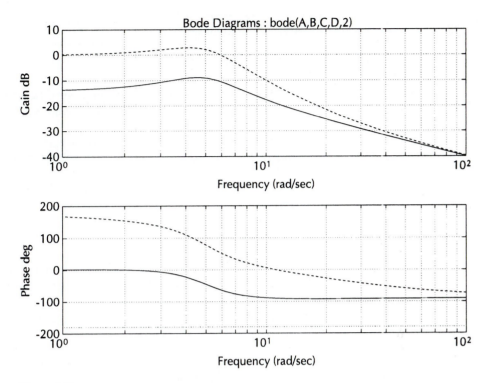

Figure 6-30

If we wish to plot two phase curves on one diagram, we need to specify a satisfactory phase-angle range. One way to do this is to plot invisible lines at, say, 220° and −100° by entering statements and command as follows:

```
pmax = 220 * ones(1,100);
pmin = −100 * ones(1,100);
semilogx(w,Y1p,'o',w,Y1p,'-',w,pmax,'--i',w,pmin,':i')
```

(Note that the number of pmax points and that of pmin points must be the same as the number of frequency points, which is 100 in this case.) The pmax line and pmin line are invisible because we used marks '--i' and ':i'.

As stated earlier, the above technique can also be used for plotting the magnitude curves. If we need a magnitude range to be at least from −100 dB to +40 dB, then we may enter invisible lines at −100 dB and +40 dB in the plot by specifying

```
dBmax = 40 * ones(1,100)
dBmin = −100 * ones(1,100)
```

and enter the command

```
semilogx(w,Y1dB,'o',w,Y1dB,'-',w,dBmax,'--i',w,dBmin,':i')
```

MATLAB Program 6-10 is a program to plot Bode diagrams for $Y_1(j\omega)/U_1(j\omega)$, $Y_2(j\omega)/U_1(j\omega), Y_1(j\omega)/U_2(j\omega)$, and $Y_2(j\omega)/U_2(j\omega)$ with user-specified frequency range and phase-angle range. The resulting Bode diagrams are shown in Figures 6-31 and 6-32.

Note that the effect of adding the invisible line at −100°, for example, may show up on the hard copy on the abscissa at −100°. If this effect is not desired, change the −100° line to a −95° line, for instance. The line at −95° will not show up on the hard copy. The effect of the invisible line appears only if such an invisible line coincides with the top or bottom abscissa.

MATLAB Program 6–10

```
% ---------- Bode diagram ----------

% ***** In this program we shall obtain Bode diagrams of system
% having two inputs (u1 and u2) and two outputs (y1 and y2) *****

% ***** Enter state matrix A, control matrix B, output
% matrix C, and direct transmission matrix D *****

A = [0   1;-25  -4];
B = [1   1;0   1];
C = [1   0;0   1];
D = [0   0;0   0];

% ***** We shall first obtain the frequency response when
% u2 = 0; that is, we obtain Y1(jw)/U1(jw) and Y2(jw)/U1(jw) *****

% ***** Specify the frequency range and enter the command
% [mag1,phase1,w] = bode(A,B,C,D,1,w) *****

w = logspace(-1,3,100);
[mag1,phase1,w] = bode(A,B,C,D,1,w);

% ***** To plot Bode diagrams, convert magnitudes Y1 and Y2
% into decibels *****

Y1 = mag1*[1;0]; Y1dB = 20*log10(Y1);
Y2 = mag1*[0;1]; Y2dB = 20*log10(Y2);

% ***** To plot Bode diagrams for Y1(jw)/U1(jw) and Y2(jw)/U1(jw)
% on one graph using hold command, plot the latter first because
% it has wider magnitude range than the former *****

semilogx(w,Y2dB,'x',w,Y2dB,'-')
grid
title('Bode Diagrams : Input = u1 (u2 = 0)')
xlabel('Frequency (rad/sec)')
ylabel('Gain dB')
text(1,2,'Y2')
hold

Current plot held

semilogx(w,Y1dB,'o',w,Y1dB,'-')
text(1,-14,'Y1')
hold

Current plot released

% ***** Next, we shall plot phase curves.  A possible
```

```
% range for phase angles for two curves is from -100
% degrees to +220 degrees.  Actual range should include
% angles -100 degrees and +220 degrees.  Enter pmax and
% pmin in the program and draw pmax line and pmin line in
% invisible color.  To plot the phase curves and invisible
% lines, enter the following pmax, pmin, Y1p, Y2p, and
% semilogx command *****

pmax = 220*ones(1,100);
pmin = -100*ones(1,100);
Y1p = phase1*[1;0];
Y2p = phase1*[0;1];
semilogx(w,Y1p,'o',w,Y1p,'-',w,pmax,'--i',w,pmin,':i')
grid
xlabel('Frequency (rad/sec)')
ylabel('Phase deg')
text(1,10,'Y1')
hold

Current plot held

semilogx(w,Y2p,'x',w,Y2p,'-')
text(1,172,'Y2')
hold

Current plot released

% ***** In the following, we shall obtain the frequency
% response when u1 = 0; that is we obtain Y1(jw)/U2(jw)
% and Y2(jw)/U2(jw) *****

[mag2,phase2,w] = bode(A,B,C,D,2,w);
YY1 = mag2*[1;0]; YY1dB = 20*log10(YY1);
YY2 = mag2*[0;1]; YY2dB = 20*log10(YY2);
semilogx(w,YY2dB,'x',w,YY2dB,'-')
grid
title('Bode Diagrams : Input = u2 (u1 = 0)')
xlabel('Frequency (rad/sec)')
ylabel('Gain dB')
text(1,2,'Y2')
hold

Current plot held

semilogx(w,YY1dB,'o',w,YY1dB,'-')
text(1,-12,'Y1')
hold

Current plot released

% ***** Next, we shall plot phase curves.  A possible
```

```
% range for phase angles for two curves is from -100
% degrees to +220 degrees.  Actual range should include
% angles -100 degrees and +220 degrees.  We use the same
% pmax and pmin as defined earlier.  Enter YY1p and YY2p
% as defined below.  Then enter the semilogx command *****

YY1p = phase2*[1;0];
YY2p = phase2*[0;1];
semilogx(w,YY1p,'o',w,YY1p,'-',w,pmax,'--i',w,pmin,':i')
grid
xlabel('Frequency (rad/sec)')
ylabel('Phase deg')
text(1,7,'Y1')
hold

Current plot held

semilogx(w,YY2p,'x',w,YY2p,'-')
text(1,170,'Y2')
hold

Current plot released
```

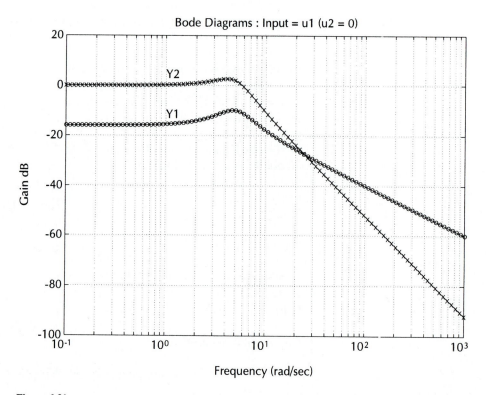

Figure 6-31

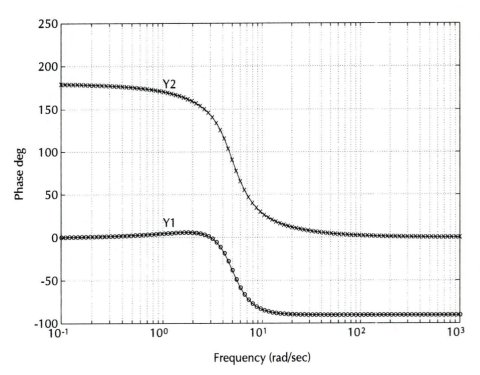

Figure 6-31 (*Continued*)

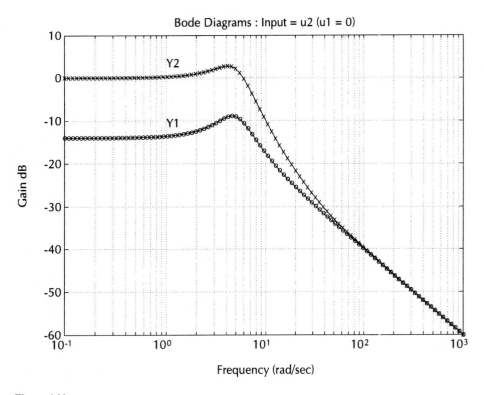

Figure 6-32

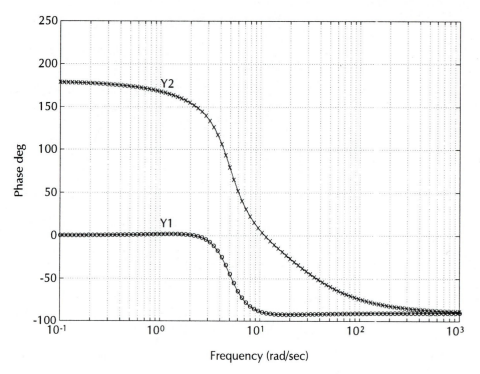

Figure 6-32 (*Continued*)

6-4 OBTAINING NYQUIST PLOTS WITH MATLAB

Nyquist plots, just like Bode diagrams, are commonly used in the frequency-response representation of linear, time-invariant, feedback control systems. Nyquist plots are polar plots, while Bode diagrams are rectangular plots. One plot or the other may be more convenient for a particular operation, but a given operation can always be carried out in either plot.

The command nyquist computes the frequency response for continuous-time, linear, time-invariant systems. When invoked without left-hand arguments, nyquist produces a Nyquist plot on the screen. nyquist can conveniently be used to determine the stability of a unity feedback system based on the Nyquist stability criterion. The closed-loop system will be stable if the Nyquist plot encircles the $-1 + j0$ point exactly P times in the counterclockwise direction, where P is the number of open-loop poles in the right-half s plane.

The command

$$\text{nyquist(num,den)}$$

draws the Nyquist plot of the transfer function

$$G(s) = \frac{\text{num}(s)}{\text{den}(s)}$$

where num and den contain the polynomial coefficients in descending powers of s.

The command

$$nyquist(num,den,w)$$

uses the user-specified frequency vector w. The vector w specifies the frequency points in radians per second at which the frequency response will be calculated. When invoked with the left-hand arguments

$$[re,im,w] = nyquist(num,den)$$

or

$$[re,im,w] = nyquist(num,den,w)$$

MATLAB returns the frequency response of the system in the matrices re, im, and w. No plot is drawn on the screen. The matrices re and im contain the real and imaginary parts of the frequency response of the system evaluated at the frequency points specified in the vector w. Note that re and im have as many columns as outputs and one row for each element in w.

EXAMPLE 6-13

Consider the following open-loop transfer function:

$$G(s) = \frac{1}{s^2 + 0.8s + 1}$$

Draw a Nyquist plot with MATLAB.
    Since the system is given in the form of the transfer function, the command

$$nyquist(num,den)$$

may be used to draw a Nyquist plot. MATLAB Program 6-11 produces the Nyquist plot shown in Figure 6-33. In this plot the ranges for the real axis and imaginary axis are automatically determined.
    If we wish to draw the Nyquist plot using manually determined ranges, for example,

MATLAB Program 6–11

num = [0   0   1];
den = [1   0.8   1];
nyquist(num,den)
grid
title('Nyquist Plot of G(s) = 1/(s^2+0.8s+1)')

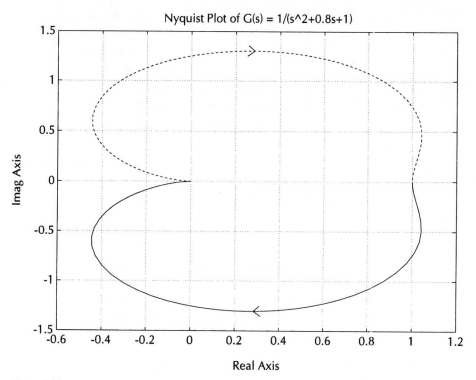

Figure 6-33

from −2 to 2 on the real axis and from −2 to 2 on the imaginary axis, enter the following command into the computer:

$$v = [-2 \quad 2 \quad -2 \quad 2];$$
$$axis(v);$$

or, combing these two lines into one,

$$axis([-2 \quad 2 \quad -2 \quad 2]);$$

See MATLAB Program 6-12 and the resulting Nyquist plot shown in Figure 6-34.

MATLAB Program 6–12

```
num = [0  0  1];
den = [1  0.8  1];
v = [-2  2  -2  2];
axis(v);
nyquist(num,den)
grid
title('Nyquist Plot of G(s) = 1/(s^2+0.8s+1)')
```

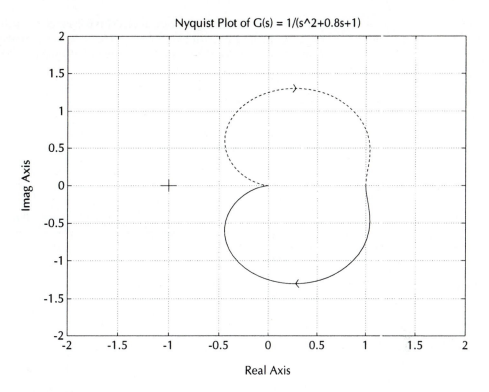

Figure 6-34

EXAMPLE 6-14

Draw a Nyquist plot for the following $G(s)$:

$$G(s) = \frac{1}{s(s + 1)}$$

If we enter MATLAB Program 6-13 into the computer, the following warning message appears:

'Divide by zero'

MATLAB Program 6–13

num = [0 0 1];
den = [1 1 0];
nyquist(num,den)
 	
Warning: Divide by zero
 	
title('Erroneous Nyquist Plot')

This corresponds to a singular case in MATLAB computations. If we use MATLAB Program 6-13, the resulting Nyquist plot, shown in Figure 6-35, is erroneous. This erroneous Nyquist plot can be corrected if we specify the axis(v). For example, if we enter the command

$$v = [-2 \quad 2 \quad -5 \quad 5];$$
$$\text{axis(v)}$$

in the computer, as given in MATLAB Program 6-14, a correct Nyquist plot can be obtained, as shown in Figure 6-36.

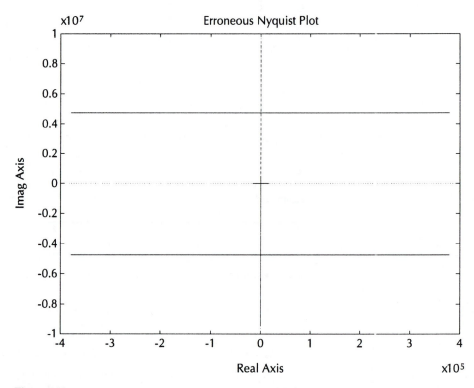

Figure 6-35

MATLAB Program 6–14

```
num = [0   0   1];
den = [1   1   0];
v = [-2   2   -5   5];
axis(v);
nyquist(num,den)

Warning: Divide by zero

grid
title('Nyquist Plot of G(s) = 1/[s(s+1)]')
```

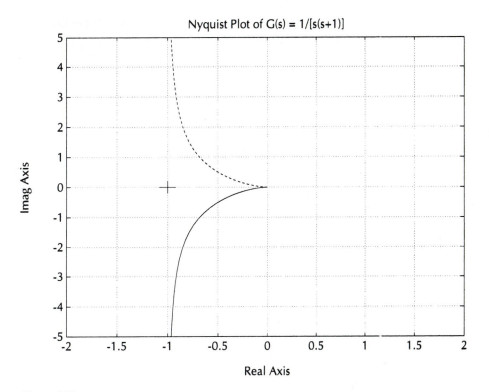

Figure 6-36

Notice that the Nyquist plot shown in Figure 6-36 includes the loci for both $\omega > 0$ and $\omega < 0$. If we wish to draw the Nyquist plot for only the positive frequency region ($\omega > 0$), then we need to use the command

$$[re,im,w] = nyquist(num,den,w)$$

A MATLAB program using this *nyquist* command is shown in MATLAB Program 6-15. The resulting Nyquist plot is presented in Figure 6-37.

MATLAB Program 6–15

```
num = [0   0   1];
den = [1   1   0];
w = 0.1:0.1:100;
[re,im,w] = nyquist(num,den,w);
v = [-2   2   -5   5];
axis(v);
plot(re,im)
grid
title('Nyquist Plot of G(s) = 1/[s(s+1)]')
xlabel('Real Axis')
ylabel('Imag Axis')
```

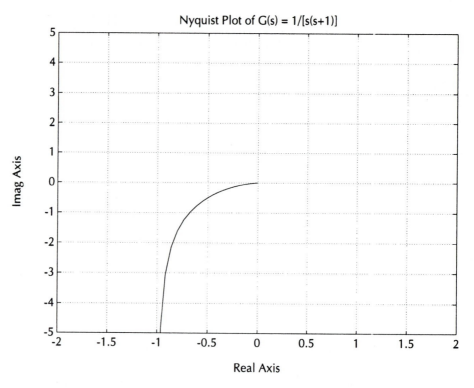

Figure 6-37

EXAMPLE 6-15

Consider a unity feedback system with the following open-loop transfer function:

$$G(s) = \frac{s^2 + 2s + 1}{s^3 + 0.2s^2 + s + 1}$$

Draw a Nyquist plot and examine the stability of the closed-loop system.

MATLAB Program 6-16 is a program to draw a Nyquist plot for the given $G(s)$. The resulting plot is shown in Figure 6-38.

Notice that the $-1 + j0$ point is encircled twice counterclockwise. To examine the locations of the three poles of $G(s)$, we may use the following MATLAB program:

```
den = [1   0.2   1   1];
roots(den)

ans =

    0.2623 + 1.1451i
    0.2623 − 1.1451i
   −0.7246
```

Clearly, there are two poles in the right-half s plane. Hence, in the Nyquist stability criterion, $P = 2$. Since the Nyquist plot of $G(s)$ encircles the $-1 + j0$ point twice counterclockwise, the closed-loop system is stable.

MATLAB Program 6–16

```
num = [0   1   2   1];
den = [1   0.2   1   1];
nyquist(num,den)
grid
title('Nyquist Plot of G(s) = (s^2+2s+1)/(s^3+0.2s^2+s+1)')
```

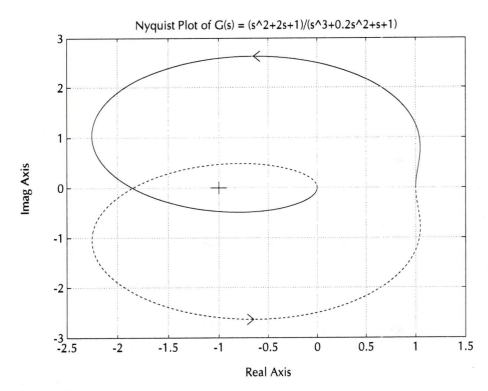

Figure 6-38

EXAMPLE 6-16

Consider a unity feedback system with the following open-loop transfer function:

$$G(s) = \frac{1}{s^3 + 0.2s^2 + s + 1}$$

Draw a Nyquist plot and examine the stability of the system.

A MATLAB program for drawing the Nyquist plot for this $G(s)$ is shown in MATLAB Program 6-17. The resulting Nyquist plot is shown in Figure 6-39.

To draw the Nyquist plot in a larger domain, that is, the real axis from -2 to 2 and the imaginary axis from -1 to 1, we may enter MATLAB Program 6-18 into the computer. The resulting plot is shown in Figure 6-40.

MATLAB Program 6–17

```
num = [0  0  0  1];
den = [1  0.2  1  1];
nyquist(num,den)
grid
title('Nyquist Plot of G(s) = 1/(s^3+0.2s^2+s+1)')
```

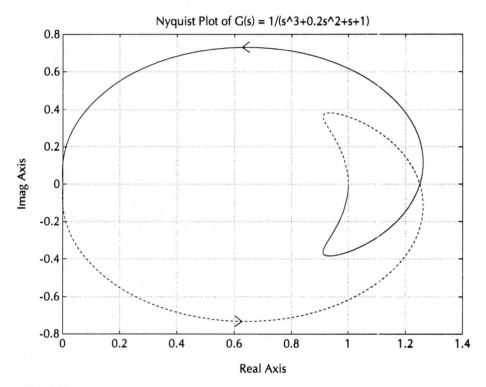

Figure 6-39

MATLAB Program 6–18

```
num = [0  0  0  1];
den = [1  0.2  1  1];
v = [-2  2  -1  1];
axis(v);
nyquist(num,den)
grid
title('Nyquist Plot of G(s) = 1/(s^3+0.2s^2+s+1)')
```

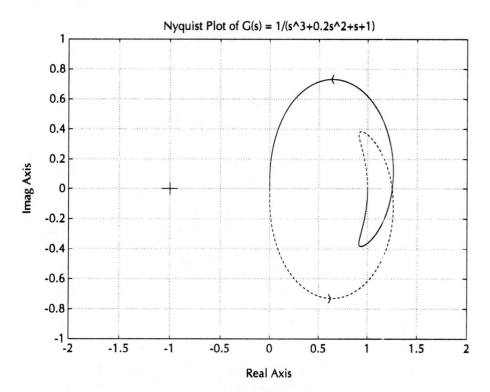

Figure 6-40

From Figure 6-39 (or 6-40), we see that the Nyquist plot does not encircle the $-1 + j0$ point. If $G(s)$ did not have right-half plane poles, then the closed-loop system would be stable. However, $G(s)$ involves two poles in the right-half s plane ($s = 0.2623 \pm j1.1451$). Thus, for stability, the Nyquist plot must encircle the $-1 + j0$ point twice counterclockwise. Since the Nyquist plot does not encircle the $-1 + j0$ point, the closed-loop system is unstable.

EXAMPLE 6-17

Consider a unity feedback system with the following open-loop transfer function:

$$G(s) = \frac{20(s^2 + s + 0.5)}{s(s + 1)(s + 10)}$$

Draw a Nyquist plot with MATLAB and examine the stability of the closed-loop system.

We first enter MATLAB Program 6-19 into the computer. The screen will show the warning message "Divide by zero" and will not produce the correct Nyquist plot. This is a singular case in MATLAB computations. Figure 6-41 shows the erroneous plot generated by MATLAB Program 6-19.

This erroneous Nyquist plot can be corrected by entering the *axis* command, as shown in MATLAB Program 6-20. The resulting Nyquist plot is shown in Figure 6-42. Since no open-loop poles lie in the right-half s plane, $P = 0$ in the Nyquist stability criterion. From Figure 6-42 we see that the Nyquist plot does not encircle the $-1 + j0$ point. Hence the closed-loop system is stable.

```
MATLAB Program 6–19
```

```
num = [0   20   20   10];
den = [1   11   10   0];
nyquist(num,den)

Warning: Divide by zero

title('Erroneous Nyquist Plot')
```

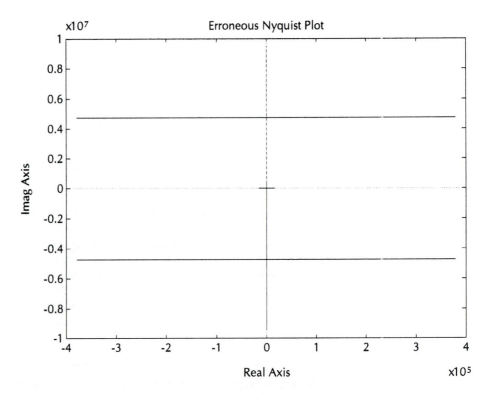

Figure 6-41

```
MATLAB Program 6–20
```

```
num = [0   20   20   10];
den = [1   11   10   0];
v = [-2   3   -3   3];
axis(v);
nyquist(num,den);

Warning: Divide by zero

grid
title('Nyquist Plot of G(s) = 20(s^2+s+0.5)/[s(s+1)(s+10)]')
```

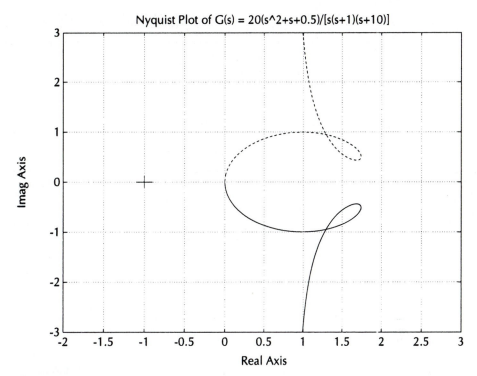

Figure 6-42

Next, let us draw the Nyquist plot for only the positive frequency region. This can be done by use of the command

$$[re,im,w] = nyquist(num,den,w)$$

The frequency region may be divided into several subregions using different increments. For example, the frequency region of interest may be divided into three subregions as follows:

$$w1 = 0.1:0.1:10;$$
$$w2 = 10:2:100;$$
$$w3 = 100:10:500;$$
$$w = [w1 \quad w2 \quad w3]$$

MATLAB Program 6-21 uses this frequency region. Using this program, we obtain the Nyquist plot shown in Figure 6-43.

```
MATLAB Program 6–21

num = [0  20  20  10];
den = [1  11  10  0];
w1 = 0.1:0.1:10; w2 = 10:2:100; w3 = 100:10:500;
w = [w1  w2  w3];
[re,im,w] = nyquist(num,den,w);
v = [-3  3  -5  1];
axis(v);
plot(re,im)
grid
title('Nyquist Plot of G(s) = 20(s^2+s+0.5)/[s(s+1)(s+10)]')
xlabel('Real Axis')
ylabel('Imag Axis')
```

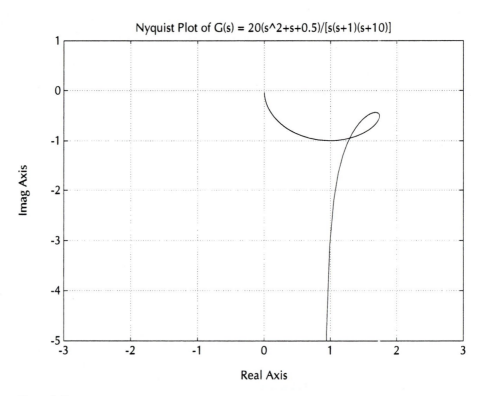

Figure 6-43

EXAMPLE 6-18

Consider a negative feedback system with the following open-loop transfer function:

$$G(s) = \frac{s^2 + 4s + 6}{s^2 + 5s + 4}$$

Draw a Nyquist plot.

MATLAB Program 6-22 will provide the Nyquist plot, which is shown in Figure 6-44. This system is stable, since there are no open-loop poles in the right-half s plane and there is no encirclement of the $-1 + j0$ point.

MATLAB Program 6–22

num = [1   4   6];
den = [1   5   4];
nyquist(num,den);
grid
title('Nyquist Plot of G(s) = (s^2+4s+6)/(s^2+5s+4)')

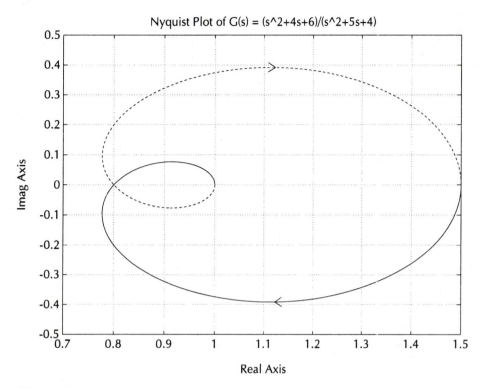

Figure 6-44

EXAMPLE 6-19

Consider a positive feedback system with the following open-loop transfer function:

$$G(s) = \frac{s^2 + 4s + 6}{s^2 + 5s + 4}$$

Draw a Nyquist plot.

The Nyquist plot of the positive feedback system can be obtained by defining num and den as

$$\text{num} = \begin{bmatrix} -1 & -4 & -6 \end{bmatrix}$$
$$\text{den} = \begin{bmatrix} 1 & 5 & 4 \end{bmatrix}$$

and using the command nyquist(num,den). MATLAB Program 6-23 produces the Nyquist plot, as shown in Figure 6-45.

MATLAB Program 6–23

```
num = [-1  -4  -6];
den = [1  5  4];
nyquist(num,den);
grid
title('Nyquist Plot of G(s) = -(s^2+4s+6)/(s^2+5s+4)')
```

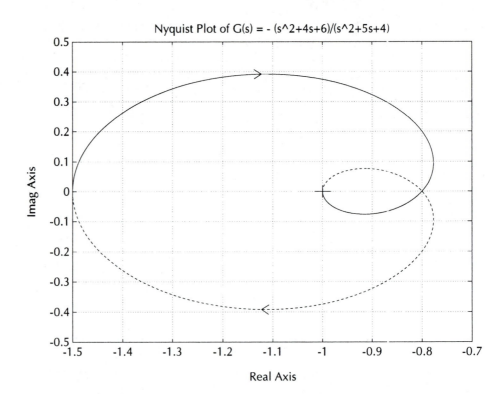

Figure 6-45

This system is unstable because the $-1 + j0$ point is encircled once clockwise. Note that this is a special case where the Nyquist plot passes through the $-1 + j0$ point and also encircles this point once clockwise. This means that the closed-loop system is degenerate; the system behaves as if it is an unstable first-order system. See the following closed-loop transfer function of the positive-feedback system:

$$\frac{C(s)}{R(s)} = \frac{s^2 + 4s + 6}{s^2 + 5s + 4 - (s^2 + 4s + 6)}$$

$$= \frac{s^2 + 4s + 6}{s - 2}$$

Note that the Nyquist plot for the positive feedback case is a mirror image about the imaginary axis of the Nyquist plot for the negative feedback case. This may be seen from Figure 6-46, which is obtained by use of MATLAB Program 6-24.

MATLAB Program 6–24

```
num1 = [1   4   6];
den1 = [1   5   4];
num2 = [-1   -4   -6];
den2 = [1   5   4];
v = [-2   2   -1   1];
axis(v);
nyquist(num1,den1);
grid
```

```
title('Nyquist Plots of G(s) and -G(s)')
text(1.05,0.45,'G(s)')
text(0.6,-0.6,'Use this Nyquist')
text(0.6,-0.7,'plot for negative')
text(0.6,-0.8,'feedback system')
hold

Current plot held

nyquist(num2,den2);
text(-1.3,0.45,'-G(s)')
text(-1.7,-0.6,'Use this Nyquist')
text(-1.7,-0.7,'plot for positive')
text(-1.7,-0.8,'feedback system')

hold

Current plot released
```

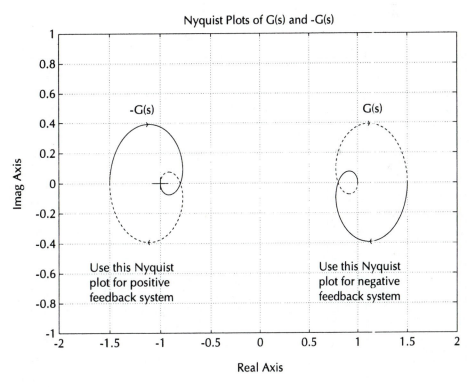

Figure 6-46

Additional examples of Nyquist plots

Several additional examples of Nyquist plots are shown in Examples 6-20 through 6-24.

EXAMPLE 6-20

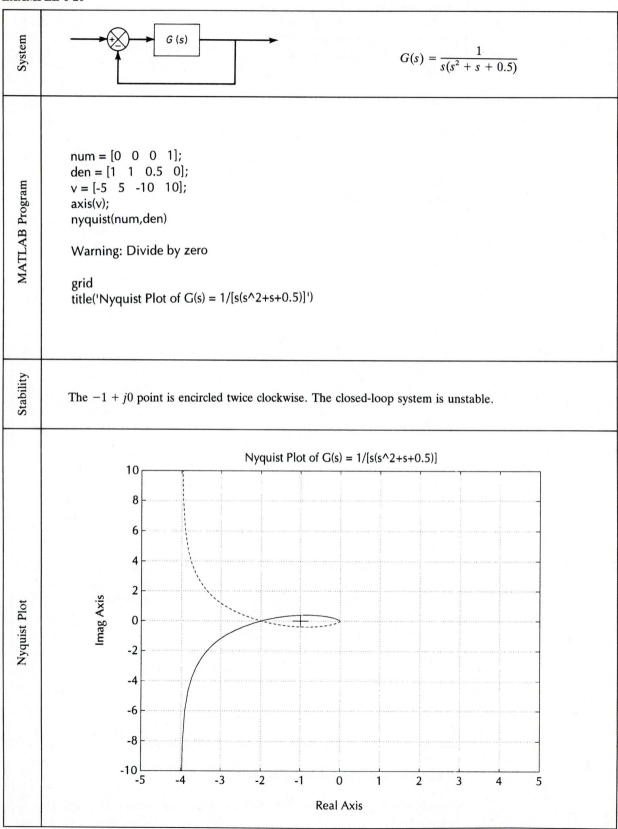

System	$$G(s) = \dfrac{1}{s(s^2 + s + 0.5)}$$

MATLAB Program

```
num = [0   0   0   1];
den = [1   1   0.5   0];
v = [-5   5   -10   10];
axis(v);
nyquist(num,den)

Warning: Divide by zero

grid
title('Nyquist Plot of G(s) = 1/[s(s^2+s+0.5)]')
```

Stability

The $-1 + j0$ point is encircled twice clockwise. The closed-loop system is unstable.

Nyquist Plot

EXAMPLE 6-21

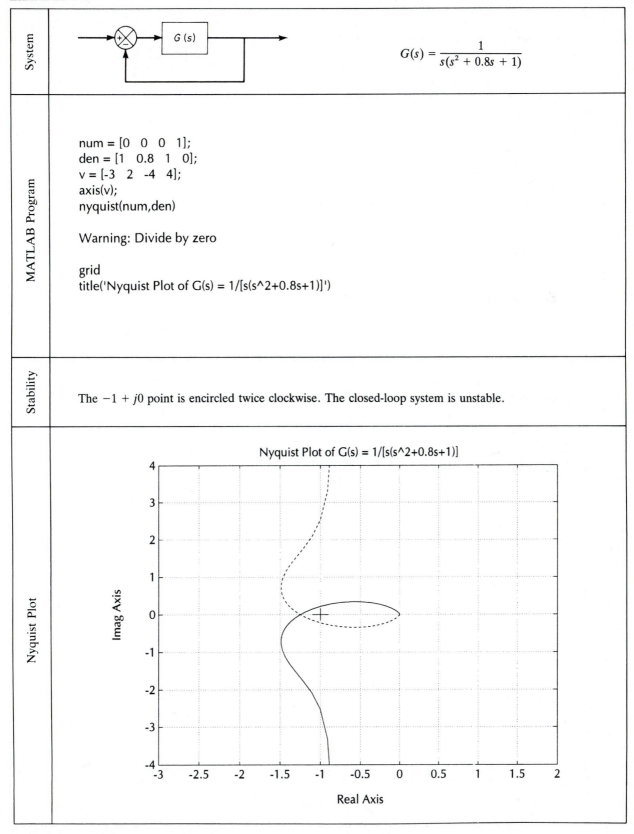

System	$$G(s) = \frac{1}{s(s^2 + 0.8s + 1)}$$

MATLAB Program	```num = [0 0 0 1];```
	```den = [1 0.8 1 0];```
	```v = [-3 2 -4 4];```
	```axis(v);```
	```nyquist(num,den)```
	
	```Warning: Divide by zero```
	
	```grid```
	```title('Nyquist Plot of G(s) = 1/[s(s^2+0.8s+1)]')```

Stability	The $-1 + j0$ point is encircled twice clockwise. The closed-loop system is unstable.
Nyquist Plot	

EXAMPLE 6-22

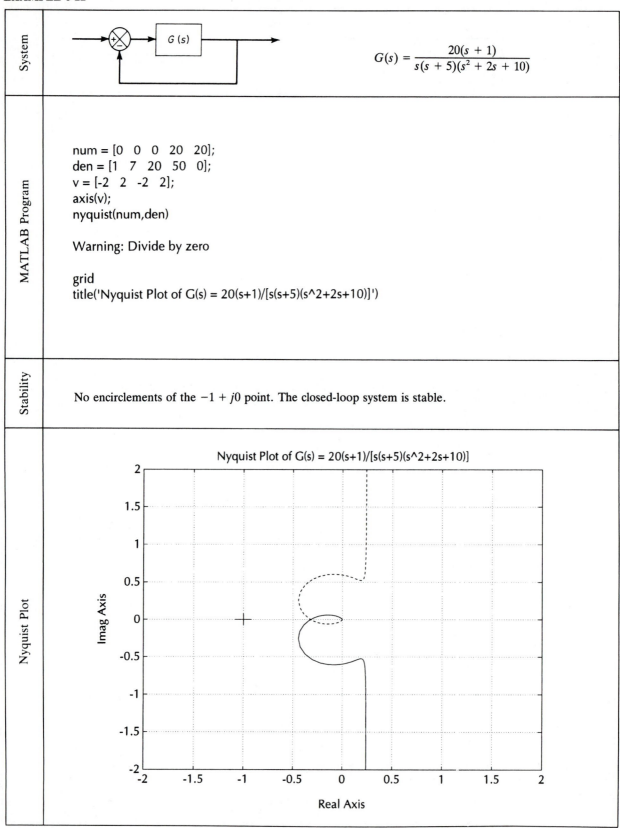

System	$$G(s) = \frac{20(s + 1)}{s(s + 5)(s^2 + 2s + 10)}$$

MATLAB Program

```
num = [0  0  0  20  20];
den = [1  7  20  50  0];
v = [-2  2  -2  2];
axis(v);
nyquist(num,den)

Warning: Divide by zero

grid
title('Nyquist Plot of G(s) = 20(s+1)/[s(s+5)(s^2+2s+10)]')
```

Stability

No encirclements of the $-1 + j0$ point. The closed-loop system is stable.

Nyquist Plot

Nyquist Plot of G(s) = 20(s+1)/[s(s+5)(s^2+2s+10)]

EXAMPLE 6-23

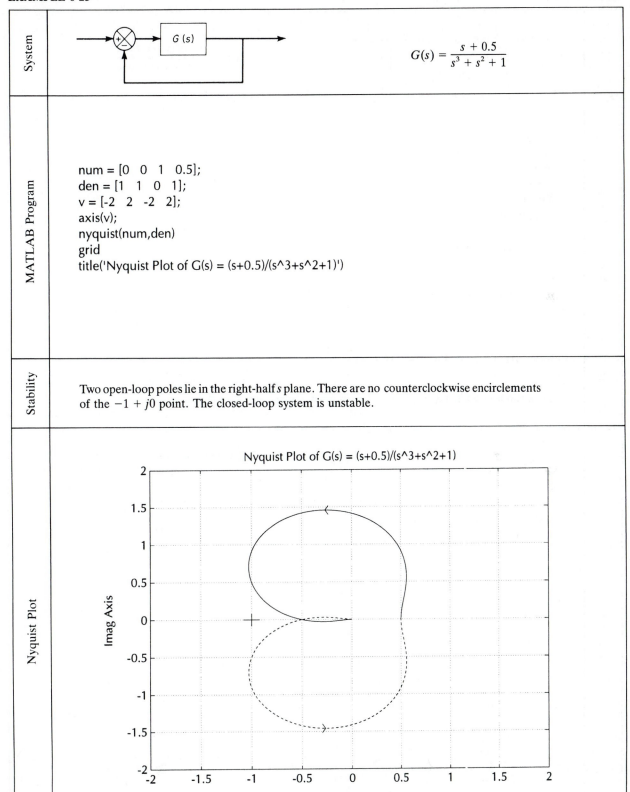

System

$$G(s) = \frac{s + 0.5}{s^3 + s^2 + 1}$$

MATLAB Program

```
num = [0   0   1   0.5];
den = [1   1   0   1];
v = [-2   2   -2   2];
axis(v);
nyquist(num,den)
grid
title('Nyquist Plot of G(s) = (s+0.5)/(s^3+s^2+1)')
```

Stability

Two open-loop poles lie in the right-half s plane. There are no counterclockwise encirclements of the $-1 + j0$ point. The closed-loop system is unstable.

Nyquist Plot

Nyquist Plot of G(s) = (s+0.5)/(s^3+s^2+1)

EXAMPLE 6-24

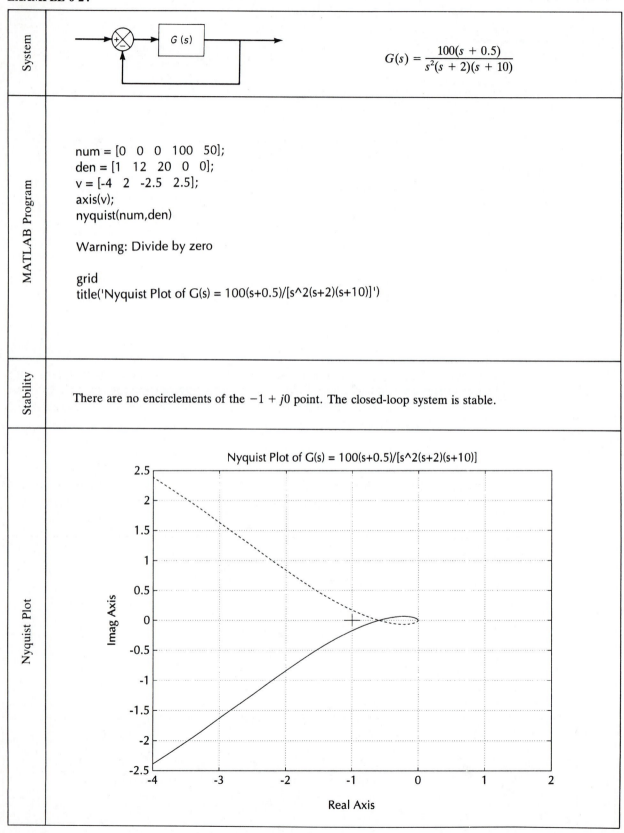

System	$$G(s) = \frac{100(s + 0.5)}{s^2(s + 2)(s + 10)}$$

MATLAB Program

```
num = [0  0  0  100  50];
den = [1  12  20  0  0];
v = [-4  2  -2.5  2.5];
axis(v);
nyquist(num,den)

Warning: Divide by zero

grid
title('Nyquist Plot of G(s) = 100(s+0.5)/[s^2(s+2)(s+10)]')
```

Stability

There are no encirclements of the $-1 + j0$ point. The closed-loop system is stable.

Nyquist Plot

Drawing Nyquist plots of system defined in state space

Consider the system defined by

$$\dot{\mathbf{x}} = \mathbf{Ax} + \mathbf{Bu}$$
$$\mathbf{y} = \mathbf{Cx} + \mathbf{Du}$$

where $\mathbf{x}$ = state vector (n-vector)
$\quad\quad \mathbf{y}$ = output vector (m-vector)
$\quad\quad \mathbf{u}$ = control vector (r-vector)
$\quad\quad \mathbf{A}$ = state matrix ($n \times n$ matrix)
$\quad\quad \mathbf{B}$ = control matrix ($n \times r$ matrix)
$\quad\quad \mathbf{C}$ = output matrix ($m \times n$ matrix)
$\quad\quad \mathbf{D}$ = direct transmission matrix ($m \times r$ matrix)

Nyquist plots for this system may be obtained by use of the command

nyquist(A,B,C,D)

This command produces a series of Nyquist plots, one for each input and output combination of the system. The frequency range is automatically determined.
The command

nyquist(A,B,C,D,iu)

produces Nyquist plots from the single input iu to all the outputs of the system, with the frequency range determined automatically. The scalar iu is an index into the inputs of the system and specifies which input to use for the frequency response.
The command

nyquist(A,B,C,D,iu,w)

uses the user-supplied frequency vector w. The vector w specifies the frequencies in radians per second at which the frequency response should be calculated.

EXAMPLE 6-25

Consider the system defined by

$$\begin{bmatrix} \dot{x}_1 \\ \dot{x}_2 \end{bmatrix} = \begin{bmatrix} 0 & 1 \\ -25 & -4 \end{bmatrix} \begin{bmatrix} x_1 \\ x_2 \end{bmatrix} + \begin{bmatrix} 0 \\ 25 \end{bmatrix} u$$

$$y = \begin{bmatrix} 1 & 0 \end{bmatrix} \begin{bmatrix} x_1 \\ x_2 \end{bmatrix} + [0]u$$

Draw a Nyquist plot.
This system has a single input u and a single output y. A Nyquist plot may be obtained by entering the command

nyquist(A,B,C,D)

or

nyquist(A,B,C,D,1)

MATLAB Program 6-25 will provide the Nyquist plot. (Note that we obtain the identical result by using either of the above two commands.) Figure 6-47 shows the Nyquist plot produced by MATLAB Program 6-25.

If we wish to draw a Nyquist plot in a larger domain, for example, [−2 2 −2 2], we may enter MATLAB Program 6-26 into the computer. The resulting Nyquist plot is shown in Figure 6-48.

MATLAB Program 6–25

```
A = [0   1;-25  -4];
B = [0;25];
C = [1   0];
D = [0];
nyquist(A,B,C,D)
grid
title('Nyquist Plot')
```

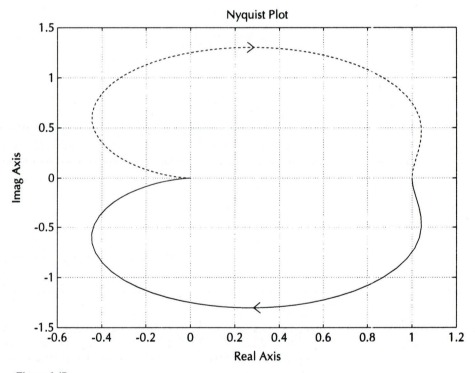

Figure 6-47

MATLAB Program 6–26

```
A = [0   1;-25  -4];
B = [0;25];
C = [1   0];
D = [0];
v = [-2  2  -2  2];
axis(v);
nyquist(A,B,C,D)
grid
title('Nyquist Plot')
```

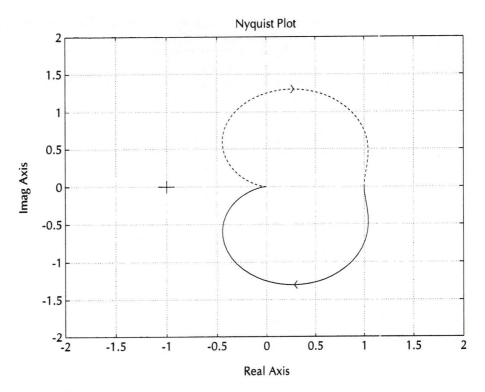

Figure 6-48

EXAMPLE 6-26

Consider the system defined by

$$\begin{bmatrix} \dot{x}_1 \\ \dot{x}_2 \end{bmatrix} = \begin{bmatrix} -1 & -1 \\ 6.5 & 0 \end{bmatrix} \begin{bmatrix} x_1 \\ x_2 \end{bmatrix} + \begin{bmatrix} 1 & 1 \\ 1 & 0 \end{bmatrix} \begin{bmatrix} u_1 \\ u_2 \end{bmatrix}$$

$$\begin{bmatrix} y_1 \\ y_2 \end{bmatrix} = \begin{bmatrix} 1 & 0 \\ 0 & 1 \end{bmatrix} \begin{bmatrix} x_1 \\ x_2 \end{bmatrix} + \begin{bmatrix} 0 & 0 \\ 0 & 0 \end{bmatrix} \begin{bmatrix} u_1 \\ u_2 \end{bmatrix}$$

This system involves two inputs and two outputs. There are four sinusoidal output–input relationships: $Y_1(j\omega)/U_1(j\omega)$, $Y_2(j\omega)/U_1(j\omega)$, $Y_1(j\omega)/U_2(j\omega)$, and $Y_2(j\omega)/U_2(j\omega)$. Draw Nyquist plots for the system. (When considering input u_1, we assume that input u_2 is zero, and vice versa.)

The four individual Nyquist plots can be obtained by use of the command

nyquist(A,B,C,D)

MATLAB Program 6-27 produces the four Nyquist plots. They are shown in Figure 6-49. [Depending on the version of MATLAB (such as Student version or Professional version 4.0) we may get slightly different plots.]

To draw two Nyquist plots for the input u_1 in one diagram and two Nyquist plots for the input u_2 in another diagram, we may use the commands

nyquist(A,B,C,D,1)

and

nyquist(A,B,C,D,2)

```
MATLAB Program 6-27

A = [-1  -1;6.5  0];
B = [1  1;1  0];
C = [1  0;0  1];
D = [0  0;0  0];
nyquist(A,B,C,D)
```

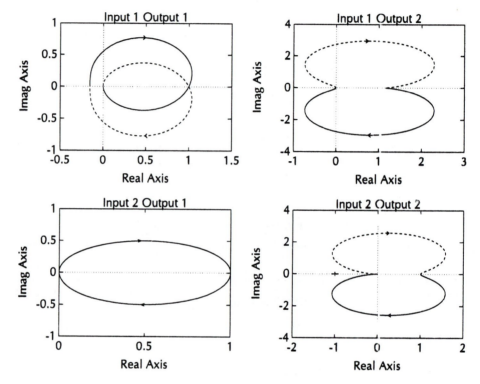

Figure 6-49

respectively. MATLAB Program 6-28 will draw two Nyquist plots for the input u_1 in one diagram and two Nyquist plots for the input u_2 in another diagram. Figure 6-50 shows the two diagrams.

The command

$$[re,im,w] = nyquist(A,B,C,D,iu)$$

returns the frequency response of the system in the matrices re, im, and w. This command does not produce plots on the screen. The matrices re and im contain the real and imaginary parts of the frequency response of the system evaluated at the frequency points in vector w. Note that re and im have as many columns as outputs and one row for each element in w.

If we wish to draw the Nyquist plot for only $Y_1(j\omega)/U_1(j\omega)$, we may use this command. That is, enter the command

$$[re,im,w] = nyquist(A,B,C,D,1)$$

In the present example system, re is a two-column matrix. The first column consists of the

---

MATLAB Program 6–28

```
% ---------- Nyquist plots ----------

% ***** In this program we obtain Nyquist plots of a system having
% two inputs (u1 and u2) and two outputs (y1 and y2) *****

% ***** We shall first obtain Nyquist plots when the input is
% u1.  Then we shall obtain Nyquist plots when the input is
% u2 *****

% ***** Enter matrices A, B, C, and D *****

A = [-1  -1;6.5   0];
B = [1   1;1   0];
C = [1   0;0   1];
D = [0   0;0   0];

% ***** To obtain Nyquist plots when the input is u1, enter
% the command 'nyquist(A,B,C,D,1)' *****

nyquist(A,B,C,D,1)
grid
title('Nyquist Plots : Input = u1 (u2 = 0)')
text(0.1,0.7,'Y1')
text(0.1,2.5,'Y2')

% ***** Next, we shall obtain Nyquist plots when the input is
% u2.  Enter the command 'nyquist(A,B,C,D,2)' *****

nyquist(A,B,C,D,2)
grid
title('Nyquist Plots : Input = u2 (u1 = 0)')
text(0.1,0.5,'Y1')
text(0.1,2.2,'Y2')
```

---

real parts of Y_1 as the frequency points move and the second column consists of the real parts of Y_2. To get the first column (real parts of Y_1, which we define as re1), enter the statement

$$re1 = re * [1;0]$$

Similarly, to obtain the imaginary part of Y_1, we enter the statement

$$im1 = im * [1;0]$$

To obtain the Nyquist plot for $Y_1(j\omega)/U_1(j\omega)$, enter the following *plot* command:

$$plot(re1,im1)$$

MATLAB Program 6-29 obtains the Nyquist plot for $Y_1(j\omega)/U_1(j\omega)$ for $\omega > 0$, which is shown in Figure 6-51. To plot the Nyquist locus for $-\infty < \omega < \infty$, replace the *plot* command plot(re1,im1) by plot(re1,im1,re1,−im1).

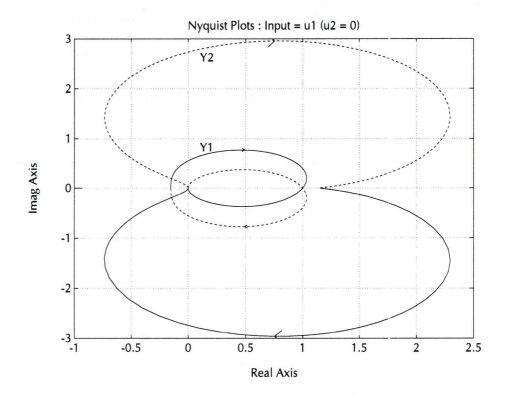

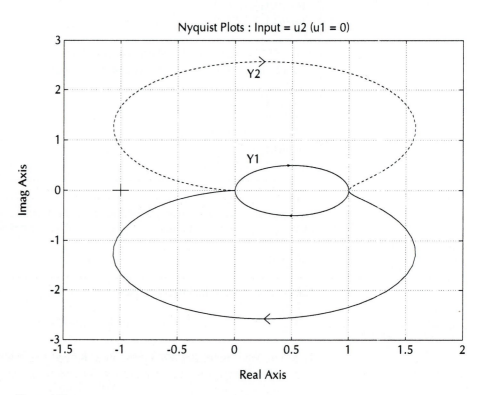

Figure 6-50

```
MATLAB Program 6–29

A = [-1   -1;6.5   0];
B = [1    1;1    0];
C = [1    0;0    1];
D = [0    0;0    0];
[re,im,w] = nyquist(A,B,C,D,1);
re1 = re*[1;0];
im1 = im*[1;0];
plot(re1,im1)
grid
title('Nyquist Plot for Y1(jw)/U1(jw)')
xlabel('Real Axis')
ylabel('Imag Axis')
```

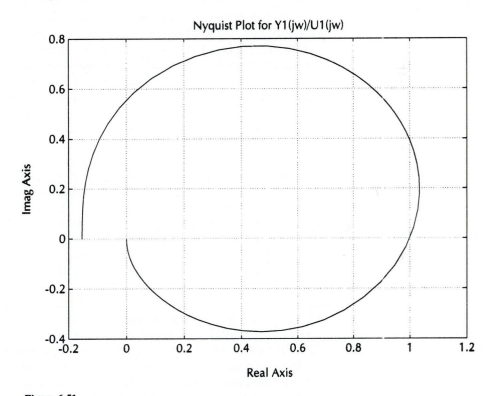

Figure 6-51

6-5 CASE STUDIES

In this section we discuss design of closed-loop systems based on the Bode-diagram approach. This approach to the design of control systems is particularly useful for the following reasons:

1. In the Bode diagram, the low-frequency asymptote of the magnitude curve is indicative of one of the static error constants K_p, K_v, or K_a.

2. Specifications of the transient response can be translated into those of the

frequency response in terms of the phase margin, gain margin, bandwidth, and so forth. These specifications can be easily handled in the Bode diagram. In particular, the phase and gain margins can be read directly from the Bode diagram.

3. The design of a compensator or controller to satisfy the given specifications (in terms of the phase margin and gain margin) can be carried out in the Bode diagram in a simple and straightforward manner.

Before we present design problems, let us review the phase-lead, phase-lag, and phase lag–lead compensation techniques.

Phase-lead compensation is commonly used for improving stability margins. The phase-lead compensation increases the system bandwidth. Thus the system has a faster speed to respond. However, such a system using phase-lead compensation may be subjected to high-frequency noise problems due to its increased high-frequency gains.

Phase-lag compensation reduces the system gain at higher frequencies without reducing the system gain at lower frequencies. The system bandwidth is reduced, and thus the system has a slower speed to respond. Because of the reduced high-frequency gain, the total system gain can be increased, and thereby low-frequency gain can be increased and the steady-state accuracy can be improved. Also, any high-frequency noises involved in the system can be attenuated.

In some applications, a phase-lag compensator is cascaded with a phase-lead compensator. The cascaded compensator is known as a *phase lag-lead* compensator. By use of the lag-lead compensator, the low-frequency gain can be increased (which means an improvement in steady-state accuracy), while at the same time the system bandwidth and stability margins can be increased.

Note that the PID controller is a special case of a phase lag-lead controller. The PD control action, which affects the high-frequency region, increases the phase-lead angle and improves system stability, as well as increasing the system bandwidth (and thus increasing the speed of response). That is, the PD controller behaves in much the same way as a phase-lead compensator. The PI control action affects the low-frequency portion and, in fact, increases the low-frequency gain and improves steady-state accuracy. Therefore, the PI controller acts as a phase-lag compensator. The PID control action is a combination of the PI and PD control actions. The design techniques for PID controllers basically follow those of phase lag-lead compensators. (In industrial control systems, however, each of the PID control actions in the PID controller may be adjusted experimentally.)

In the following we first discuss a simple gain-adjustment problem in Example 6-27. Example 6-28 treats the design of a lead compensator. Example 6-29 deals with the design of a lag-lead compensator. Here we use Bode diagrams and Nyquist plots to verify the design based on conventional methods. The scope of this section is limited to the use of MATLAB to check the results of the designed systems. Automatic MATLAB design of compensators is not discussed here.

EXAMPLE 6-27: Gain-Adjustment Problem

Consider the control system shown in Figure 6-52. Determine the value of gain K such that the phase margin is 60°.

The open-loop transfer function is

$$G(s) = K\frac{s + 0.1}{s + 0.5}\frac{10}{s(s + 1)}$$

$$= \frac{K(10s + 1)}{s^3 + 1.5s^2 + 0.5s}$$

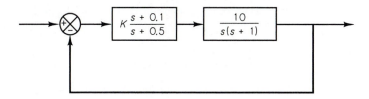

Figure 6-52

Let us plot the Bode diagram of $G(s)$ when $K = 1$. MATLAB Program 6-30 may be used for this purpose. Figure 6-53 shows the Bode diagram produced by this program. From this diagram the required phase margin of 60° occurs at the frequency $\omega = 1.15$ rad/sec. The magnitude of $G(j\omega)$ at this frequency is found to be 14.5 dB. Then gain K must satisfy the following equation:

$$20 \log K = -14.5 \text{ dB}$$

or

$$K = 0.188$$

MATLAB Program 6–30

```
num = [0  0  10  1];
den = [1  1.5  0.5  0];
bode(num,den)
title('Bode Diagram of G(s) = (10s+1)/[s(s+0.5)(s+1)]');
```

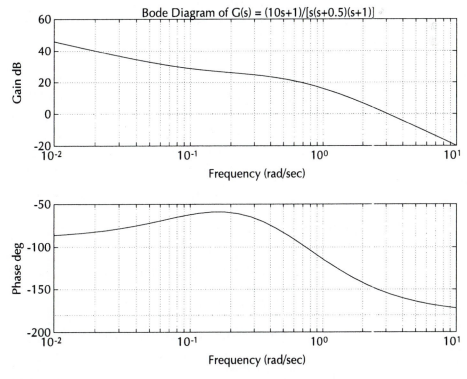

Figure 6-53

Thus we have determined the value of gain K.

To verify the results, let us draw a Nyquist plot of G for the frequency range

$$w = 0.1{:}0.01{:}1.15$$

The end point of the locus (w = 1.15 rad/sec) will be on a unit circle in the Nyquist plane. To check the phase margin, it is convenient to draw the Nyquist plot on a polar diagram, using polar grids.

To draw the Nyquist plot on a polar diagram, first define a complex vector z by

$$z = re + i*im = re^{i\theta}$$

where r and θ (theta) are given by

$$r = abs(z)$$
$$theta = angle(z)$$

The abs means the square root of the sum of the real part squared and imaginary part squared. angle means $\tan^{-1}$ (imaginary part/real part).

If we use the command

$$polar(theta,r)$$

```
MATLAB Program 6–31

% ---------- Nyquist Plot in Polar Coordinates ----------

num = [0   0   1.88   0.188];
den = [1   1.5   0.5   0];
w = 0.1:0.05:1.15;
v = [-2   2   -2   2];
axis(v); axis ('square')
[re,im,w] = nyquist(num,den,w);

% ***** Convert rectangular coordinates into polar
% coordinates by difinig z, r, theta as follows *****

z = re+i*im;
r = abs(z);
theta = angle(z);

% ***** To draw polar plot, enter command 'polar(theta,r)' *****

polar(theta,r)
grid
title('Check of Phase Margin');
text(-1.65,1.8,'Nyquist plot')
text(-3,1.5,'Phase margin')
text(-2.9,1.6,'is 60 degrees.')

% ***** Restore normal graphics perspective *****

axis ('normal')
```

MATLAB will produce a plot in the polar coordinates. Subsequent use of the *grid* command draws polar grid lines and grid circles.

MATLAB Program 6-31 produces the Nyquist plot of $G(j\omega)$, where ω is between 0.1 and 1.15 rad/sec. The resulting plot is shown in Figure 6-54. Notice that point $G(j1.15)$ lies on the unit circle and the phase angle of this point is $-120°$. Hence the phase margin is 60°. The fact that point $G(j1.15)$ is on the unit circle verifies that at $\omega = 1.15$ rad/sec the magnitude is equal to 1 or 0 dB. (Thus $\omega = 1.15$ is the gain crossover frequency.) Thus $K = 0.188$ gives the desired phase margin of 60°.

Note that in writing 'text' in the polar diagram we enter the *text* command as follows:

$$\text{text(angle in radians, radius, ' ')}$$

For example, to write 'Nyquist plot' starting at point (angle $= -1.65$ rad, radius $= 1.8$), enter the command

$$\text{text}(-1.65,1.8,\text{'Nyquist plot'})$$

The text is written horizontally on the screen.

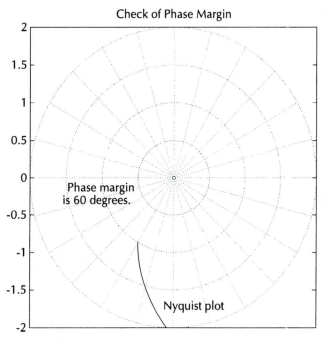

Figure 6-54

EXAMPLE 6-28: Design of Lead Compensator

Consider the system shown in Figure 6-55(a). We wish to design a compensator such that the closed-loop system will satisfy the following requirements:

$$\text{static velocity error constant} = K_v = 20 \text{ sec}^{-1}$$
$$\text{phase margin} = 50°$$
$$\text{gain margin} \geq 10 \text{ dB}$$

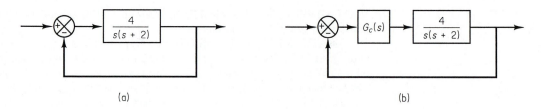

(a)   (b)

Figure 6-55

We shall design a lead compensator $G_c(s)$ of the form

$$G_c(s) = K_c\alpha\frac{Ts + 1}{\alpha Ts + 1} = K_c\frac{s + \dfrac{1}{T}}{s + \dfrac{1}{\alpha T}}$$

The compensated system is shown in Figure 6-55(b).
Define

$$G_1(s) = KG(s) = \frac{4K}{s(s + 2)}$$

where $K = K_c\alpha$.

The first step in the design is to adjust the gain K to meet the steady-state performance specification or to provide the required static velocity error constant. Since the static velocity error constant K_v is given as 20 sec^{-1}, we have

$$K_v = \lim_{s \to 0} sG_c(s)G(s) = \lim_{s \to 0} s\frac{Ts + 1}{\alpha Ts + 1}G_1(s)$$
$$= \lim_{s \to 0}\frac{s4K}{s(s + 2)} = 2K = 20$$

or

$$K = 10$$

With $K = 10$, the compensated system will satisfy the steady-state requirement.
We shall next plot the Bode diagram of

$$G_1(s) = \frac{40}{s(s + 2)}$$

MATLAB Program 6-32 produces the Bode diagram shown in Figure 6-56. From this plot, the phase margin is found to be 17°. The gain margin is +∞ dB.

Since the specification calls for a phase margin of 50°, the additional phase lead necessary to satisfy the phase-margin requirement is 33°. A lead compensator can contribute this amount.

Noting that the addition of a lead compensator modifies the magnitude curve in the Bode diagram, we realize that the gain crossover frequency will be shifted to the right. We must offset the increased phase lag of $G_1(j\omega)$ due to this increase in the gain crossover frequency. Taking the shift of the gain crossover frequency into consideration, we may assume that ϕ_m, the maximum phase lead required, is approximately 38°. (This means that approximately 5° has been added to compensate for the shift in the gain crossover frequency.) Since

$$\sin\phi_m = \frac{1 - \alpha}{1 + \alpha}$$

```
MATLAB Program 6–32

num = [0   0   40];
den = [1   2   0];
w = logspace(-1,1,100);
bode(num,den, w)
title('Bode Diagram of G1(s) = 40/[s(s+2)]')
```

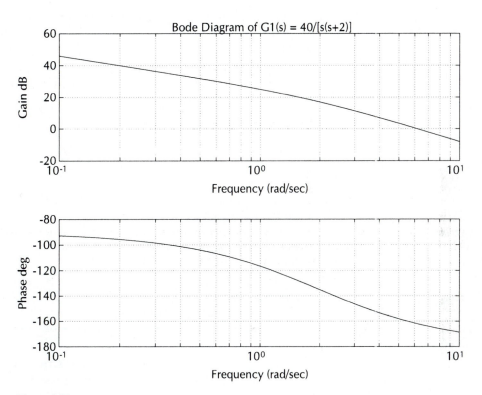

Figure 6-56

$\phi_m = 38°$ corresponds to $\alpha = 0.2379$. Note that $\alpha = 0.24$ corresponds to $\phi_m = 37.8°$. Whether we choose $\phi_m = 38°$ or $\phi_m = 37.8°$ does not make much difference in the final solution. Hence let us choose $\alpha = 0.24$.

Once the attenuation factor α has been determined on the basis of the required phase-lead angle, the next step is to determine the corner frequencies $\omega = 1/T$ and $\omega = 1/(\alpha T)$ of the lead compensator. Notice that the maximum phase-lead angle ϕ_m occurs at the geometric mean of the two corner frequencies, or $\omega = 1/(\sqrt{\alpha}T)$.

The amount of the modification in the magnitude curve at $\omega = 1/(\sqrt{\alpha}T)$ due to the inclusion of the term $(Ts + 1)/(\alpha Ts + 1)$ is

$$\left|\frac{1 + j\omega T}{1 + j\omega\alpha T}\right|_{\omega = \frac{1}{\sqrt{\alpha}T}} = \left|\frac{1 + j\dfrac{1}{\sqrt{\alpha}}}{1 + j\alpha\dfrac{1}{\sqrt{\alpha}}}\right| = \frac{1}{\sqrt{\alpha}}$$

Note that

$$\frac{1}{\sqrt{\alpha}} = \frac{1}{\sqrt{0.24}} = 0.2041 = 6.2 \text{ dB}$$

We need to find the frequency point where, when the lead compensator is added, the total magnitude becomes 0 dB.

From Figure 6-56 we see that the frequency point where the magnitude of $G_1(j\omega)$ is -6.2 dB occurs between $\omega = 1$ and 10 rad/sec. Hence we plot a new Bode diagram of $G_1(j\omega)$ in the frequency range between $\omega = 1$ and 10 to locate the exact point where $G_1(j\omega) = -6.2$ dB. MATLAB Program 6-33 produces the Bode diagram in this frequency range, which is shown in Figure 6-57. From this diagram, we find the frequency point where $\left|G_1(j\omega)\right| = -6.2$ dB occurs at $\omega = 9$ rad/sec. Let us select this frequency to be the new gain crossover frequency, or $\omega_c = 9$ rad/sec. Noting that this frequency corresponds to $1/(\sqrt{\alpha}T)$, or

$$\omega_c = \frac{1}{\sqrt{\alpha}T}$$

we obtain

$$\frac{1}{T} = \omega_c\sqrt{\alpha} = 9\sqrt{0.24} = 4.409$$

and

$$\frac{1}{\alpha T} = \frac{\omega_c}{\sqrt{\alpha}} = \frac{9}{\sqrt{0.24}} = 18.371$$

MATLAB Program 6–33

num = [0 0 40];
den = [1 2 0];
w = logspace(0,1,100);
bode(num,den,w)
title('Bode Diagram of G1(s) = 40/[s(s+2)]')

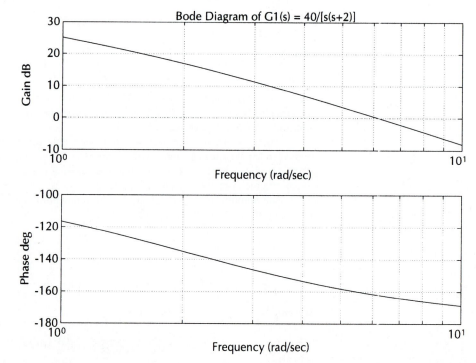

Figure 6-57

The lead compensator thus determined is

$$G_c(s) = K_c \frac{s + 4.409}{s + 18.371} = K_c\alpha \frac{0.227s + 1}{0.0544s + 1}$$

where K_c is determined as

$$K_c = \frac{K}{\alpha} = \frac{10}{0.24} = 41.667$$

Thus the transfer function of the compensator becomes

$$G_c(s) = 41.667 \frac{s + 4.409}{s + 18.371} = 10 \frac{0.227s + 1}{0.0544s + 1}$$

MATLAB Program 6-34 produces the Bode diagram of this lead compensator, which is shown in Figure 6-58. Note that

$$\frac{G_c(s)}{K} G_1(s) = \frac{G_c(s)}{10} 10G(s) = G_c(s)G(s)$$

MATLAB Program 6–34

```
numc = [41.667   183.71];
denc = [1   18.371];
w = logspace(-1,3,100);
bode(numc,denc,w)
title('Bode Diagram of Gc(s) = 41.667(s+4.409)/(s+18.371)')
```

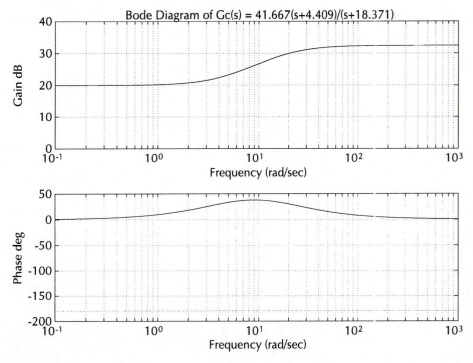

Figure 6-58

The open-loop transfer function of the designed system is

$$G_c(s)G(s) = 41.667\frac{s + 4.409}{s + 18.371}\frac{4}{s(s + 2)}$$

$$= \frac{166.668s + 734.839}{s^3 + 20.371s^2 + 36.742s}$$

MATLAB Program 6-35 will produce the Bode diagram of $G_c(s)G(s)$, which is shown in Figure 6-59.

Also, MATLAB Program 6-36 may be used to draw Nyquist plots of $G(j\omega)$, $G_1(j\omega)$, and $G_c(j\omega)G(j\omega)$ on a polar plane. The resulting plots are shown in Figure 6-60.

MATLAB Program 6–35

```
num = [0  0  166.668  734.839];
den = [1  20.371  36.742  0];
w = logspace(-1,3,100);
bode(num,den,w)
title('Bode Diagram of Gc(s)G(s)')
```

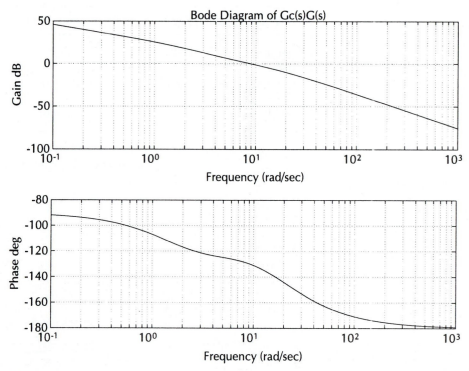

Figure 6-59

MATLAB Program 6–36

```
% ---------- Nyquist plots ----------

% ***** We shall draw Nyquist plots of G(jw), G1(jw), and
% Gc(jw)G(jw) *****
```

```
num1 = [0   0   4];
den1 = [1   2   0];
num2 = [0   0   40];
den2 = [1   2   0];
num3 = [0   0   166.668   734.839];
den3 = [1   20.371   36.742   0];
v = [-5   5   -5   5];
axis(v); axis ('square')
[re1,im1,w] = nyquist(num1,den1);
```

Warning: Divide by zero

```
z1 = re1+i*im1;
r1 = abs(z1);
theta1 = angle(z1);
polar(theta1,r1)
grid
hold
```

Current plot held

```
[re2,im2,w] = nyquist(num2,den2);
```

Warning: Divide by zero

```
z2 = re2+i*im2;
r2 = abs(z2);
theta2 = angle(z2);
polar(theta2,r2)
[re3,im3,w] = nyquist(num3,den3);
```

Warning: Divide by zero

```
z3 = re3+i*im3;
r3 = abs(z3);
theta3 = angle(z3);
polar(theta3,r3)
title('Nyquist Plots of G(jw), G1(jw), and Gc(jw)G(jw)')
text(-1.9,3,'G(jw)')
text(-2.35,5.6,'Gc(jw)G(jw)')
text(-2.8,3.5,'G1(jw)')

hold
```

Current plot released

```
% ***** Restore normal graphics perspective *****

axis ('normal')
```

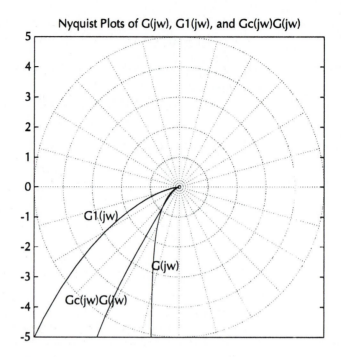

Figure 6-60

```
MATLAB Program 6–37

% ---------- Unit-step responses ----------

% ***** In this program we shall obtain unit-step responses
% of uncompensated system and compensated system *****

num1 = [0   0   4];
den1 = [1   2   4];
num2 = [0   0   166.668   734.839];
den2 = [1   20.371   203.41   734.839];
v = [0   6   0   1.6];
axis(v);
t = 0:0.05:6;
c1 = step(num1,den1,t);
c2 = step(num2,den2,t);
plot(t,c1,t,c2)
grid
title('Unit-Step Responses of Uncompensated and Compensated Systems')
xlabel('t Sec')
ylabel('Outputs c1 and c2')
text(2.5,1.1,'Uncompensated system')
text(0.3,1.25,'Compensated system')
```

Unit-step response   We shall check the unit-step response of the designed system. We shall plot both the unit-step response of the designed system and that of the original uncompensated system.

The closed-loop transfer function of the original uncompensated system is

$$\frac{C_1(s)}{R_1(s)} = \frac{4}{s^2 + 2s + 4}$$

The closed-loop transfer function of the compensated system is

$$\frac{C_2(s)}{R_2(s)} = \frac{41.667(s + 4.409) \times 4}{(s + 18.371)s(s + 2) + 41.667(s + 4.409) \times 4}$$

$$= \frac{166.668s + 734.839}{s^3 + 20.371s^2 + 203.41s + 734.839}$$

MATLAB Program 6-37 produces the unit-step responses of the uncompensated and compensated systems. The resulting response curves are shown in Figure 6-61.

Unit-ramp response   It is worthwhile to check the unit-ramp response of the compensated system. Since $K_v = 20 \text{ sec}^{-1}$, the steady-state error following the unit-ramp input will be $1/K_v = 0.05$. The static velocity error constant of the uncompensated system is 2 sec^{-1}. Hence the original uncompensated system will have a large steady-state error following the unit-ramp input.

MATLAB Program 6-38 produces the unit-ramp response curves. [Note that the unit-ramp response is obtained as the unit-step response of $C_i(s)/sR(s)$, where $i = 1, 2$.] The resulting curves are shown in Figure 6-62. The compensated system has a steady-state error equal to one-tenth that of the original uncompensated system.

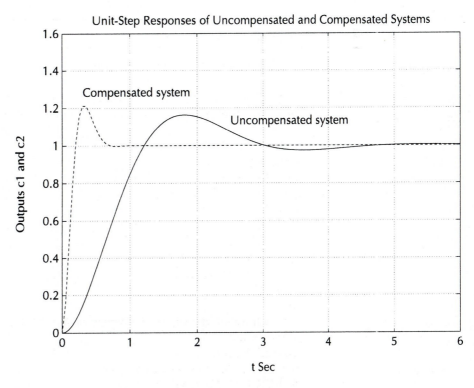

Figure 6-61

```
MATLAB Program 6-38

% ---------- Unit-ramp responses ----------

% ***** In this program we shall obtain unit-ramp responses
% of uncompensated system and compensated system *****

num1 = [0   0   0   4];
den1 = [1   2   4   0];
num2 = [0   0   0   166.668   734.839];
den2 = [1   20.371   203.41   734.839   0];
t = 0:0.1:4;
c1 = step(num1,den1,t);
c2 = step(num2,den2,t);
plot(t,c1,t,c2,t,t,'-')
grid
title('Unit-Ramp Responses of Uncompensated and Compensated Systems')
xlabel('t Sec')
ylabel('Outputs c1 and c2')
text(2.5,1.75,'Uncompensated')
text(2.5,1.6,'system')
text(1.65,2.5,'Compensated')
text(1.65,2.35,'system')
```

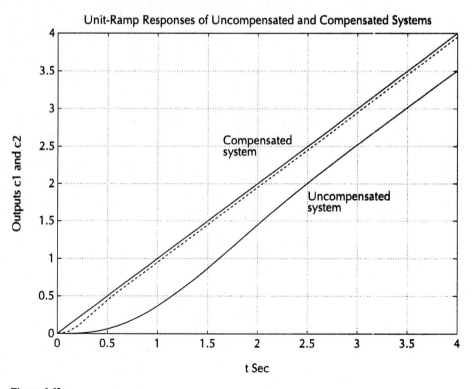

Figure 6-62

EXAMPLE 6-29: Design of Lag–Lead Compensator

Consider the unity feedback system whose open-loop transfer function is

$$G(s) = \frac{K}{s(s + 1)(s + 4)}$$

Design a compensator $G_c(s)$ such that the static velocity error constant is 10 sec^{-1}, the phase margin is $50°$, and the gain margin is 10 dB or more.

We shall design a lag–lead compensator of the form

$$G_c(s) = K_c \frac{\left(s + \dfrac{1}{T_1}\right)\left(s + \dfrac{1}{T_2}\right)}{\left(s + \dfrac{\beta}{T_1}\right)\left(s + \dfrac{1}{\beta T_2}\right)}$$

Then the open-loop transfer function of the compensated system is $G_c(s)G(s)$. Since the gain K of the plant is adjustable, let us assume that $K_c = 1$. Then $\lim_{s \to 0} G_c(s) = 1$. From the requirement on the static velocity error constant, we obtain

$$K_v = \lim_{s \to 0} sG_c(s)G(s) = \lim_{s \to 0} sG_c(s) \frac{K}{s(s + 1)(s + 4)}$$

$$= \frac{K}{4} = 10$$

Hence

$$K = 40$$

We shall first plot a Bode diagram of the uncompensated system with $K = 40$. MATLAB Program 6-39 may be used to plot this Bode diagram. The diagram obtained is shown in Figure 6-63.

From Figure 6-63, the phase margin of the uncompensated system is found to be $-16°$, which indicates that the uncompensated system is unstable. The next step in the design of a lag–lead compensator is to choose a new gain crossover frequency. From the phase-angle curve for $G(j\omega)$, we notice that the phase crossover frequency is $\omega = 2$ rad/sec. We may choose the new gain crossover frequency to be 2 rad/sec so that the phase-lead angle required at $\omega = 2$ rad/sec is about $50°$. A single lag–lead compensator can provide this amount of phase-lead angle quite easily.

Once we choose the gain crossover frequency to be 2 rad/sec, we can determine the corner frequencies of the phase-lag portion of the lag–lead compensator. Let us choose the corner frequency $\omega = 1/T_2$ (which corresponds to the zero of the phase-lag portion of the compensator) to be 1 decade below the new gain crossover frequency, or at $\omega = 0.2$ rad/sec. For another corner frequency $\omega = 1/(\beta T_2)$, we need the value of β. The value of β can be determined from the consideration of the lead portion of the compensator, as shown next.

MATLAB Program 6–39

```
num = [0  0  0  40];
den = [1  5  4  0];
w = logspace(-1,1,100);
bode(num,den,w)
title('Bode Diagram of G(s) = 40/[s(s+1)(s+4)]')
```

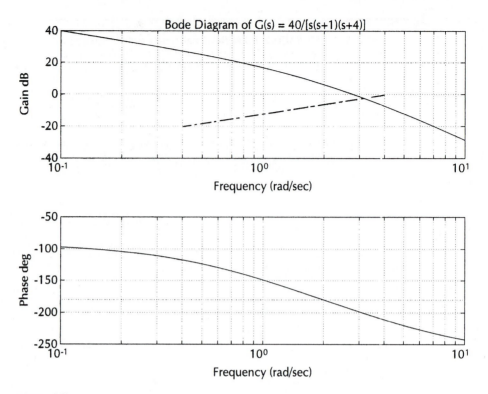

Figure 6-63

For the lead compensator, the maximum phase-lead angle ϕ_m is given by

$$\sin \phi_m = \frac{\beta - 1}{\beta + 1}$$

Notice that $\beta = 10$ corresponds to $\phi_m = 54.9°$. Since we need a 50° phase margin, we may choose $\beta = 10$. (Note that we will be using several degrees less than the maximum angle, 54.9°.) Thus

$$\beta = 10$$

Then the corner frequency $\omega = 1/(\beta T_2)$ (which corresponds to the pole of the phase-lag portion of the compensator) becomes

$$\omega = 0.02$$

The transfer function of the phase-lag portion of the lag–lead compensator becomes

$$\frac{s + 0.2}{s + 0.02} = 10\left(\frac{5s + 1}{50s + 1}\right)$$

The phase-lead portion can be determined as follows: Since the new gain crossover frequency is $\omega = 2$ rad/sec, from Figure 6-63, $|G(j2)|$ is found to be 6 dB. Hence, if the lag–lead compensator contributes -6 dB at $\omega = 2$ rad/sec, then the new gain crossover frequency is as desired. From this requirement, it is possible to draw a straight line of slope 20 dB/decade passing through the point (-6 dB, 2 rad/sec). (Such a line has been manually drawn on Figure 6-63.) The intersections of this line and the 0 dB line and -20-dB line determine the corner frequencies. From this consideration, the corner frequencies for the lead portion can be determined as $\omega = 0.4$ rad/sec and $\omega = 4$ rad/sec. Thus the transfer function of the lead portion of the lag–lead compensator becomes

$$\frac{s + 0.4}{s + 4} = \frac{1}{10}\left(\frac{2.5s + 1}{0.25s + 1}\right)$$

Combining the transfer functions of the lag and lead portions of the compensator, we can obtain the transfer function $G_c(s)$ of the lag–lead compensator. Since we chose $K_c = 1$, we have

$$G_c(s) = \frac{s + 0.4}{s + 4}\frac{s + 0.2}{s + 0.02} = \frac{(2.5s + 1)(5s + 1)}{(0.25s + 1)(50s + 1)}$$

The Bode diagram of the lag–lead compensator $G_c(s)$ can be obtained by entering MATLAB Program 6-40 into the computer. The resulting plot is shown in Figure 6-64.

MATLAB Program 6–40

```
num = [1   0.6   0.08];
den = [1   4.02   0.08];
bode(num,den)
title('Bode Diagram of Lag-Lead Compensator')
```

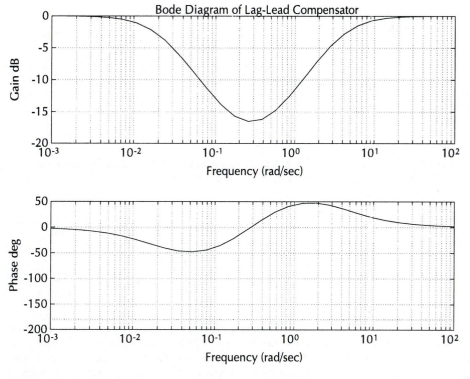

Figure 6-64

The open-loop transfer function of the compensated system is

$$G_c(s)G(s) = \frac{(s + 0.4)(s + 0.2)}{(s + 4)(s + 0.02)} \frac{40}{s(s + 1)(s + 4)}$$

$$= \frac{40s^2 + 24s + 3.2}{s^5 + 9.02s^4 + 24.18s^3 + 16.48s^2 + 0.32s}$$

The magnitude and phase-angle curves of the designed open-loop transfer function $G_c(s)G(s)$ are shown in the Bode diagram of Figure 6-65. This diagram is obtained using MATLAB Program 6-41. Note that the denominator polynomial den was obtained using the conv command, as follows:

```
a = [1   4.02   0.08];
b = [1   5   4   0];
conv(a,b)

ans =

    1.0000    9.0200    24.1800    16.4800    0.3200    0
```

```
MATLAB Program 6–41

num = [0  0  0  40  24  3.2];
den = [1  9.02  24.18  16.48  0.32  0];
bode(num,den)
title('Bode Diagram of Gc(s)G(s)')
```

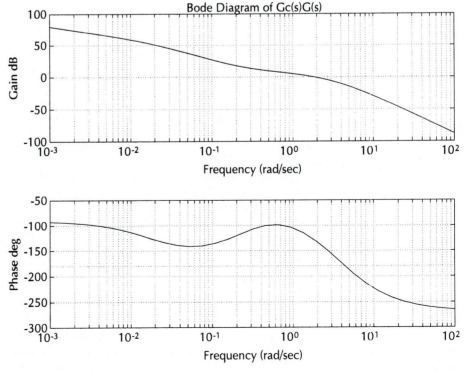

Figure 6-65

From Figure 6-65, we see that the actual gain crossover frequency is slightly shifted from 2 rad/sec to a lower value. The actual gain crossover frequency can be found by plotting the Bode diagram in the region $1 \le \omega \le 10$. It is found to be $\omega = 1.86$ rad/sec. [Such a small shift of the gain crossover frequency from the assumed gain crossover frequency (2 rad/sec in this case) always occurs in the present method of design.]

MATLAB Program 6-42 will draw the Nyquist plot on a polar plane. The resulting polar plot is shown in Figure 6-66.

MATLAB Program 6–42

```
num = [0  0  0  40  24  3.2];
den = [1  9.02  24.18  16.48  0.32  0];
w = 0.1:0.01:1.86;
v = [-2  2  -2  2];
axis(v); axis ('square')
[re,im,w] = nyquist(num,den,w);
z = re+i*im;
r = abs(z);
theta = angle(z);
polar(theta,r)
grid
title('Check of Phase Margin');
text(-1.75,1.8,'Nyquist plot')
text(-3,1.5,'Phase margin')
text(-2.9,1.6,'is 50 degrees.')

% ***** Restore normal graphics perspective *****

axis ('normal')
```

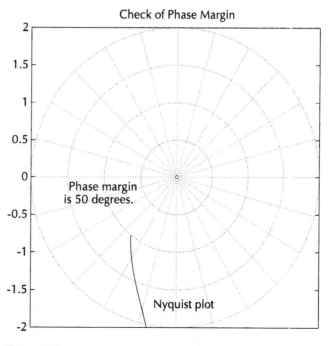

Figure 6-66

Since the phase margin of the compensated system is 50°, the gain margin is 12.5 dB, and the static velocity error constant is 10 sec^{-1}, all the requirements are met.

Figure 6-67 shows the Nyquist plots of $G(j\omega)$ (uncompensated case) and $G_c(j\omega)G(j\omega)$ (compensated case). The MATLAB program to obtain Figure 6-67 is shown in MATLAB Program 6-43.

If it is desired to plot Bode diagrams of $G(j\omega)$, $G_c(j\omega)$, and $G_c(j\omega)G(j\omega)$ on the same graph, MATLAB Program 6-44 may be used. Figure 6-68 shows the plots produced by this MATLAB program.

We shall next investigate the transient response characteristics of the designed system.

Unit-step response   Noting that

$$G_c(s)G(s) = \frac{40(s + 0.4)(s + 0.2)}{(s + 4)(s + 0.02)s(s + 1)(s + 4)}$$

we have

$$\frac{C(s)}{R(s)} = \frac{G_c(s)G(s)}{1 + G_c(s)G(s)}$$

$$= \frac{40(s + 0.4)(s + 0.2)}{(s + 4)(s + 0.02)s(s + 1)(s + 4) + 40(s + 0.4)(s + 0.2)}$$

To determine the denominator polynomial with MATLAB, we may proceed as follows. Define

$$a(s) = (s + 4)(s + 0.02) = s^2 + 4.02s + 0.08$$

$$b(s) = s(s + 1)(s + 4) = s^3 + 5s^2 + 4s$$

$$c(s) = 40(s + 0.4)(s + 0.2) = 40s^2 + 24s + 3.2$$

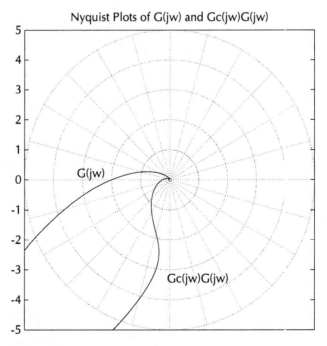

Figure 6-67

```
MATLAB Program 6–43

num1 = [0   0   0   40];
den1 = [1   5   4   0];
num2 = [0   0   0   40   24   3.2];
den2 = [1   9.02   24.18   16.48   0.32   0];
v = [-5   5   -5   5];
axis(v); axis ('square')
[re1,im1,w] = nyquist(num1,den1);


Warning: Divide by zero


z1 = re1+i*im1;
r1 = abs(z1);
theta1 = angle(z1);
polar(theta1,r1)
grid
hold


Current plot held


[re2,im2,w] = nyquist(num2,den2);


Warning: Divide by zero


z2 = re2+i*im2;
r2 = abs(z2);
theta2 = angle(z2);
polar(theta2,r2)
title('Nyquist Plots of G(jw) and Gc(jw)G(jw)');
text(3.14,3.2,'G(jw)')
text(-1.6,3.5,'Gc(jw)G(jw)')


hold


Current plot released


% ***** Restore normal graphics perspective *****


axis ('normal')
```

Then we have

$$a = [1 \quad 4.02 \quad 0.08]$$
$$b = [1 \quad 5 \quad 4 \quad 0]$$
$$c = [40 \quad 24 \quad 3.2]$$

MATLAB Program 6–44

```
% ---------- Bode diagrams ----------

% ***** In this program we plot Bode diagrams of G(w), Gc(w), and
% Gc(w)G(w) *****

num = [0   0   0   40];
den = [1   5   4   0];
numc = [1   0.6   0.08];
denc = [1   4.02   0.08];
w = logspace(-3,2,100);
[mag,phase,w] = bode(num,den,w);
magdB = 20*log10(mag);
[magc,phasec,w] = bode(numc,denc,w);
magcdB = 20*log10(magc);

% ***** Define the magnitude of Gc(w)G(w) in decibels as mgdB.
% mgdB is given by mgdB = magdB + magcdB *****

mgdB = magdB + magcdB;

% ***** We shall first plot magnitude curves *****

semilogx(w,magdB,'o',w,magdB,'-',w,magcdB,'x',w,magcdB,'-',...
  w,mgdB,'--')
grid
title('Bode Diagrams of G(w), Gc(w), and Gc(w)G(w)')
xlabel('Frequency (rad/sec)')
ylabel('Gain dB')
text(0.1,40,'G(w)')
text(0.1,-25,'Gc(w)')
text(0.03,12,'Gc(w)G(w)')

% ***** We shall next plot phase-angle curves *****

% ***** Define the phase angle of Gc(w)G(w) as pha.  pha is
% given by pha = phase + phasec *****

pha = phase + phasec;

% ***** Draw a line at -180 degrees by entering the following
% statement *****

ph180 = -180*ones(1,100);

% ***** Enter the following plot command *****

semilogx(w,phase,'o',w,phase,'-',w,phasec,'x',w,phasec,'-',...
  w,pha,'--',w,ph180,'-')
grid
xlabel('Frequency (rad/sec)')
```

```
ylabel('Phase deg')
text(0.01,-85,'G(w)')
text(0.01,-20,'Gc(w)')
text(0.01,-160,'Gc(w)G(w)')
```

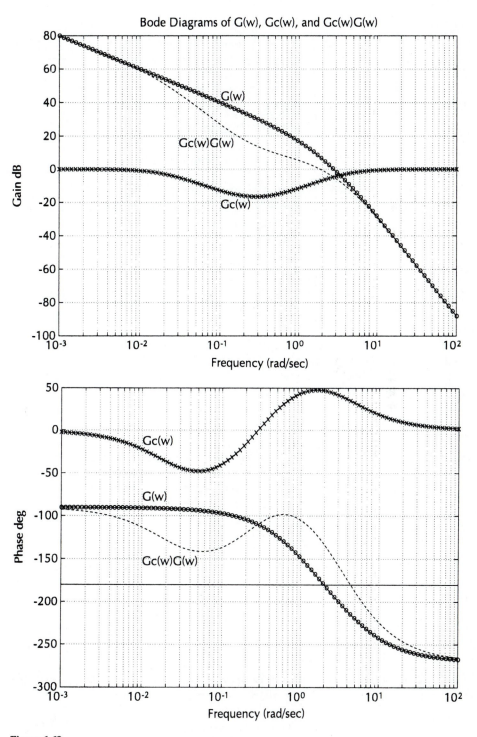

Figure 6-68

Using the following MATLAB program, we obtain the denominator polynomial.

```
a = [1   4.02   0.08];
b = [1   5   4   0];
c = [40   24   3.2];
p = [conv(a,b)] + [0   0   0   c]

p =

     1.0000    9.0200    24.1800    56.4800    24.3200    3.2000
```

```
MATLAB Program 6–45

% ---------- Unit-step response ----------

num = [0   0   0   40   24   3.2];
den = [1   9.02   24.18   56.48   24.32   3.2];
t = 0:0.2:40;
v = [0   40   0   1.4];
axis(v);
step(num,den,t)
grid
title('Unit-Step Response of Designed System')
```

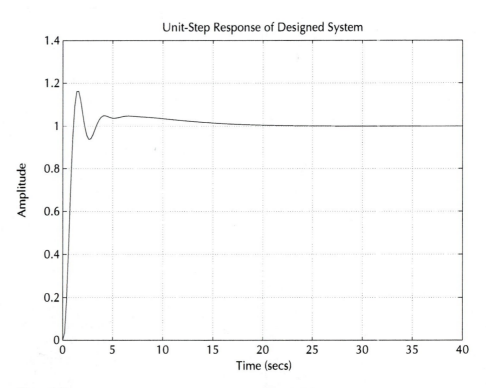

Figure 6-69

To obtain the unit-step response, we may use MATLAB Program 6-45, which produces the unit-step response curve shown in Figure 6-69.

Unit-ramp response The unit-ramp response of this system may be obtained by entering MATLAB Program 6-46 into the computer. Here we converted the unit-ramp response of $G_cG/(1 + G_cG)$ into the unit-step response of $G_cG/[s(1 + G_cG)]$. The unit-ramp response curve obtained using this program is shown in Figure 6-70.

MATLAB Program 6–46

```
% ---------- Unit-ramp response ----------

num = [0  0  0  0  40  24  3.2];
den = [1  9.02  24.18  56.48  24.32  3.2  0];
t = 0:0.2:20;
c = step(num,den,t);
plot(t,c,t,t,'--')
grid
title('Unit-Ramp Response of Designed System')
xlabel('Time (secs)')
ylabel('Amplitude')
```

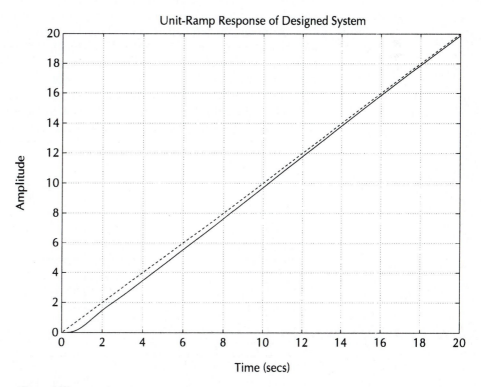

Figure 6-70

6-6 FREQUENCY RESPONSE OF DISCRETE-TIME CONTROL SYSTEMS

The z transformation maps the primary and complementary strips of the left half of the s plane into the unit circle in the z plane. Since conventional frequency-response methods deal with the entire left half-plane, they do not apply to the z plane.

The difficulty, however, can be overcome by transforming the pulse transfer function in the z plane into that in the w plane. The transformation, commonly called the w transformation, a bilinear transformation, is defined by

$$z = \frac{1 + (T/2)w}{1 - (T/2)w} \qquad (6\text{-}15)$$

where T is the sampling period involved in the discrete-time control system under consideration. By converting a given pulse transfer function in the z plane into a rational function of w, the frequency-response methods can be extended to discrete-time control systems. By solving Eq. (6-15) for w, we obtain the inverse relationship

$$w = \frac{2}{T} \frac{z - 1}{z + 1} \qquad (6\text{-}16)$$

Through the z transformation and the w transformation, the primary strip of the left half of the s plane is first mapped into the inside of the unit circle in the z plane and then mapped into the entire left half of the w plane. The two mapping processes are depicted in Figure 6-71. (Note that in the s plane we consider only the primary strip.) Notice that the origin of the z plane is mapped into the point $w = -2/T$ in the w plane. Notice also that, as s varies from 0 to $j\omega_s/2$ along the $j\omega$ axis in the s plane, z varies from 1 to -1 along the unit circle in the z plane, and w varies from 0 to ∞ along the imaginary axis in the w plane.

Although the left half of the w plane corresponds to the left half of the s plane, and the imaginary axis of the w plane corresponds to the imaginary axis of the s plane, there are differences between the two planes. The chief difference is that the behavior in the s plane over the frequency range $-\frac{1}{2}\omega_s \le \omega \le \frac{1}{2}\omega_s$ maps to the range $-\infty < \nu < \infty$, where ν is the fictitious frequency in the w plane.

Once the pulse transfer function $G(z)$ is transformed into $G(w)$ by means of the w transformation, it may be treated as a conventional transfer function in w. By

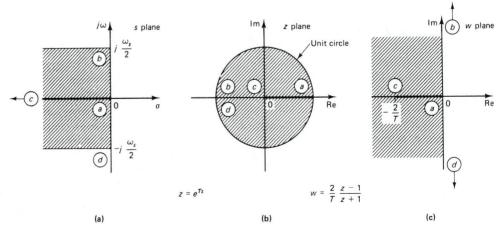

(a)   (b)   (c)

Figure 6-71

replacing w by $j\nu$, conventional frequency-response techniques may be used to draw the Bode diagram for the transfer function in w. Since $G(w)$ is a rational function of w, the Nyquist stability criterion can be applied to $G(w)$. Thus the concepts of the phase margin and gain margin apply to $G(w)$.

Although the w plane resembles the s plane geometrically, the frequency axis in the w plane is distorted. The fictitious frequency ν and the actual frequency ω are related as follows:

$$\left. w \right|_{w=j\nu} = j\nu = \frac{2}{T}\frac{z-1}{z+1}\bigg|_{z=e^{j\omega T}} = \frac{2}{T}\frac{e^{j\omega T}-1}{e^{j\omega T}+1}$$

$$= \frac{2}{T}\frac{e^{j(1/2)\omega T}-e^{-j(1/2)\omega T}}{e^{j(1/2)\omega T}+e^{-j(1/2)\omega T}} = \frac{2}{T}j\tan\frac{\omega T}{2}$$

or

$$\nu = \frac{2}{T}\tan\frac{\omega T}{2} \tag{6-17}$$

Equation (6-17) gives the relationship between the actual frequency ω and the fictitious frequency ν. Note that, as the actual frequency ω moves from $-\frac{1}{2}\omega_s$ to 0, the fictitious frequency ν moves from $-\infty$ to 0, and as ω moves from 0 to $\frac{1}{2}\omega_s$, ν moves from 0 to ∞.

Referring to Eq. (6-17), the actual frequency ω can be translated into the fictitious frequency ν. For example, if the bandwidth is specified as ω_b, then the corresponding bandwidth in the w plane is $(2/T)\tan(\omega_b T/2)$. Figure 6-72 shows the relationship between the fictitious frequency ν times $\frac{1}{2}T$ and the actual frequency ω for the frequency range between 0 and $\frac{1}{2}\omega_s$.

Notice in Eq. (6-17) that if ωT is small then

$$\nu \doteq \omega$$

This means that for small ωT the transfer functions $G(s)$ and $G(w)$ resemble each other. Note that this is the direct result of the inclusion of the scale factor $2/T$ in

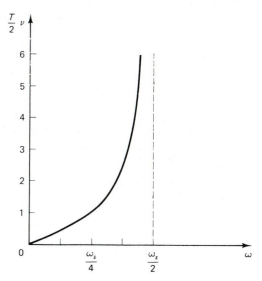

Figure 6-72

Eq. (6-16). The presence of this scale factor in the transformation enables us to maintain the same error constants before and after the w transformation. (This means that the transfer function in the w plane will approach that in the s plane as T approaches zero. See Example 6-30.)

Some remarks concerning frequency-response tests on discrete-time systems

In performing frequency-response tests on a discrete-time system, it is important that the system have a low-pass filter before the sampler so that sidebands are filtered out. Then the response of the linear time-invariant system to a sinusoidal input preserves the frequency and modifies only the amplitude and phase of the input signal. Thus the amplitude and phase are the only two quantities that must be dealt with.

EXAMPLE 6-30

Consider the transfer-function system shown in Figure 6-73. The sampling period T is assumed to be 0.1 sec. Obtain $G(w)$.

The z transform of $G(s)$ is

$$G(z) = Z\left[\frac{1 - e^{-Ts}}{s}\frac{10}{s + 10}\right]$$

$$= (1 - z^{-1})Z\left[\frac{10}{s(s + 10)}\right]$$

$$= \frac{0.6321}{z - 0.3679}$$

By use of the bilinear transformation given by Eq. (6-15), or

$$z = \frac{1 + (T/2)w}{1 - (T/2)w} = \frac{1 + 0.05w}{1 - 0.05w}$$

$G(z)$ can be transformed into $G(w)$ as follows:

$$G(w) = \frac{0.6321}{\dfrac{1 + 0.05w}{1 - 0.05w} - 0.3679} = \frac{0.6321(1 - 0.05w)}{0.6321 + 0.06840w}$$

$$= 9.241\frac{1 - 0.05w}{w + 9.241}$$

Notice that the location of the pole of the plant is $s = -10$ and that of the pole in the w plane is $w = -9.241$. The gain value in the s plane is 10 and that in the w plane is 9.241. (Thus both the pole locations and the gain values are similar in the s plane and the w plane.) However, $G(w)$ has a zero at $w = 2/T = 20$, although the plant does not have any zero. As

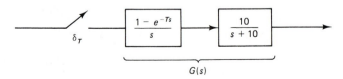

Figure 6-73

the sampling period T becomes smaller, the w plane zero at $w = 2/T$ approaches infinity in the right half of the w plane. Note that we have

$$\lim_{w \to 0} G(w) = \lim_{s \to 0} \frac{10}{s + 10}$$

This fact is very useful in checking the numerical calculations when transforming $G(s)$ into $G(w)$.

G(w) is a nonminimum-phase transfer function

As seen in Example 6-30, in general, one or more zeros of $G(w)$ lie in the right half of the w plane. The presence of a zero or zeros in the right half of the w plane means that $G(w)$ is a nonminimum-phase transfer function. Therefore, we must be careful in drawing the phase-angle curve in the Bode diagram.

Some remarks on the coefficient quantization problem

From the viewpoint of microprocessor implementation of the phase-lead, phase-lag, and phase lag–lead compensators, phase-lead compensators present no coefficient quantization problem, because the locations of poles and zeros are widely separated. However, in the case of phase-lag compensators and phase lag–lead compensators, the phase-lag network presents a coefficient quantization problem because the locations of poles and zeros are close to each other. (They are near the point $z = 1$.)

Since the filter coefficients must be realized by binary words that use limited numbers of bits, if the number of bits employed is insufficient, the pole and zero locations of the filter may not be realized exactly as desired, and the resulting filter will not behave as expected.

Since small deviations in the pole and zero locations from the desired locations can have significant effects on the frequency-response characteristics of the compensator, the digital version of the compensator may not perform as expected. To minimize the effect of the coefficient quantization problem, it is necessary to structure the filter so that it is least subject to coefficient inaccuracies due to quantization.

Because the sensitivity of the roots of polynomials to the parameter variations becomes severe as the order of the polynomial increases, direct realization of a higher-order filter is not desirable. It is preferable to place lower-order elements in cascade or in parallel. As a matter of course, from the outset, if we choose poles and zeros of the digital compensator from allowable discrete points, then the coefficient quantization problem can be avoided. (The important thing to remember is that the poles and zeros of the filter in the z plane must lie on a finite number of allowable discrete points.)

Transformation from G(s) to G(z)

Transforming a continuous-time transfer function $G(s)$ to a discrete-time transfer function (pulse transfer function) $G(z)$ may be performed by the following procedure: First define

$$G(s) = \frac{\text{num}}{\text{den}}$$

Then use the following commands:

$$[A,B,C,D] = \text{tf2ss(num,den)}$$
$$[G,H] = \text{c2d(A,B,Ts)}$$
$$[\text{numz, denz}] = \text{ss2tf(G,H,C,D)}$$

where Ts is the sampling period in seconds. Row vectors numz and denz specify the coefficients of the numerator and denominator of $G(z)$ (in descending powers of z). Thus

$$G(z) = \frac{numz}{denz}$$

See Examples 6-31 and 6-32 for details.

EXAMPLE 6-31

Assuming the sampling period T to be 0.1 sec, transform

$$G(s) = \frac{10}{s + 10}$$

into $G(z)$.

MATLAB Program 6-47 produces $G(z)$, the z transform of $G(s)$ preceded by the zero-order hold. Thus we obtain

$$G(z) = \frac{0.6321}{z - 0.3679}$$

```
MATLAB Program 6–47

% ---------- Transforming G(s) into G(z) ----------

% ***** Enter the numerator and denominator of G(s) *****

num = [0   10];
den = [1   10];

% ***** The numerator (numz) and denominator (denz) of G(z)
% can be obtained by entering the following commands *****

[A,B,C,D] = tf2ss(num,den);
[G,H] = c2d(A,B,0.1);
[numz,denz] = ss2tf(G,H,C,D)

numz =

          0        0.6321


denz =

    1.0000     -0.3679
```

which is correct. The intermediate outputs, such as matrices A, B, C, D, G, and H, are shown in the following:

```
num = [0   10];
den = [1   10];
[A,B,C,D] = tf2ss(num,den)

A =

      -10


B =

      1


C =

      10


D =

      0

[G,H] = c2d(A,B,0.1)

G =

      0.3679


H =

      0.0632
```

EXAMPLE 6-32

Assuming the sampling period T to be 0.2 sec, transform

$$G(s) = \frac{1}{s(s + 1)}$$

into $G(z)$.

MATLAB Program 6-48 produces $G(z)$. Row vectors numz and denz give the coefficients of the numerator polynomial and denominator polynomial of $G(z)$ as follows:

$$G(z) = \frac{0.01873z + 0.01752}{z^2 - 1.8187z + 0.8187}$$

MATLAB Program 6–48

% ---------- Transforming G(s) into G(z) ----------

% ***** Enter the numerator and denominator of G(s) *****

num = [0   0   1];
den = [1   1   0];

% ***** The numerator (numz) and denominator (denz) of G(z)
% can be obtained by entering the following commands *****

[A,B,C,D] = tf2ss(num,den);
[G,H] = c2d(A,B,0.2);
[numz,denz] = ss2tf(G,H,C,D)

numz =

              0   0.0187   0.0175

denz =

       1.0000   -1.8187   0.8187

% ***** To increase accuracy we may use 'format long' *****

format long
[numz,denz] = ss2tf(G,H,C,D)

numz =

                    0   0.01873075307798   0.01752309630642

denz =

       1.00000000000000   -1.81873075307798   0.81873075307798

% ***** Thus we obtained G(z) as follows
%   G(z) = (0.01873z + 0.01752)/(z^2 - 1.8187z + 0.8187) *****

% ***** Restore normal format *****

format short

Bilinear transformation

The bilinear transformation is a mathematical mapping of variables. The command bilinear transforms $G(w)$ to $G(z)$ such that

$$G(z) = G(w)\Big|_{w = 2f_s \frac{z-1}{z+1}}$$

where $f_s = 1/T$. (T is the sampling period in seconds.) Define

$$G(w) = \frac{\text{num}}{\text{den}}$$

Then the command

$$[\text{numz,denz}] = \text{bilinear(num,den,fs)}$$

where fs = 1/T = sampling frequency in hertz, will produce

$$G(z) = \frac{\text{numz}}{\text{denz}}$$

Note that the design of digital controllers based on the Bode-diagram approach involves two different bilinear transformations. One is the transformation from $G(z)$ to $G(w)$ with the bilinear transformation defined by

$$z = \frac{1 + \dfrac{T}{2}w}{1 - \dfrac{T}{2}w} \tag{6-18}$$

where T is the sampling period involved in the discrete-time control system. Once the plant transfer function is transformed into $G(w)$, we may design the digital controller $G_c(w)$ in the w plane.

The other transformation involved in the design process is to transform $G_c(w)$ back to $G_c(z)$. Transformation from the w plane to the z plane is performed with the following transformation:

$$w = \frac{2}{T}\frac{z-1}{z+1} = 2f_s\frac{z-1}{z+1} \tag{6-19}$$

MATLAB performs the bilinear transformation defined by Eq. (6-19). Therefore, the command bilinear can be used to transform $G(w)$ into $G(z)$. However, this command cannot be used to transform $G(z)$ into $G(w)$.

It is, however, possible to utilize the command bilinear to transform $G(z)$ to $G(w)$ with certain modifications in the command statements. See Examples 6-33 and 6-34 for details.

EXAMPLE 6-33

Transform

$$G(z) = \frac{0.6321}{z - 0.3679}$$

into $G(w)$, where the transformation between z and w is given by

$$z = \frac{1 + \dfrac{T}{2}w}{1 - \dfrac{T}{2}w} = \frac{1 + 0.05w}{1 - 0.05w} \tag{6-20}$$

where $T = 0.1$ sec.

Since the command bilinear uses the transformation

$$z = 2f_s \frac{v - 1}{v + 1}$$

we first set $f_s = 0.5$ so that

$$z = \frac{v - 1}{v + 1}$$

Then transform v to w by the equation

$$v = -0.05w$$

Then we have

$$z = \frac{-0.05w - 1}{-0.05w + 1} = \frac{-(1 + 0.05w)}{1 - 0.05w}$$

or

$$-z = \frac{1 + 0.05w}{1 - 0.05w} \qquad\qquad (6\text{-}21)$$

Notice that the right side of Eq. (6-21) is the same as that of Eq. (6-20).

From the above analysis, to transform $G(z)$ into $G(w)$ using the *bilinear* command, we may proceed as follows:

1. Replace z by $-z$ in $G(z)$ and define

$$\text{num} = [0 \quad 0.6321];$$
$$\text{den} = [-1 \quad -0.3679];$$

2. Use the following *bilinear* command:

$$[\text{numv,denv}] = \text{bilinear(num,den,fs)}$$

where fs = 0.5. Note that numv and denv can be obtained as shown in the following MATLAB output.

```
num = [0   0.6321];
den = [−1   −0.3679];
[numv,denv] = bilinear(num,den,0.5)

numv =

   −0.4621      −0.4621


denv =

    1.0000      −0.4621
```

Hence

$$G(v) = \frac{\text{numv}}{\text{denv}} = \frac{-0.4621v - 0.4621}{v - 0.4621}$$

3. Substitute $v = -0.05w$ into the numerator and denominator of $G(v)$. Then we get

$$G(w) = \frac{-0.4621(-0.05w) - 0.4621}{-0.05w - 0.4621}$$

This operation of substituting $v = -0.05w$ into the numerator and denominator of $G(v)$ can be done by MATLAB as follows: First note that

$$\text{numerator in } w = -0.4621(-0.05w) - 0.4621$$

Thus

$$\text{numw} = [-0.4621 \quad -0.4621]. *[-0.05 \quad 1] \qquad (6\text{-}22)$$

Here the operation '.∗' means that this multiplication is done entrywise. Similarly,

$$\text{denominator in } w = -0.05w - 0.4621$$

from which we get

$$\text{denw} = [1 \quad -0.4621]. *[-0.05 \quad 1] \qquad (6\text{-}23)$$

Equations (6-22) and (6-23) can be written as

$$\text{numw} = [\text{numv}]. *[-0.05 \quad 1]$$
$$\text{denw} = [\text{denv}]. *[-0.05 \quad 1]$$

Entering these commands into the computer, we obtain $G(w)$. See the following MATLAB output.

```
numw = [numv]. *[-0.05   1], denw = [denv]. *[-0.05   1]

numw =

    0.0231    -0.4621


denw =

   -0.0500    -0.4621
```

The first term in numw is printed as 0.0231. To check the accuracy of this printed number, let us print the number in *format long*.

```
format long
numw = [numv]. *[-0.05   1], denw = [denv]. *[-0.05   1]

numw =

    0.02310475911982    -0.46209518239637


denw =

   -0.05000000000000    -0.46209518239637
```

From this *format long* output, we obtain

$$G(w) = \frac{0.023105w - 0.462095}{-0.05w - 0.462095} \tag{6-24}$$

Although this expression is correct, it is convenient if the coefficient of the highest-degree term in w of the denominator be unity, or

$$G(w) = \frac{-0.4621w + 9.2419}{w + 9.2419}$$

This can be done by multiplying -20 to the numerator and denominator of $G(w)$ given by Eq. (6-24). Hence, if we enter the program

$$\text{numw} = [\text{numv}].*[1 \quad -20]$$
$$\text{denw} = [\text{denv}].*[1 \quad -20]$$

then the output of the computer will have the desired form, as seen from the following MATLAB output.

```
numw = [numv].*[1   −20], denw = [denv].*[1   −20]

numw =

    −0.4621      9.2419


denw =

     1.0000      9.2419
```

MATLAB Program 6-49 shows a series of commands to transform $G(z)$ into $G(w)$.

```
MATLAB Program 6–49

% ---------- Transforming G(z) into G(w) ----------

% ***** First substitute -z for z in pulse transfer function G(z)
% and enter numerator and denominator *****

num = [0  0.6321];
den = [-1  -0.3679];

% ***** Then enter command 'bilinear' with fs = 0.5 *****

[numv,denv] = bilinear(num,den,0.5);

% ***** Transform G(v) into G(w) where v and w are related by
% v = -0.05w.  This can be done by entering the following
% commands *****
```

```
numw = [numv].*[1   -20], denw = [denv].*[1   -20]

numw =

    -0.4621     9.2419


denw =

     1.0000     9.2419

% ***** Thus we obtained G(w) as follows
%   G(w) = (-0.4621w + 9.2419)/(w + 9.2419) *****
```

EXAMPLE 6-34

Transform

$$G(z) = \frac{0.01873z + 0.01752}{z^2 - 1.8187z + 0.8187}$$

into $G(w)$, where the transformation between z and w is given by

$$z = \frac{1 + \dfrac{T}{2}w}{1 - \dfrac{T}{2}w} = \frac{1 + 0.1w}{1 - 0.1w}$$

where $T = 0.2$ sec.

To get $G(w)$, we may proceed as follows:

1. Replace z by $-z$ in $G(z)$ and define

$$\text{num} = [0 \quad -0.01873 \quad 0.01752];$$
$$\text{den} = [1 \quad 1.8187 \quad 0.8187];$$

2. Use the following *bilinear* command:

$$[\text{numv, denv}] = \text{bilinear(num,den,0.5)}$$

The MATLAB output is as follows:

```
[numv,denv] = bilinear(num,den,0.5)

numv =

    -0.0003     0.0096     0.0100


denv =

     1.0000    -0.0997     0.0000
```

3. To convert $G(v)$ into $G(w)$, note that v and w are related by $v = -0.1w$. Since

$$\text{numerator in } v = -0.0003v^2 + 0.0096v + 0.0100$$

we have

$$\text{numerator in } w = -0.0003(-0.1w)^2 + 0.0096(-0.1w) + 0.0100$$

Hence

$$\text{numw} = [-0.0003 \quad 0.0096 \quad 0.0100].*[(-0.1)^\wedge 2 \quad -0.1 \quad 1]$$

Similarly,

$$\text{denominator in } v = v^2 - 0.0997v$$

and

$$\text{denominator in } w = (-0.1w)^2 - 0.0997(-0.1w)$$

Hence

$$\text{denw} = [1 \quad -0.0997 \quad 0].*[(-0.1)^\wedge 2 \quad -0.1 \quad 1]$$

To make the coefficient of the highest-power term in the denominator unity, multiply 100 to

$$[(-0.1)^\wedge 2 \quad -0.1 \quad 1]$$

and write numw and denw as follows:

$$\text{numw} = [\text{numv}].*[1 \quad -10 \quad 100];$$
$$\text{denw} = [\text{denv}].*[1 \quad -10 \quad 100]$$

Based on the discussions above, we may enter MATLAB Program 6-50 to obtain $G(w)$.

The transfer function $G(w)$ obtained by use of MATLAB Program 6-50 can be written as follows:

$$G(w) = \frac{-0.000333w^2 - 0.09633w + 0.9966}{w^2 + 0.9969w}$$

$$\doteq \frac{\left(1 + \dfrac{w}{300}\right)\left(1 - \dfrac{w}{10}\right)}{w(w + 1)} \tag{6-25}$$

Note that $G(z)$ in this example was obtained from the following $G(s)$:

$$G(s) = \frac{1}{s(s + 1)} \tag{6-26}$$

(See Example 6-32.) Comparing Eqs. (6-25) and (6-26), the transfer functions $G(w)$ and $G(s)$ are similar in that both have the same dc gain and have the poles at the same locations. The difference appears in the locations of the zeros. $G(s)$ has no finite zeros, while $G(w)$ has two zeros, one at $w = -300$ (which is located very far from the origin so that this zero is insignificant in the transient response) and the other located in the right half-plane at $w = 10$.

MATLAB Program 6–50

```
% ---------- Transforming G(z) into G(w) ----------

% ***** First substitute -z for z in pulse transfer function G(z)
% and enter numerator and denominator *****

num = [0  -0.01873  0.01752];
den = [1   1.8187   0.8187];

% ***** Then enter command 'bilinear' with fs = 0.5 *****

[numv,denv] = bilinear(num,den,0.5);

% ***** Transform G(v) into G(w) where v and w are related by
% v = -0.1w.  This can be done by entering the following
% commands *****

numw = [numv].*[1  -10  100], denw = [denv].*[1  -10  100]

numw =

   -0.0003     -0.0963      0.9966


denw =

    1.0000      0.9969      0.0000

% ***** To increase accuaracy, we may use 'format long' *****

format long
numw = [numv].*[1  -10  100], denw = [denv].*[1  -10  100]

numw =

    -0.00033265519327     -0.09633254522461      0.99659097157309


denw =

     1.00000000000000      0.99686589322043      0.00000000000000

% ***** Thus we obtained G(w) as follows
%   G(w) = (-0.000333w^2 - 0.09633w + 0.9966)/(w^2 + 0.9969w) *****

% ***** Restore normal format *****

format short
```

Therefore, $G(w)$ is a nonminimum-phase transfer function. Differences in the Bode diagram of $G(s)$ and that of $G(w)$ may be seen from Figure 6-74, which is obtained by use of MATLAB Program 6-51.

Notice that the magnitude curves are about the same for both $G(s)$ and $G(w)$ for $0 < \omega < 6$ rad/sec. Separation of magnitude curves occurs around $\omega = 6$ rad/sec. The mag-

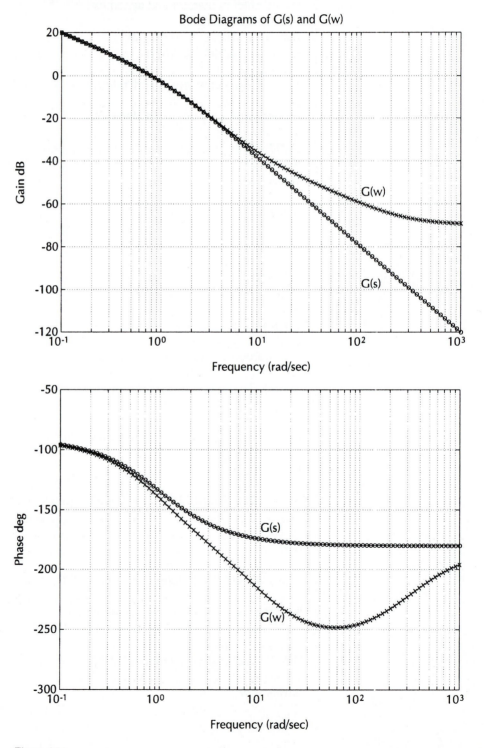

Figure 6-74

MATLAB Program 6–51

```
% ---------- Bode diagrams ----------

% ***** We shall plot Bode diagrams of G(s) and G(w) *****

nums = [0   0   1];
dens = [1   1   0];
numw = [-0.000333   -0.09633   0.9966];
denw = [1   0.9969   0];
w = logspace(-1,3,100);
[mags,phases,w] = bode(nums,dens,w);
magsdB = 20*log10(mags);
[magw,phasew,w] = bode(numw,denw,w);
magwdB = 20*log10(magw);

% ***** We shall first plot magnitude curves *****

semilogx(w,magsdB,'o',w,magsdB,'-')
hold

Current plot held

semilogx(w,magwdB,'x',w,magwdB,'-')
grid
title('Bode Diagrams of G(s) and G(w)')
xlabel('Frequency (rad/sec)')
ylabel('Gain dB')
text(100,-100,'G(s)')
text(100,-57,'G(w)')
hold

Current plot released

% ***** We shall next plot phase-angle curves *****

% ***** We choose phase-angle range to be from -300
% degrees to -50 degrees.  This can be done by plotting
% invisible lines at -290 degrees and -60 degrees *****

pmax = -60*ones(1,100);
pmin = -290*ones(1,100);
semilogx(w,phases,'o',w,phases,'-',w,pmax,'--i',w,pmin,':i')
hold

Current plot held

semilogx(w,phasew,'x',w,phasew,'-')
grid
xlabel('Frequency (rad/sec)')
ylabel('Phase deg')
text(10,-170,'G(s)')
```

```
text(10,-245,'G(w)')

% ***** Remove hold on graphics *****

hold

Current plot released
```

nitude $|G(s)|$ approaches $-\infty$ dB as the frequency increases, while the magnitude $|G(w)|$ approaches a constant value at about -69.5 dB as the frequency increases. The phase curves are the same for $0 < \omega < 0.2$ and $10^4 < \omega < \infty$. For $0.2 < \omega < 10^4$, a significant difference appears because one is a minimum-phase system and the other is a nonminimum-phase system. [The angle contribution of the zero in the right-half w plane is negative (phase lag).]

EXAMPLE 6-35

Consider the digital control system shown in Figure 6-75. Design a digital controller in the w plane such that the phase margin is $50°$, the gain margin is at least 10 dB, and the static velocity error constant K_v is 2 sec^{-1}. Assume that the sampling period T is 0.2 sec.

The pulse transfer function $G(z)$ of the plant is

$$G(z) = Z\left[\frac{1 - e^{-0.2s}}{s}\frac{K}{s(s + 1)}\right]$$

$$= (1 - z^{-1})Z\left[\frac{K}{s^2(s + 1)}\right]$$

$$= \frac{K(0.01873z + 0.01752)}{z^2 - 1.8187z + 0.8187}$$

This result (when $K = 1$) was obtained in Example 6-32.

To apply the Bode-diagram approach to the design, we need to transform $G(z)$ into $G(w)$. The transformation from z to w is given by

$$z = \frac{1 + \frac{T}{2}w}{1 - \frac{T}{2}w} = \frac{1 + 0.1w}{1 - 0.1w}$$

Then $G(w)$ is given by

$$G(w) = \frac{K(0.01873z + 0.01752)}{z^2 - 1.8187z + 0.8187}\bigg|_{z = \frac{1 + 0.1w}{1 - 0.1w}}$$

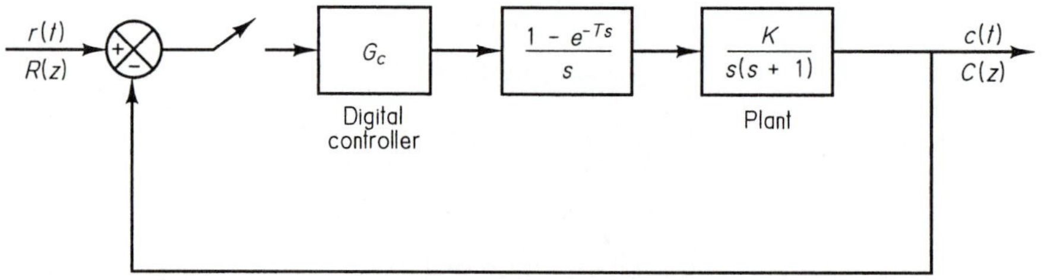

Figure 6-75

This transformation from $G(z)$ to $G(w)$ when $K = 1$ was carried out by MATLAB in Example 6-34. Referring to the result obtained there, we have

$$G(w) = \frac{K(-0.000333w^2 - 0.09633w + 0.9966)}{w^2 + 0.9969w}$$

$$\doteq \frac{K\left(1 + \dfrac{w}{300}\right)\left(1 - \dfrac{w}{10}\right)}{w(w + 1)}$$

The factored form of $G(w)$ tells us where the corner frequencies are located. Notice that one zero is located in the right-half w plane ($w = 10$). $G(w)$ is therefore a nonminimum-phase transfer function.

Now let us assume that the transfer function of the digital controller $G_c(w)$ has unity gain for the low-frequency range and has the following form:

$$G_c(w) = \frac{1 + \tau w}{1 + \alpha \tau w}$$

(Note that this is one of the simplest forms for the digital controller transfer function. Other forms may be assumed as well.) The open-loop transfer function is

$$G_c(w)G(w) = \frac{1 + \tau w}{1 + \alpha \tau w} \frac{K(-0.000333w^2 - 0.09633w + 0.9966)}{w^2 + 0.9969w}$$

The static velocity error constant K_v is specified as 2 sec^{-1}. Hence

$$K_v = \lim_{w \to 0} wG_c(w)G(w) \doteq K = 2$$

The gain K is thus determined as 2, or

$$K = 2$$

Next, by setting $K = 2$, we shall plot the Bode diagram of $G(w)$:

$$G(w) = \frac{-0.000666w^2 - 0.19266w + 1.9932}{w^2 + 0.9969w}$$

MATLAB Program 6-52 may be used to produce the Bode diagram of $G(w)$ with $K = 2$.

Figure 6-76 shows the Bode diagram of $G(w)$ with $K = 2$. The phase margin may be read from the diagram as 30° and the gain margin as 14.5 dB.

The given specifications require, in addition to $K_v = 2$, the phase margin of 50° and a gain margin of at least 10 dB. Let us design a digital controller to satisfy these specifications. We shall use the conventional design technique as given next.

MATLAB Program 6–52

```
num = [-0.000666  -0.19266  1.9932];
den = [1  0.9969  0];
w = logspace(-1,3,100);
bode(num,den,w)
title('Bode Diagram of Plant G(w) with K = 2')
```

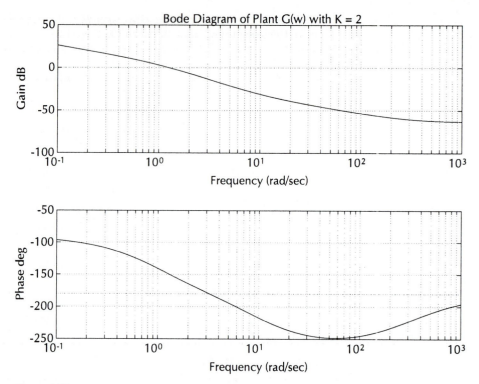

Figure 6-76

Design of lead compensator: Since the specification calls for a phase margin of 50°, the additional phase-lead angle necessary to satisfy this requirement is 20°. To achieve a phase margin of 50° without decreasing the value of K, the lead compensator must contribute the required phase-lead angle.

Noting that the addition of a lead compensator modifies the magnitude curve in the Bode diagram, the gain crossover frequency will be shifted to the right. Considering the shift of the gain crossover frequency, we may assume that ϕ_m, the maximum phase-lead angle required, is approximately 28°. (This means that 8° has been added to compensate for the shift in the gain crossover frequency.) Since

$$\sin \phi_m = \frac{1 - \alpha}{1 + \alpha}$$

$\phi_m = 28°$ corresponds to $\alpha = 0.361$.

Once the attenuation factor α has been determined on the basis of the required phase-lead angle, the next step is to determine the corner frequencies $\omega = 1/\tau$ and $\omega = 1/(\alpha\tau)$ of the lead compensator. To do so, we first note that the maximum phase-lead angle ϕ_m occurs at the geometric mean of the two corner frequencies, or $\omega = 1/(\sqrt{\alpha}\tau)$. The amount of the modification in the magnitude curve at $\omega = 1/(\sqrt{\alpha}\tau)$ due to the inclusion of the term $(1 + \tau w)/(1 + \alpha\tau w)$ is

$$\left| \frac{1 + \tau w}{1 + \alpha\tau w} \right|_{w = \frac{1}{\sqrt{\alpha}\tau}} = \frac{1}{\sqrt{\alpha}}$$

Next we find the frequency where the magnitude of the uncompensated system is equal to $-20 \log(1/\sqrt{\alpha})$. Note that

$$-20 \log \frac{1}{\sqrt{0.361}} = -20 \log 1.6643 = -4.425 \text{ dB}$$

To find the frequency point where the magnitude is −4.425 dB, we may plot the Bode diagram in the frequency range $1 \leq \omega \leq 10$ rad/sec. See MATLAB Program 6-53 and the resulting plot shown in Figure 6-77. From this diagram, we find that at $\omega = 1.7$ rad/sec the magnitude becomes approximately −4.4 dB.

We select this frequency to be the new gain crossover frequency ω_c. Noting that this frequency corresponds to $1/(\sqrt{\alpha}\tau)$, or

$$\omega_c = \frac{1}{\sqrt{\alpha}\tau} = 1.7$$

we obtain

$$\tau = \frac{1}{1.7\sqrt{\alpha}} = 0.9790$$

and

$$\alpha\tau = 0.3534$$

MATLAB Program 6–53

```
num = [-0.000666  -0.19266  1.9932];
den = [1  0.9969  0];
w = logspace(0,1,100);
bode(num,den,w)
title('Bode Diagram of Plant G(w) with K = 2')
```

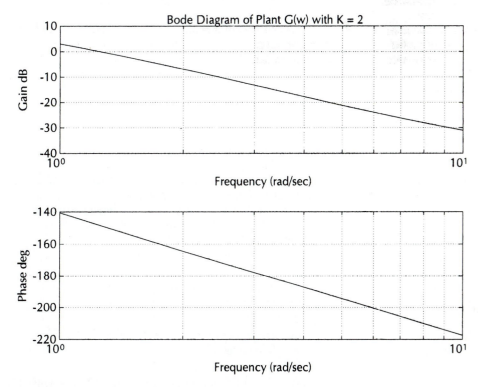

Figure 6-77

The lead compensator thus determined is

$$G_c(w) = \frac{1 + \tau w}{1 + \alpha \tau w} = \frac{1 + 0.9790w}{1 + 0.3534w} \tag{6-27}$$

The Bode diagram of this lead compensator is shown in Figure 6-78. It is obtained by use of MATLAB Program 6-54.

To plot Bode diagrams of $G(w)$, $G_c(w)$, and $G_c(w)G(w)$, MATLAB Program 6-55 may be used. Three magnitude curves are plotted on one graph and three phase-angle curves are plotted on another graph. These curves are shown in Figure 6-79.

From the magnitude and phase-angle curves of $G_c(w)G(w)$, we find that the phase margin is approximately 50° and the gain margin is approximately 14 dB.

Since the gain K is adjusted to satisfy the requirement on K_v, the compensated system satisfies all the requirements. Hence the digital controller $G_c(w)$ as designed is satisfactory. [If $G_c(w)G(w)$ did not satisfy all the requirements, it would be necessary to shift the corner frequencies of $G_c(w)$.]

Note that the solution to such a design problem is not unique. Many other $G_c(w)$'s will satisfy all the requirements.

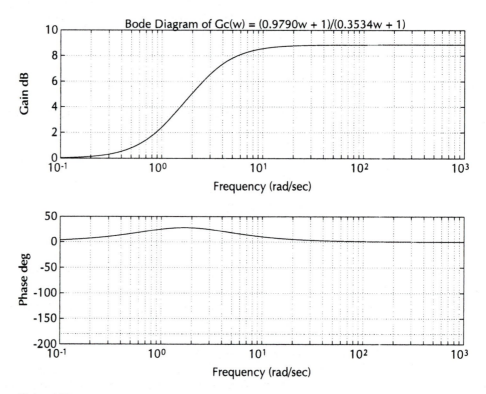

Figure 6-78

MATLAB Program 6–54

```
numc = [0.9790  1];
denc = [0.3534  1];
w = logspace(-1,3,100);
bode(numc,denc,w)
title('Bode Diagram of Gc(w) = (0.9790w + 1)/(0.3534w + 1)')
```

MATLAB Program 6–55

```
% ---------- Bode diagrams ----------

% ***** In this program we plot Bode diagrams of G(w), Gc(w), and
% Gc(w)G(w) *****

num = [-0.000666  -0.19266  1.9932];
den = [1   0.9969   0];
numc = [0.9790   1];
denc = [0.3534   1];
w = logspace(-1,3,100);
[mag,phase,w] = bode(num,den,w);
magdB = 20*log10(mag);
[magc,phasec,w] = bode(numc,denc,w);
magcdB = 20*log10(magc);

% ***** Define the magnitude of Gc(w)G(w) in decibels as mgdB.
% mgdB is given by mgdB = magdB + magcdB *****

mgdB = magdB + magcdB;

% ***** We shall first plot magnitude curves *****

semilogx(w,magdB,'o',w,magdB,'-',w,magcdB,'x',w,magcdB,'-',...
  w,mgdB,'--')
grid
title('Bode Diagrams of G(w), Gc(w), and Gc(w)G(w)')
xlabel('Frequency (rad/sec)')
ylabel('Gain dB')
text(10,-42,'G(w)')
text(10,10,'Gc(w)')
text(10,-20,'Gc(w)G(w)')

% ***** We shall next plot phase-angle curves *****

% ***** Define the phase-angle of Gc(w)G(w) as pha.  pha is
% given by pha = phase + phasec *****

pha = phase + phasec;

% ***** We choose phase-angle range to be from -300 degrees
% to +50 degrees.  This can be done by plotting invisible
% lines at -290 degrees and +40 degrees.  Also, we draw a
% line at -180 degrees *****

pmax = 40*ones(1,100);
pmin = -290*ones(1,100);
ph180 = -180*ones(1,100);

% ***** Enter the following plot command *****
```

```
semilogx(w,phase,'o',w,phase,'-',w,phasec,'x',w,phasec,'-',...
  w,pha,'--',w,pmax,'-i',w,pmin,'-i',w,ph180,'-')
grid
xlabel('Frequency (rad/sec)')
ylabel('Phase deg')
text(1,-177,'G(w)')
text(1,4,'Gc(w)')
text(1,-115,'Gc(w)G(w)')
```

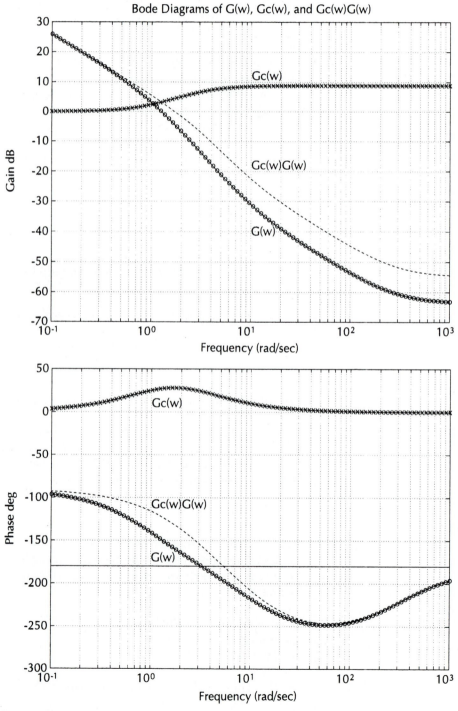

Figure 6-79

The controller transfer function given by Eq. (6-27) will now be transformed back to the z plane by use of the following bilinear transformation:

$$w = \frac{2}{T}\frac{z - 1}{z + 1} = 10\frac{z - 1}{z + 1}$$

The computation

$$G_c(z) = G_c(w)\Big|_{w = 10\frac{z-1}{z+1}} = \frac{1 + 0.9790w}{1 + 0.3534w}\Big|_{w = 10\frac{z-1}{z+1}}$$

can be easily handled by the following *bilinear* command:

$$[\text{numcz, dencz}] = \text{bilinear(numc,denc,fs)}$$

where fs in this case is

$$\text{fs} = \frac{1}{T} = \frac{1}{0.2} = 5$$

MATLAB Program 6-56 may be used to transform $G_c(w)$ into $G_c(z)$. The controller pulse transfer function $G_c(z)$ is now given by

$$G_c(z) = \frac{2.3798z - 1.9387}{z - 0.5589}$$

The open-loop pulse transfer function of the compensated system is

$$G_c(z)G(z) = \frac{2.3798z - 1.9387}{z - 0.5589}\frac{0.03746z + 0.03504}{z^2 - 1.8187z + 0.8187}$$

The multiplication of the two polynomials involved in both the numerator and denominator

---

MATLAB Program 6–56

```
% ---------- Transformation from Gc(w) to Gc(z) ----------

numc = [0.9790  1];
denc = [0.3534  1];
[numcz,dencz] = bilinear(numc,denc,5)

numcz =

    2.3798    -1.9387


dencz =

    1.0000    -0.5589
```

of this function can be easily done by use of the *convolution* command in MATLAB, as follows:

```
a = [2.3798    −1.9387];
b = [0.03746    0.03504];
p = conv(a,b)

p =

      0.0891        0.0108       −0.0679

c = [1   −0.5589];
d = [1   −1.8187   0.8187];
q = conv(c,d)

q =

      1.0000      −2.3776       1.8352       −0.4576
```

Hence

$$G_c(z)G(z) = \frac{0.0891z^2 + 0.0108z - 0.0679}{z^3 - 2.3776z^2 + 1.8352z - 0.4576}$$

The closed-loop pulse transfer function of the designed system is

$$\frac{C(z)}{R(z)} = \frac{0.0891z^2 + 0.0108z - 0.0679}{z^3 - 2.2885z^2 + 1.8460z - 0.5255}$$

The zeros and poles of the closed-loop pulse transfer function can be obtained as shown in the following MATLAB output.

```
num = [0   0.0891   0.0108   −0.0679];
den = [1   −2.2885   1.8460   −0.5255];

roots(num)

ans =

   −0.9357
    0.8145

roots(den)

ans =

    0.8126
    0.7379 + 0.3196i
    0.7379 − 0.3196i
```

Notice that the closed-loop pulse transfer function involves two zeros located at $z = -0.9357$ and $z = 0.8145$. The zero at $z = 0.8145$ almost cancels with the closed-loop pole at $z = 0.8126$. The effect of another zero at $z = -0.9357$ on the transient and frequency responses is very small, since it is located on the negative real axis of the z plane between 0 and -1 and is close to point $z = -1$.

To check the transient-response characteristics, we shall obtain the unit-step response of the designed system using MATLAB Program 6-57. The resulting response curve is shown in Figure 6-80. The unit-step response curve exhibits a maximum overshoot of 20% and a settling time of approximately 4 sec.

Note that for the present system the sampling period T is chosen as 0.2 sec. From Figure 6-80 it can be seen that the number of samples per cycle of sinusoidal oscillation is about 14.

MATLAB Program 6–57

```
% ---------- Unit-step response of designed system ----------

num = [0   0.0891   0.0108   -0.0679];
den = [1   -2.2885   1.8460   -0.5255];
x = ones(1,41);
v = [0   40   0   1.6];
axis(v);
k = 0:40;
y = filter(num,den,x);
plot(k,y,'o')
grid
title('Unit-Step Response of Designed System')
xlabel('k     (Sampling period T = 0.2 sec)')
ylabel('Output c(k)')
```

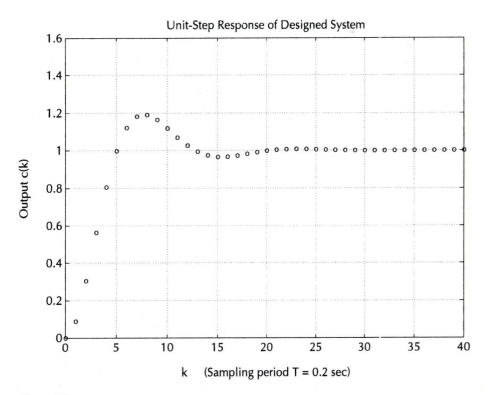

Figure 6-80

Thus the sampling frequency is 14 times the damped natural frequency and the sampling period is satisfactory under normal circumstances.

If the system had neither digital controller nor zero-order hold, but the gain K was simply adjusted to 2, the closed-loop system would have had the transfer function

$$\frac{C(s)}{R(s)} = \frac{2}{s^2 + s + 2}$$

and the maximum overshoot would have been 30% and the settling time 8 sec. Thus the designed system shows considerable improvement of the response.

Comments

The advantage of the w transformation is that the conventional frequency-response method using Bode diagrams can be used for the design of discrete-time control systems.

Remember that the w transformation may generate one or more right-half-plane zeros in $G(w)$. If one or more right-half-plane zeros exist, then $G(w)$ is a nonminimum-phase transfer function. Because the zeros in the right half-plane are generated by the sample-and-hold operation, the locations of these zeros depend on the sampling period T. The effects of these zeros in the right half-plane on the response become smaller as the sampling period T becomes smaller. (A smaller sampling period means a higher sampling frequency.)

References

1. MathWorks, Inc., *The Student Edition of MATLAB*. Englewood Cliffs, N.J.: Prentice Hall, 1992.

2. MathWorks, Inc., *MATLAB User's Guide*. Natick, Mass.: MathWorks, Inc., 1990.

3. Ogata, K., *Discrete-Time Control Systems*. Englewood Cliffs, N.J.: Prentice Hall, 1987.

4. Ogata, K., *Modern Control Engineering*, 2nd ed. Englewood Cliffs, N.J.: Prentice Hall, 1990.

Index

The MATH WORKS Inc.

Ogata

BUSINESS REPLY MAIL

FIRST CLASS   PERMIT NO. 82   NATICK, MA

POSTAGE WILL BE PAID BY ADDRESSEE

THE MATHWORKS, INC.
24 Prime Park Way
Natick, MA 01760-9889